A
VOICE
WAS
SOUNDING

SELECTIONS FROM *THIS LAND*

VOL

3

THIS LAND
PRESS

Works appearing in this anthology were originally published between January and December 2012 in *This Land*, Tulsa, OK.

Vincent LoVoi, Publisher; Michael Mason, Editor

WWW.THISLANDPRESS.COM

Book designed by This Land Press.
Printed in the United States of America.

First Edition, November 2014

ISBN: 978-0-9858487-7-4

PRAISE FOR *THIS LAND*

"A rare example of literary journalism... *The New Yorker* with balls."

—*Columbia Journalism Review*

"I first discovered This Land Press in 2012, and I am so glad that I did. In just a short time, they have created something special not just for readers in Tulsa, but for the rest of us around the world. With outstanding storytelling, thoughtful reporting, and truly diverse voices, they've become a model for the future of journalism with a real sense of place."

— Mark Armstrong, *Longreads*

"*This Land* suggests the kind of pioneering spirit that Woody Guthrie would likely approve."

—*Monocle* magazine

"Nobody tells our story like *This Land*. In this eclectic and compulsively readable volume, essays of character and place, portrait and memoir, tightly researched journalism, and delectable fiction all combine to create a whole that is much larger than its parts. *A Voice Was Sounding* is a tapestry, a feast, a tamed cacophony that evokes not merely the heartland of America but its very heart: bitter, self-obsessed, self-deprecating, glorious. Here is a collection of writings from the center of America that is as disparate and wild and strange as the land from which it springs."

— Rilla Askew, *Fire in Beulah*

"I love this!"

—David Carr, *The New York Times*

A VOICE WAS SOUNDING

SELECTIONS FROM
THIS LAND VOL **3**

Reports, essays, and
fiction that broaden
our understanding of
life and culture in the
middle of America

EDITED BY
Michael Mason
& Mark Brown

CONTENTS

5   FICTION

A
VOICE
WAS
SOUNDING

SELECTIONS FROM *THIS LAND*

VOL

3

INTRODUCTION

By *Mark Brown*

Only two roads go through Archer City, Texas, and one of them goes through Wichita Falls. I'll see any town once. We blew by Oklahoma City, a capital place but, on this trip, just another frontier outcropping. The Devon Tower was a rocket awaiting liftoff. We talked about looking in on Anadarko, home of that dark star of crime noir, James Myers Thompson, but it was all talk.

"Next time," Lee said.

We were headed to Archer City, Texas, in search of a lost text of erotica anonymously written by Anaïs Nin and Henry Miller and whatever poor poets and flailing novelists they could recruit to help them satiate the softcore appetites of a long-dead Tulsa oilman who paid by the page. As I drove, he read to me from the opening lines of what would be titled—rather, the ripe seeds that would sprout the sleeping germ of—"The Strange Love of Dr. Billy James Hargis."

"Two words," he made sure to remind me at press time. "*Strange* and *love*."

The more he read, the more thread he unraveled, until I could hardly see how anything publishable could ever be stitched from it. But publish it did, three months after that road trip. It came together the way all the good ones do, with much selling and pleading and slaving and pain and luck. You don't polish diamonds in a jewelry store, but in deep darkness, applying much pressure, when no one is looking.

———————

Near Randlett, barely a hamlet, the H.E. Bailey Turnpike fades off into Texas. This is the old Comancheria, a land of mangy mesquite and dry gulches, in August anyway. The few towns out here cower in the face of drought and desertion. You cross the Red River near Burkburnett. The banks are low and nothing flows. In the Texas-Oklahoma water wars, it's desolate ground.

This lost text was among the 300,000 books for sale, across four warehouses, in Larry McMurtry's "Last Book Sale." McMurtry, an unstoppable force of a writer, is also an Amazon, and Archer City his Alexandria. A missile strike on Archer City could set literacy in America back a thousand years. The erotica was the last title in the so-called "100," a hundred titles that would be auctioned off as singles instead of lots.

Lee found the book in the stacks of the store labeled Booked Up No. 2. He also found a copy of Larry Clark's *Tulsa*, not an easy find anywhere. We were photographing the pages of a story titled "The Hostelry of the Prick" when McMurtry arrived to do an interview for a Houston rag. He wore sandals with white socks, and eyeglasses on a strap. His denim was held in check by a belt *and* suspenders. "That's Texas," Lee said with a grin.

We told him our intentions and he told us all he knew of the text. Only in this version, the oilman was from Ardmore.

"Ardmore?" I said. "You wrote online that he was a Tulsa oilman."

"Yes," McMurtry said, eyes floating off. "The research goes on." Then he wished us good luck and wandered off.

The 1,139 pages had been bound in a bolted ledger. The only bylines we came across in a terse thumbing were obviously suspect—children's poets Eugene Field and James Whitcomb Riley, the real-life author of such ditties as "When the Frost is on the Punkin," "Leedle Dutch Baby," and "The Happy Little Cripple."

The auction wasn't until Saturday, so we joined the rest of the early bidders at the Royal Theater for some brisket and cold Shiner. We left before they screened *The Last Picture Show* on the same street they shot it 40 years earlier, but not before McMurtry shared with our small band something that the writer Frank O'Connor had told him at Stanford: "You can't make art out of unredeemed pain."

Then, with the only inn in Archer City booked up, we drove back to Wichita Falls.

———————

I checked in to the shithole, two other cars parked in the mushy asphalt lot. Two room keys. "Bring them back in the morning," the manager said, scolding me ahead of time. "And please rate us on TripAdvisor."

Before retiring to our lagers and laptops, we leaned across the balcony rail and tried to get our story straight. We'd been given a limit of $2,500, but I didn't feel confident bidding on an unauthenticated text, however good the backstory. "The provenance is real," Lee said. While he smoked a cigarette, I stared down into the robin-egg depths of the unused swimming pool. I had a vision, true or imagined, of just such a room I'd shared with Lee in a past life.

On the bed, after much Googling and little luck, I turned off the machine. My third Dos Equis was down an X. I lay back on the pillow, wondering, waiting. The window unit kicked out a humid breeze. Lee clacked away on his keyboard. I would have killed for something printed to read.

Some 300,000 books for sale and we hadn't bought a one.

———————

Here's what you do on drives back: You face facts. Lawton heading west looks like Lawton heading east. Hargis and his Christian Crusade were a right-wing propaganda machine, a talk-radio pulpit. A long, hot drive is fueled on cola and petrol. Lee Harvey Oswald did fire at and miss retired General Edwin Walker, the man who tried to quell the Little Rock Nine, through the window of his Turtle Creek Boulevard home. Direct-mail proselytizing was a cottage industry of Tulsa invention. Some were saved, but many were lost.

We left without the erotica, outbid by a New Jersey rare book dealer, no less—an inveterate Yankee in King Archer's court. A fact: It takes love *and* money. Sitting among the soon-to-be-sold stacks, the going and gone titles of a literary yesteryear—Swinburne's *Poems and Ballads*,

Synge's *Playboy of the Western World*, Stein's *Tender Buttons*, Churchill's *A History of the English-Speaking Peoples*—I grew antsy. It was hot enough for McMurtry, when he took the stage for an intro, to offer apologies. "And thanks to Sep's, for the beer," he said, announcing the beginning of the auction, the end of a book-gathering life.

We did our bidding and then went and ate another barbecued lunch. Afterward, Lee wandered off. "Pick me up on the square," he said. I went to get the car, parked under a shade tree out back of the Royal. It wouldn't start. It was high sun on a Saturday. Stranded in a city of books. A heavenly fate on a day from hell, until I found the one mechanic in town, who jumped my Toyota and told me that I'd blown a belt. While I got the car fixed, Lee went back to Booked Up No. 1 and bought a hardcover first edition of McMurtry's *Books: A Memoir*. He got it autographed when he looked up and saw the man himself walking between warehouses. A *flâneur* in his own hometown.

Fact: We had two stories to write. Lee's hands were full with Hargis, so I said I'd take the reins on the great erotica caper, my own playboys-of-the-Western-world. His you'll find inside, sharing a byline with his editor. Some stories, like tangos, take two. Mine never did get written. Somebody has to drive.

Down in the southern bowl of the Great Plains, the expanse can be deafening, even at 70 miles an hour. We didn't play music, just talked, if that. I try not to fill the space in the air with needless chat, knowing that the silence can sometimes release genius. And damned if it didn't—a tune that had been in my head, one by Karen Dalton, Bob Dylan's favorite singer, the Billie Holiday of the prairie, Enid's own. The melody bounced around in my head, untethered to the sequences of digital or analog. And on it a lyric of reproach:

> Didn't you know, you can't make it without
> ever even trying?

We'd filled the tank at Walters, but I was driving on fumes. Texas in my rear-view mirror. A line straddled. Who is H.E. Bailey, and why so many turnpikes in Oklahoma? As often as I safely could, I averted my eyes from the pavement lines to the lone prairie. Out there, a voice was sounding, again, sweeping down the plains, raw and free and star-crossed.

Mark Brown was This Land's *managing editor for two years.*

ONE

EXAMINING OUR PAST, NEAR AND FAR

A WEEK WITH THE BOYS

How a 1954 psychology experiment turned Robbers Cave
into 'Lord of the Flies'

By *Gene Perry*

In May of 1919, Greek soldiers occupied the Ottoman province
of Smyrna, in what is modern-day Turkey. During the initial invasion,
they massacred somewhere between dozens and hundreds of civilians.
The exact number was lost in the chaos of war.

A Turkish teenager, Muzafer Sherif, witnessed many killed that day,
and nearly became a casualty himself. Standing by as a Turk was run
through by a Greek bayonet, Muzafer thought for certain that he would
be next. The soldier readied his weapon and looked at the boy, but then
turned and walked away.

It was one more bloody day between these two lands in a sequence
as long as recorded history, going back to when Alexander the Great
quarreled with the Persians. Muzafer likely would have known this
history, but on that particular day the reality of human conflict jumped
out of books to burn itself vividly into his mind. In one of the few times
that he ever discussed those years, Muzafer wrote that he had seen great
compassion and self-sacrifice within human groups, matched only by
their hatred and "bestial destructiveness" toward outsiders. It became
his life's work to understand why.

Fast forward to 1954, when two dozen Oklahoma City public schools received visitors wielding credentials from "higher educational authorities." The guests asked to observe the fifth-graders at recess and examine their school records. They were looking for "normal" boys—white, Protestant, middle class, with similar IQ scores, no physical abnormalities or problems in school, and living in two-parent families. Boys from foster care or "broken homes"—divorces were still a relative anomaly—were absolutely excluded.

Selected boys were offered the chance to go to a three-week summer camp at Robbers Cave State Park. A man whom the boys would know only as the "camp director" met with their families. He collected a $25 nominal fee for tuition and made the parents promise not to visit, saying it would contribute to homesickness. To further ensure seclusion, "Restricted" and "No Trespassing" signs were posted around the 200-acre campgrounds.

The camp was planned by a husband-and-wife team from the University of Oklahoma, well-known experts in social psychology: Muzafer and Carolyn Sherif. It would be the third boys' camp arranged by the Sherifs to study group dynamics. Two others had previously been held in Connecticut. In the earlier camps, the psychologists had watched in-groups of boys spontaneously emerge and begin to develop tensions with outsiders. With this camp, they would go much further.

The psychologists' research into social groups revolved around goals. They believed that "in-groups" naturally emerge when people must work together to solve a common problem. As part of this process, a group will develop its own culture and hierarchy. If the "in-group" then finds itself in competition with an "out-group," tensions and stereotypes will develop. These tensions are "functional" because they motivate a group to defeat the others and achieve its goal. But once stereotypes become part of the shared cultural beliefs of a group, they may persist beyond the point when they served any useful function. It is then only by a shared goal requiring cooperation between groups that they consider reconciliation.

Muzafer's life had been only slightly less eventful since he escaped World War I. He had earned degrees from Harvard and Columbia, and before World War II he returned to Turkey—to teach psychology at Ankara University. Turkey stayed neutral during the Second World

War, but some officials held sympathies for Nazi Germany. Muzafer wrote several books and helped publish a periodical with anti-Nazi messages, and in 1944 he was jailed for "actions inimical to the national interest." The prosecutor sought a 27-year sentence, but thanks to pressure from some of his Harvard schoolmates (now high-ranking State Department officials), as well as the increasing likelihood that Germany would lose the war, Muzafer was released after 40 days in solitary confinement. He had spent his prison time developing the outline for a social psychology textbook.

In 1949, Muzafer came to the University of Oklahoma with Carolyn Wood Sherif, his wife and close collaborator. Carolyn wrote of their introduction, "I had decided that I wanted to marry an intellectual, as well as sexual and emotional partner, who would encourage my being a social psychologist. The idea was based on literature I had read, not realities I saw, and it was romantic in the extreme. The impact of meeting Muzafer Sherif, already a well-known contributor who espoused social psychology and male-female equality with equal fervor, and whose work had already inspired me, cannot be overdrawn. He asked me how far I wanted to go in social psychology, and I replied, 'All the way.'"

By all accounts, theirs was an equal partnership, though Carolyn would be frustrated much of her life when her contributions were not acknowledged in the larger academic world. As she put it, "A careful historian will recognize that both of us were involved in everything published under the name of Sherif after 1945." A new research institute was created at OU for Muzafer, who served as director. Though the Sherifs worked side by side there for 17 years, Carolyn was never given a regular faculty appointment.

Muzafer's passion for his work was great enough that his research assistants were terrified of letting him drive. He would engage in emphatic discussions about social psychology while behind the wheel, often at the expense of safety. As colleague O.J. Harvey recalled, Muzafer "would first hint, intensify the hint, and then insist on being allowed to drive." Once in the driver's seat, he might go "from 10 miles per hour to 90, and on either side of the road with both arms waving if he was making some big point."

With grant funding from the Rockefeller Foundation, the Sherifs had reserved an isolated Boy Scout campground. The building of these campgrounds was described in a 1931 edition of *The Daily Oklahoman*, under the headline "A Kingdom for Boys." The labor of fifteen inmates was donated by the warden of the state penitentiary at McAlester. They spent months constructing water lines, camp houses, kitchens, and other buildings. As the *Oklahoman* described it, "Four white men and 11 Negroes make up the construction gang. They have their own tent camp with fireplaces of their own making. They do their own cooking, washing and maintain themselves as a separate construction company. They have not been under supervision of even a guard from the penitentiary." This "Tom Hale Camp"—named for the president of the Choctaw council who donated $1,000 for its development—is still used by the Boy Scouts today.

It was an ideal location for the Sherifs' research. They could study small groups in situations that were carefully manipulated, yet more realistic than a psychology lab. The boys, all between the ages of 11 and 12, were picked for the camp to have similar race, religion, class, and family backgrounds, so there would be no major reasons for conflict besides those introduced by the experimenters. They brought only one boy from each school so that none would know any of the others beforehand. With a homogeneous group of young boys in an isolated environment, they hoped to exclude the variables of race, class, and history to uncover a more pure example of human conflict.

The psychologists went to great lengths to keep the boys from knowing they were in an experiment. (Research ethics were less strict at the time.) The Sherifs and their assistants posed as ordinary camp staff, and they took down notes only when the children were not present. Hidden tape recorders were scattered throughout the campgrounds, and when the kids first arrived, staff members acted like shutterbugs, conspicuously taking pictures of everything they saw, so this would not attract attention later. Muzafer himself played the role of the camp janitor.

Groups of eleven boys each were set up on opposite sides of the campground. For the first week of camp, the groups remained isolated and unaware of the other's presence. Because the experimenters wanted groups to emerge with as little interference as possible, the boys were given free rein to explore and form a society in miniature: they scouted hideouts, built diving boards and rope bridges at nearby swimming holes, had run-ins with rattlesnakes and copperheads.

———————————

Leaders emerged. In Group 1, a boy called Mills often made himself the center of attention by clowning (all of the names are fictional, given to the boys by the researchers). In one incident, he started a pine cone fight that ended with him in a tree being pelted by all of the others. "Where's my fellow men?" Mills shouted, and a boy replied, "Look at our leader!"

In honor of several rattlesnake encounters, the boys dubbed themselves the "Tom Hale Rattlers." Mills created a stencil to decorate group t-shirts, hats, and a flag. On the third day, Mills hurt his toe but did not reveal it until bedtime. From then on, it was established that the Rattlers were "tough" and did not complain. As part of this "tough" persona, cursing grew rampant.

In the second group, a boy called Craig took charge at first. He introduced a song on the bus ride to camp that was soon called "our song." Another popular boy was Mason, who stood out as the most capable baseball player. A boy swam without trunks one day and was called "Nudie," but after Mason took it up, the rest followed suit.

A couple of boys in Group 2, Boyd and Davis, struggled with homesickness. Boyd would frequently break into tears. Davis would try to comfort him, only to end up crying himself. The researchers decided they could not help the boys without distorting the experiment, so Boyd and Davis were sent home.

The rest of the group rallied. After discovering they were gone, Craig said, "Things are going to be better around here now." Another boy, Wilson, gibed, "They chickened out." Mason, who had himself struggled with homesickness, replied, "They are the only boys who will."

After the boys naturally coalesced into tribes, the experiment moved on to Stage 2. The Sherifs introduced rivals. Near the end of week one, they arranged for the two groups to be within earshot for the first time. The reaction was immediately negative. Without seeing the other group, Wilson referred to "those nigger campers."

After learning of the Rattlers' existence, Group 2 decided it also needed a name. One boy suggested Rattlesnake Biters, but they settled on the Eagles.

The Sherifs then ramped up the conflict. Counselors told the boys there would be a series of contests: baseball, touch football, tug of war, tent pitching, skits and music, cabin inspections, and, as the grand finale, a treasure hunt—the more subjective events were included so the researchers could pick winners that kept the competition close if one team proved much better at athletics. Each boy on the winning team would get a four-bladed pocket knife, among other prizes. Throughout the tournament, the running score was displayed in the mess hall in the form of rising thermometers.

The contests began with baseball, a pastime the boys took very seriously. The Rattlers arrived at the field first, and then the Eagles approached, singing the notes of the *Dragnet* theme ("Dun da-dun dun ...dun da-dun dun daaaa!") and carrying a flag with the motto: "You may win but we will give you a hell of a fight."

Despite the Eagles' bravado, the Rattlers took an early lead, winning the first baseball game and tug-of-war. After their defeats, the frustrated Eagles noticed the Rattlers' flag had been left on the diamond backstop. They rushed to the flag and tore it down. "Let's burn it," someone suggested. Another boy found matches. They hung the scorched remains back up for the Rattlers to find, a few letters and a picture of a snake still visible. Then they sang "Taps."

As the research report put it, in the restrained language of academic psychology, "This flag-burning episode started a chain of events which made it unnecessary for the experimenters to introduce special situations of mutual frustration for the two groups."

The Rattlers discovered their desecrated flag the next morning. The boys clustered around, shouting excitedly. Simpson, the baseball captain, came up with a plan. When the Eagles arrived, he would demand an accounting. When the Eagles confessed (no one doubted they would), he would throw the first punch, and the others would back him up. A boy called Martin volunteered to grab the Eagle flag and burn it.

It went as planned. Martin took off with the Eagle flag, with several Eagles and Rattlers in pursuit. Remaining Eagles grabbed another Rattler flag and tore it apart. Rattler Swift put Craig in a wrestling hold, demanding, "Which one of you guys burned our flag?" Craig shouted back: "We all did!"

Fistfights broke out, and the staff intervened to stop it. Then Mason returned, after witnessing the Rattlers burn the Eagle flag. He was "crying mad" and yelling for someone "my size" to fight. "Here I am!" responded Mills. The staff had to pull them apart again.

Eventually the groups settled down enough to play another game of baseball, with plenty of jeering on both sides. Among the epithets thrown between teams: "stinkers," "cheats," "damn niggers," "communists," "fatty," "tubby," and "Little Black Sambo."

This time, the Eagles won. Mason said the victory was due to their prayers, and another boy suggested the Rattlers lost because they cuss so much. "Hey, you guys!" he shouted over everyone. "Let's not do any more cussing, and I'm serious, too."

Things escalated that night. The Eagles took the second tug-of-war match, and the increasingly frustrated Rattlers planned a raid. They covered their faces and arms with warpaint. At 10:30 p.m., they charged into the rival cabin. The Eagles, torn from their sleep, sat stunned as the Rattlers flipped over beds and ripped down mosquito nets.

When they recovered from the shock, the Eagles were ready to retaliate, but the researchers posing as camp staff stepped in "when it was mentioned that rocks would be used." Celebrations ensued back at the Rattlers' cabin. Mills had stolen comic books and a pair of Mason's blue jeans. He painted "The Last of the Eagles" in orange down each leg and carried them like a flag.

The retaliatory raid came the next morning. After making sure the Rattlers were at the mess hall, the Eagles broke into their cabin armed with sticks and bats. They trashed the place and returned to their own cabin, where they prepared socks filled with rocks in case the Rattlers returned.

———————————

Tensions had risen alongside the now red-hot thermometers that kept the scores. With some help from the researchers, the Rattlers and

Eagles stayed close to the very end. On the last day, counselors gathered both groups together with the prizes between them. They announced the results for each contest one by one. It came down to the final event: the treasure hunt. Staff read out the times. Rattlers: 10 minutes, 15 seconds. Eagles: 8 minutes, 38 seconds.

The Eagles had won. (The boys didn't know that the experimenters had made sure of it by giving the Eagles an easier route.) The winners hugged, shouted, and jumped in the air. Mason broke into happy tears. The losers sat silently on the ground.

It didn't take long for the Rattlers to have their revenge. When the Eagles left to swim in a nearby creek, the Rattlers again raided their cabin. They ransacked the room, untied boats from the dock, and stole the prize knives and medals.

When the Eagles discovered what had happened, several boys rushed to the Rattler cabin. The groups lined up across from each other, shouting over an invisible line. The Rattlers said they would return the knives and medals if the Eagles got down on their bellies and crawled. Mason again demanded someone his size to fight, but the Rattlers refused to take out their two biggest boys. When fights did break out among some of the others, the experimenters decided to intervene to avoid serious injuries.

Just two weeks into camp, and a mere week since the groups first engaged, the Sherifs had expertly created a situation that turned young boys into bitter enemies. In the last week, they would try to make them friends.

Conciliation came slowly. With any contact, the boys would yell slurs and hold their noses. They complained about eating in the same mess hall, and multiple meals descended into food and garbage fights. When contact by itself did not reduce tensions, the experiment moved to the next stage: introduce problems that would require group cooperation to resolve, what the researchers called "superordinate goals." So they turned off the water.

The experimenters disabled a valve going to the camp's water main and covered it with boulders. They stuffed sacking into the faucet at the water tower that fed the main. Then staff announced they were having problems with the water system. To cover themselves, they mentioned that vandals had damaged it in the past.

After turning off the water in the morning, the experimenters waited until 4 p.m. The high that day was close to 100 degrees. The boys had almost used up their canteens and were growing parched. A staff member made an announcement.

"Fellows, we haven't been able to find the trouble yet," he said. "It may be at the tank; it may be the valves, or in the pump or intake; or it may be a leak in the line. We just don't know. Now we need your help to find the trouble."

The boys split up and examined the whole system before finally converging at the tank, partway up a mountain more than a mile from the campsite. It took 45 minutes of work by multiple boys digging out the sacking with their knives to finally access the water.

Tensions remained, but there were signs of a thaw. At breakfast the next day, a few boys exchanged howdys. The experimenters introduced more situations requiring cooperation: they rented a movie with donations from both groups; they revived a "stalled" truck that was needed to retrieve food by pulling it with a rope. Celebrating together, the boys announced they had "won the tug-of-war with the truck."

For the Sherifs, the experiment was a resounding success. It was not any innate difference between the Rattlers and the Eagles, or the Greeks and Turks, that set them at each other's throats—just a coincidence of geography. Their results were described in an influential report, "Intergroup Conflict and Cooperation: The Robbers Cave Experiment." This became the basis for realistic conflict theory, a tool to better understand prejudice and discrimination—how even similar groups could so easily fall into conflict and violence, but also how it might be resolved.

By the end of week three, the efforts had gone so well that the boys chose to ride back to Oklahoma City on the same bus. They took turns singing the favorite songs of both groups. Towards the end of the trip, some boys began to sing "Oklahoma!", and everyone rushed to the front of the bus to join in.

THE GENESIS OF VAGABOND

A behind-the-scenes look at the making of a photographic
masterpiece—Gaylord Herron's 'Vagabond'

By *Grant McClintock*

IN THE EARLY 1970S, Tulsa delivered two of the world's most promising young photographers, Larry Clark and Gaylord Herron. One of
them, Clark, went on to international fame. The other, after early acclaim
for his 1975 book *Vagabond*, seemingly disappeared. Now nearly four
decades later, he is re-emerging with a body of new work—one that
could reshape the artistic landscape of Tulsa. This current work, along
with a renewed appreciation of *Vagabond,* may finally garner Herron
the attention and appreciation he has long deserved. Where has he been
hiding? In plain sight, it turns out.

When the art book *Vagabond* came out in 1975, I was running a
photo gallery in the French Quarter of New Orleans. The art community was stunned into a pensive silence of admiration and envy by the
sheer power of Larry Clark's 1971 book *Tulsa*—one of the more evocative
and influential photography books ever published. Suddenly people
were interested in my hometown.

"Did you know these guys?" they would ask. To New Orleanians,
Tulsa was a cozy village up in the plains where surely everyone
knew everyone.

When *Vagabond* arrived on my doorstep, I lent my copy to my partner in the gallery. He took it home to check it out. The next morning he handed it back to me.

"Incredible," he said. "What the hell's going on up there?"

What indeed. In the early 1970s, Tulsa arts yielded up three legitimate international stars: Larry Clark, Leon Russell, and J.J. Cale, along with an extensive cast of supporting talent. David Gates, Mary Kay Place, and Gailard Sartain were hitting their stride, and what they had in common was Tulsa. Gaylord Herron fell into no easy category, neither leading man nor supporting cast. *Vagabond* was a true one-off—there's been nothing like it before or since.

Whereas Clark's *Tulsa* rolled into the room like a live grenade, *Vagabond* was quiet, subtle, and not readily decoded. *Vagabond* was warmly received by critics and other photographers. Bill Burke at the Museum of Fine Arts in Boston listed *Vagabond* as one of the most important photography books of 1975. English critic William Messer labeled it a "contemporary masterpiece."

"Photographer Larry Clark named a powerful book *Tulsa*, but he only scratched the city's skin while mainlining in another vein that might have gone down similarly in a hundred other locales," wrote Messer. "In the Tulsa of *Vagabond*, Herron leans into the place's chest and makes it breathe back."

But the book never made that leap into the public consciousness necessary to become a commercial success. Over the years it disappeared from book lists and faded into obscurity. In an interview 15 years after its publication, Robert Frank, the godfather of American social landscape photography, said, "There was a book, *Vagabond*. I liked him a lot. A guy from Oklahoma? Not Larry Clark. I think he's very good. It's a wonderful book. I think it's hard to get now."

Since publishing *Tulsa*, Larry Clark has directed movies (*Kids* and *Wassup Rockers*, among others) and recently released a new collection of work, *Kiss the Past Hello*, which debuted at Musee d'Art Moderne de la Ville de Paris. Clark's muse, Tiffany Limos, is preparing to release a documentary about the making of *Tulsa*. The Gaylord Herron story, on the other hand, remains nearly as obscure as *Vagabond* itself.

Herron has been right here in Tulsa for the last four decades, diligently photographing and documenting his hometown with hardly a note of fanfare, nor a care for it. You've probably driven past his business downtown, or walked by him as he hid behind a camera. Now, after four decades of shirking the spotlight, Herron is re-emerging with a body of new work, one that could reshape the artistic landscape of Tulsa. In order to fully understand Herron's significance, though, you first have to know *Vagabond*.

"Behold, thou has driven me out this day from the face of the earth; and from thy face shall I be hid; and I shall be a fugitive and a vagabond in the earth."

Vagabond opens with Cain's words from Genesis 4:14. The quote supplies both the title of the book and the maypole around which Herron entwines his work.

In a fit of breathtaking jealously, Cain killed his brother Abel after God rejected Cain's offering of produce while accepting Abel's offering of sheep. God cursed Cain for the deed, sentencing him to endlessly wander the earth, in search of peace, redemption, and a return to the father. Even by Old Testament standards this comes off as grim stuff. As Herron interprets it, we are all thrust like boomerangs out into the world, straining to return to the purity and simplicity of original existence. The story of Cain and Abel provides the author an apt metaphor with which to examine this universal journey.

The genesis of *Vagabond* seems almost as improbable as the genesis of man as depicted in the Bible. *Vagabond* is indisputably Gaylord Herron's book, but without the contributions of two additional characters—Dan Mayo and Bill Rabon—it would have been, at the very least, greatly altered and, more probably, nonexistent.

Herron has depicted his childhood home in *Vagabond*. In 1970 he photographed his mother standing on the front porch of their house. Her face is lost in a monotone of gray grain. A light by the door bleeds down into the house number, 1024. This is North Florence Street in Tulsa. Herron refers to that part of town as "near northeast." This small area of Tulsa has been fertile ground for artists, yielding up Johnny Cale,

Leon Russell, Elvin Bishop, and David Gates—not to mention such polarizing notables as Bobby Dean Morris (one of Clark's *Tulsa* players) and Anita Bryant.

I cannot cite a page number for this or any photograph in the book because, in a nod to the ongoing lighthearted eccentricity of *Vagabond*, only one page in the book is numbered, the last, 132. These little oddities and visual jokes run throughout *Vagabond*. Near the end of the book Herron had written, "I have one son, one wife, one car … " The typesetter mistakenly converted this to, " … one wife, one ear … " The boys, ever disciples of the happy accident, liked the typo better than the original and just left it. So Herron arrived on the world stage shy one ear.

Herron attended Cleveland Junior High School on North Birmingham, where he became fast friends with one Buster Craft. They sang duets at the Nazarene Church at 12th and Delaware and wrestled in Buster's backyard after Sunday school, swapping take-downs. They set pins at Huckett's Bowling Alley, trading out labor for lane time.

One afternoon Buster brought along another kid who lived somewhere around 15th and Peoria. He and Herron wrestled. A bit over a decade later, Lustrum Press would publish this kid's book, *Tulsa*—by one Larry Clark.

Herron attended Webster High School. He had good SAT scores and, in 1961, he was accepted at the University of Tulsa to study engineering. He flunked out and joined the Army, which shipped him to Korea for two and a half years beginning in 1962. There he was transformed into a devoted photographer.

"I was just like everyone else," he says. "I bought a camera as soon as I got there."

But unlike everyone else, Herron became a shutterbug extreme. He pored over *Popular Photography* magazine, checking out the new gear, trying to duplicate the work of Art Kane or Eugene Smith. He first upgraded to a Pentax and then to a medium format Mamiyaflex. He learned to print in the base darkroom. He shot rolls and rolls of Tri-X, the black-and-white film *de rigeur* at the time. The world became an endless photo op. He showed his buddies the pics. They nodded. They liked them. So he shot more film, lots more film. By the time he returned to the states in 1964, Herron was, and always would be, a dedicated photographer. Totally hooked.

While in Korea, Herron wrote a poem to this father, "Bits and Pieces." He had a vague idea of delivering this poem on his return home as a first step in the long overdue reconciliation he envisioned. The original, complete with corrections and the circular swirl to get the ink flowing, is reproduced in *Vagabond*. "Bits and Pieces" is a cry from the heart of a man who never acknowledged nor even recognized the worth of his father, the love he felt for him nor the debt he owed him:

> I observe, of course, the Irish face,
> The auburn hair,
> The sharp blue hunters' eyes,
> I observe the forearms bare and sweat,
> Working the tools, Breaking the lids
> Too tight for a woman's hand....
>
> I apologize for being an ingrate,
> moreover I apologize for being
> something I can never retrieve.

The poem was not delivered, the reconciliation and return to the father never achieved. Herron's father died just ten days after his return to the states in 1964.

"*Vagabond* had to do with the death of my father more than any other aspect of my life," Herron says.

He set up a little darkroom in his garage and began cranking out his Korea work. After his stint overseas, a garage darkroom in his hometown began to feel a little unimaginative. Growing restless, he finally packed what belongings he had into a 1957 Desoto and headed for the buzz of New York City. He landed a good job as studio assistant for Vincent Lisanti, lugging around an 8x10 Deardorff, reflectors, tripods, all manner of gear. Lisanti primarily shot interiors for high-end magazines—*Better Homes and Gardens, Ladies' Home Journal*. The scenes were fully lighted, the perspectives corrected and everything front to back in focus. Lisanti schooled Herron in the peculiarities of the view camera. Herron would use a view camera for the rest of his life, producing with it many of his most compelling images.

At one point down the road Herron ran short of cash so he began using paper, in place of more costly film, in his 8x10. These paper negatives yield soft, other-worldly prints that glow like 19th century work—perhaps Julia Margaret Cameron. For a fine example of this technique, see the shot of the Arkansas River in the Washington Irving spread in *Vagabond*. I'd give you a page number, but there isn't one.

Herron slept in the back of Lisanti's studio. He schlepped equipment, set lights, took meter readings. He subsisted on a diet of English muffins and street food. But he was still broke all the time.

"Even paying no rent I couldn't afford to live in New York," he says. "I don't know how people do it." He returned to Oklahoma.

Herron moved into the Vogue Apartments next door to Bob Hawks photography studio on Main Street. (A half a century, Herron's bicycle shop and studio is now located in that very building.) Herron dropped by Hawks' studio looking for work. By chance, Hawks had gone to Brooks Institute with Lisanti. After a phone call to Lisanti, Herron had a job as photo assistant to The Hawk.

Bob Hawks was a tree-shaking money-maker. He and Herron shot product for Zebco, massive amounts for ORU, architecture of all sorts, anything that paid. One of Hawks' dependable income streams came from the Sweet Adelines Conventions—a women's barbershop quartet singing convention. The Adelines were big on Lawrence Welk. Herron traveled the country photographing these songbirds. He sent the negatives back to Hawk who then peddled them to the Adelines. One of these images, in scary living color, appears in *Vagabond*. After a while, Herron left Hawks.

"For some reason I applied to TU," says Herron, meaning that he reapplied.

The university offered him a scholarship in the journalism school in exchange for shooting the yearbook. The *Tulsa Tribune* noticed his photos and asked him to join the staff. Happy to be shed of school, he readily joined the *Tribune* staff. He stayed with the *Tribune* from '67 to '69. Here, Herron's photography appeared before the public for the first time. Much of the "landscape of the absurd" perfume of *Vagabond* derives from photos he produced for the *Tribune*: the fat man looking very pleased having shot himself in the gut; "Jerk," the straining weightlifter; the surreal opening of Sheridan Lanes. At the *Tribune* Herron found his voice, or at least he began to share it. The *Tribune* proved an ideal landing pad. Herron was forced to produce every day, and his work was being published.

Larry Silvey was the editor at *Tulsa Magazine* at the time. He hired Herron to photograph numerous spreads for the publication.

"Larry was a perfect editor," remembers Herron. "He picked interesting and relevant subjects and turned me loose." Among many other jobs for *Tulsa Magazine*, three spreads stand out. Silvey assigned Herron to photograph two Tulsa landmarks before their destruction—the Orpheum Theater and the Cimarron Ballroom. These, and so many other elegant (or at least intriguing) buildings in Tulsa, have fallen in the name of progress. What remains of the Orpheum are Herron's photographs to remind us that we will never again slip by the "Balcony Closed" rope and sneak up into that particular paradise. Neither will future generations do the funky chicken on that supremely funky dance floor of the Cimarron, depicted in its decay in *Vagabond*.

On the positive side, the *Tulsa Magazine* photo essay of the Union Station played a role in saving that iconic building.

In 1969, Herron moved over to KOTV, taking up the feature-reporting slot created by Dino Economis. It was a colorful crew. Gailard Sartain operated a camera at the station before transmogrifying into "Mazeppa" and achieving Tulsa immortality. Bob Brown was an investigative reporter. He advanced to "20/20" on ABC News. Then you had "Lee and Lionel," Mac Krieger and Bill Pitcock. To Tulsans of a certain age, you might as well say Penningtons, the Will Rogers and Jack's Barber Shop. These people and places defined our town and sense of well-being.

Herron produced about 900 stories for KOTV over three years. I asked him to sum up the KOTV experience. He gazed off into middle distance for a moment, considering. He came back with one word: "Frantic."

————————

As Herron was spreading his images across town in print and broadcasting his words through the televised ether, a young photographer named Dan Mayo was lurking. "I followed Gaylord's work for years," says Mayo. "Finally I decided I had to meet him."

Attempting to reconstruct the initial meeting of Herron, Mayo, and Rabon compounds the geometric confusion of three aging minds, innate good manners, and chemical reorganization—a seemingly impossible task. The memory of three fellows crowded around either side of seventy years old is slippery by definition. But then, of course, Herron has a photograph, and who can argue with a photograph? As Susan Sontag observed, "Photographs are a way of imprisoning reality."

Mayo, Herron, and I gaze at the photo. This particular one imprisons a winter day in 1973. Judy Herron, Gaylord's wife, is building a fire in the background. An out-of-focus woman no one can identify stands to the side of the frame. She has arranged this meeting at Herron's house. Who is she? Several guesses lead us to no definitive identification.

Mayo spent the next three days going through boxes of prints at Herron's house. He remembers, "It was an incredible turn-on. I really wanted to do something."

Herron approached *Vagabond* from North Tulsa, passing through public schools, fundamental Christianity, and the Army. Mayo came from the other pole—the south side, through Holland Hall, secular humanism, and Southern Hills. Mayo, heir to the eponymous hotel and Okie oil money, grew up in privilege. But as Leon Russell said to him many years later from behind the wheel of his Rolls Royce, "Dan, you and I have something in common now. I'm rich too … Ain't so easy, is it?"

Great photography first arrived in Mayo's life through the pages of his mother's subscription to *Vogue*. These were the tasty years with Alexander Liberman at the helm of Condé Nast. In *Vogue*, Mayo discovered the images of Richard Avedon. The Avedon influence was to emerge in Mayo's portrait series from the late '70s, which was the match of anything anyone was doing anywhere.

After Holland Hall, Mayo went to Bard College in Annadale-on-Hudson, New York, and promptly failed out. In New York City he saw Steichen's *Family of Man* show at MoMA and was dazzled. He came across Rousseau's *Sleeping Gypsy*—in Herron's view, the ultimate vagabond.

Mayo shipped out to chilly Colorado Alpine College, which he loved, and then back to TU, which he did not. He dropped out of TU, unable to hack the requirements.

"No science, no math," Mayo recalls. "I liked literature. I didn't even like history—just fantasy and alcohol."

In the summer of 1970, Mayo discovered Cartier-Bresson through his book *The Decisive Moment*. No artist had a greater influence on photographers of the Mayo's generation than did Henri Cartier-Bresson. His ability to perfectly frame his images time after time approached the miraculous. When Mayo first opened *The Decisive Moment*, a card advertising a Minor White workshop at the Hotchkiss School fell from it. In the pantheon of photo heavy-hitters, Minor White got in line right behind Ansel Adams and Edward Weston, and he was becoming recognized as the bossman of Zen photography. "Sensitivity awareness," he called it. Mayo said, "That's for me." Minor White was the first in a string of major photographic artist under whom Mayo studied.

He learned of the Apeiron Workshops in Millerton, New York, through White. Apeiron was of prime importance to the development of Mayo's work and to the birth of *Vagabond*. Apeiron was opened in 1970 by Peter Schlessinger, a former assistant editor at *Aperture Magazine* (Minor White was a founder). Schlessinger gathered an A-list of art photography talent to demonstrate their craft to the hungry few at Apeiron. The leaders included such luminaries as Berenice Abbott, Diane Arbus, Paul Camponigro, Judy Dater, Robert Frank, Burk Uzzle, Ralph Gibson, Lee Friedlander, on and on. It was like working out with the Yankees at spring training.

In 1971 Mayo signed up for a workshop with Diane Arbus, but Arbus killed herself shortly before the workshop was to begin. "Crushing blow," recalls Mayo. "I was so excited to get to meet her."

Paul Camponigro filled Arbus' spot, and a felicitous substitution it was. Camponigro, an acknowledged master photographer, was Italian-handsome, confident, and open. Like Ansel Adams, he was a classically trained pianist. He and Mayo hit it off immediately and remained friends long after Apeiron ended. Camponigro took at engaging portrait of Mayo while they were at Apeiron. Mayo owns an admirable collection of photography and art—nothing dearer to him than that portrait by Camponigro.

That summer, Mayo also took workshops from George Tice and Emmet Gowin.

Mayo returned to Tulsa and *Mad Dogs and Englishmen*. Heady times. Leon Russell was emerging as the genius he proved to be. The Tulsa Sound was going national. Great musicians were thick on the ground: Cale, Karstein, Raffensperger, Tripplehorn, Radle, Simms, "Taco" Ryan, Blackwell, Mike Bruce, Keltner, Oldaker. Heady times, indeed.

Emily Smith introduced Mayo to Russell. Something like, "Hey, this is a good kid who loves photography. You ought to give him a try."

And he did. Mayo eventually shot the covers for *Carney, Hank Wilson's Back* (Emily Smith contributed the art work), and *Stop All that Jazz*. Mayo also photographed the St. Louis gospel duo nonpareil, The O'Neal Twins, when they recorded for Shelter Records.

Mayo became the court photographer of the Mad Dogs and Shelter Records movable celebration—the MDAE party at Mayo's parents' house, the Kool-Aid acid picnic. Denny Cordell, who had started Shelter Records with Leon Russell, arranged for Mayo to print his material at the superb Capitol Records darkroom in Los Angeles. Mayo ended up with hundreds of images from the period, which still appear from time to time in music publications.

Even in the throes of rock 'n' roll, Mayo was keeping track of another Tulsa photographer. He had admired this guy's stills in the *Tribune* and in *Tulsa Magazine*. Now he was on TV. There's something happening here, thought Mayo. And it's not all music.

Mayo and Herron agree that Tulsa painter Bill Rabon played an important role in the creation of *Vagabond,* but neither is certain what that role was.

"Muse?" says one. They consider this.

"No, that wasn't really it." Another pause.

"Bill is a poet. Mostly it was just the things he said … " They nod.

When I put the question of his role in *Vagabond* to Rabon, he answered, "Appreciator."

The book is dedicated "to Cain and to Bill Rabon," which in Rabon's mind is redundant. "I'm a vagabond, a Cain, a gypsy." He should know.

Herron's dramatic portrait of Rabon appears on the dedication page—a visage that might well belong to a vagabond, a Cain, or a gypsy.

"It was an honor having this book dedicated to me," says Rabon.

Rabon was born in Muskogee on the 4th of July, 1938, into a fundamentalist, Bible-reading home. Along with the requisite prodigious party skills, Rabon brought to the project a thorough, almost encyclopedic, knowledge of the good book. I asked him to run down the Cain and Abel story for me, expecting a couple of minutes of Wikipedia. Not at all. The main events were supported by off-shoots of twisting chronicle and fascinating factoids. The troubling issue of Cain's wife was settled with conviction. Various theories regarding the nature of the mark of Cain were put forth and batted around.

"Cain built the city of Enoch to stop the judgment," says Rabon. "We have to become aware of the city today. We must work with the city or it will overwhelm us. Tulsa is an exact model of Enoch."

"A model city?" I ask.

"Not *a* model city. Tulsa is *the* model city. Big things can happen here," Rabon says. "We are given to abstract thinking."

Rabon's educational pedigree is as Tulsa as you can get: Eliot, Central, and TU. He liked to hang out at Skaggs smoking cigs and watching the downtown bustle. In 1961, he began painting and fell in with a group known as the Bohemes. They gathered at the Bob and Barbara Bartholic's gallery on Cincinnati. Or at Id, Inez Running-rabbit's gallery on Carson. There was Alice Price, John Kennedy, Paul England, and a gaggle of other painters, poets, and folks just hanging out. Cigarettes and booze. Joe Brainard and his crew were walking up and down 11th Street eating candy bars and looking ragtag. Art and talk—all suspended in that idyllic interlude between the Beatnik era and the drugged-driven hippie onslaught. Rabon remembers the Tulsa art world of the early '60s with real fondness and gratitude.

Rabon's reputation as a painter and hipster expanded with the decade. He and Mayo became friends. Herron met Rabon separately. The three came together for *Vagabond*.

Mayo went through Herron's work for three days.

"We should do a book," he told Herron.

This wistful sentence is uttered millions of times a year across the country, usually without result. But this was different. Mayo had the funds not only to produce a book, but to produce a book of the highest quality.

"I wanted the finest printer, the most beautiful paper, everything," he says. "I had a lust for ink."

Herron was certainly ready. He had been casting about for an artistic project to give expression to the loss he felt at the death of his father—his grief over the unresolved dual abandonment. Now Mayo was throwing a book deal in his lap. And God knows, Herron had the work to fill it.

Herron was all-in immediately.

"Nobody was knocking down my door," he says. Judy Herron's enthusiasm was tempered and, well, rational. Herron had a solid job. He was gaining a local reputation. She thought the book was a fine idea but don't quit the day job, honey.

He quit the day job.

In a flurry of fast talk and high excitement, the boys loaded up Dan's Volvo with boxes of prints and such supplies as a couple of Okies might need in the big city, and they headed off for New York. One moment in the trip is chronicled in *Vagabond*. Mayo sits behind the wheel of the Volvo consulting a map. The clock shows 1:15 a.m. They are in Indianapolis, driving straight through from Tulsa. It's raining.

This was the fall of 1974. Between this time and the publication of *Vagabond* in 1975 there were five or six trips back east all involving some combination four people—Herron, Mayo, Rabon, and Judy. The triangle route was always the same: Manhattan to visit the printer and raise hell, Apeiron to seek advice from the gurus, and Tulsa to resupply and work on the photo selection, layout, and the concept.

First they traveled to Apeiron to get the opinion of the heavy hitters—something of a nervous moment. The possibility of rejection was not so farfetched. "Sorry fellows. This stinks." But when they showed the photos to Paul Camponigro and Peter Schlessinger, both men loved them and were enthusiastic about the concept. Schlessinger ran Mayo and Herron through the gauntlet of potential problems that lie ahead. He provided some much needed practical advice. Camponigro put a small "P" on the back of the prints he especially liked. Herron, who seems to know where every photo he has ever taken is located, has since lost them.

The boys contacted Ralph Gibson. Gibson opened a decade of remarkable photography books with *The Somnambulist* in 1970. His Lustrum Press then published Larry Clark's *Tulsa*. These two books hit the photo art world like *Sgt. Pepper's*. Everyone was looking at them, carrying them around, talking about them. Ralph Gibson was the man.

When Gibson was consulted about *Vagabond's* potential, he answered, "Yeah, it should be a great book, but don't expect to make any money." Prophetic on both counts.

Mayo insisted that Sidney Rappaport in New York print the book. Rappaport worked on all the most important photography books. He was the best in the business. Mayo contacted Rappaport and set things up. They then returned to Tulsa and began to assemble a dummy.

The photo book design convention at the time demanded a certain look, a style that announced, "This isn't just photography, this is *art*." It was known as Aperture monograph—clean and simple, one photo per page, lots of Helvetica. Even the iconoclastic Gibson held to the Aperture monograph standard. Herron wanted to go a different way. He envisioned an "artist's book" more along the lines of Dieter Roth and Ed Ruscha—more free-form, less constrained.

At this point, the influence of Mayo and Rabon came into play. Although the book was Herron's vision, Mayo contributed significantly to the overall aesthetic, for example, designing the collage on the right side of the "Bits and Pieces" spread. And Rabon was on hand to help Herron flesh out the Cain metaphor and keep the vibe on the tracks.

In New York, Mayo rented Eugene O'Neill's old suite in the Hotel Chelsea, home at one time or another to wild variety of artists, musicians, actors, and writers—a real Bohemian sanctuary perfect for the *Vagabond* crew.

"Great hotel," recalls Rabon. "You could pass out flat on the sidewalk and they'd pick you up and carry you to your room. Larry Rivers paintings all over the lobby."

Herron spent as much time as he could with Sidney Rappaport, at the shoulder of the master. He was absorbing the printing and composition side of bookmaking. *Vagabond* was coming together.

"Gaylord was working hard while Bill and I partied," says Mayo.

But here and there Herron did manage an evening out. One grueling night found them at the Carlyle digging Bobby Short with New York café society. Mayo knew Short through his hotelier dad, Birch, who knew everybody. Now and then Mayo barked out, "Play it, Bobby." Bobby nodded. The boys were fried. Okies on the loose in the big city. They left the Carlyle and headed for the Chelsea, but overcome by drink, they decided to bed down uptown at the Plaza. "Could you bring me a room?"

"*Vagabond* was very much about fun," says Mayo.

In 1975 the book was finished and in hand. It was boxed and sent to Light Impressions, the company in charge of the distribution. The books sat in the Light Impressions warehouse for years, a relatively small number of copies sold. Eventually Peter Schlessinger picked up the unsold *Vagabonds* and drove them to Tulsa where they took up residence in Mayo's house. Some years later Herron retrieved the boxes from Mayo's and carried back them his studio and that's where most of them they can be found today.

Distance anoints a work with historical significance. This is true of *Vagabond*. These photographs arrive from the lost past, from *our* lost past. Photographs are documents. One of the prime values of Herron's work will be to serve as an accurate record for future generations to examine, not unlike the Beryl Ford Collection. That alone gives them value.

But these photographs move far beyond documentation. Herron's work unveils the unseen, not just what we observe but how what we observe works on us—not just the world as it appears but what it feels like underneath. The people, the place, are familiar but they exist at the level of dreamscape, pared down to a wobbly essence. One hesitates to trot out that shop-worn word, but in Herron's case, it applies ... mystical.

Today, Mayo shoots more than ever, but now with an iPhone. His primary subjects are those close at hand: his granddaughter, his home, his garden, himself. His primary gallery is the Internet. His work remains fresh and untethered to convention.

Rabon lives in a very modest north side apartment. A cat wanders in and out. He willingly shares his wealth of Tulsa anecdotes, cosmic theory, and good cheer. He owns one coffee cup and an antique micro-wave on the floor to heat things up.

"I've got all I need," he says. "I get up every morning and paint."

Despite the accolades Herron's work has received over the years, his photography is rarely seen in Tulsa. Instead of attending art openings, Herron has been running a bike shop, G. Oscar, in the old Bob Hawks studio where he learned a few tricks of the trade. He has recently finished a monumental work, photographing 250 Tulsa buildings with his much loved 8x10 paper negative technique.

Herron pours over his old photographs in the studio above his shop. He is undertaking the daunting task of converting a lifetime of solid silver prints into insubstantial pixels. He scans the past for hours each day after work. I asked him if he could sum up his thoughts on the entire body of his work from 1962 to the present.

He answered, "The older I get, the less I know. The work leading up to *Vagabond* was freer, more inspired than that which came after '75. Artists learn to imitate themselves and that drags them down. The inspiration of youth is like a dream now—a dream I sometime wish I could return to."

You can't blame Herron's yearning for the energies of youth. His unique vision and talent set *Vagabond* apart and assures it a place among the most important art books of the last half of the last century. *Vagabond* was a spot in time, a distinctive gem dropped in our laps. With a new body of work forthcoming, the vagabond behind *Vagabond* may yet come to be appreciated as one of Oklahoma's most important and enigmatic artists.

THE STRANGE LOVE OF DR. BILLY JAMES HARGIS

When the radio evangelist Billy James Hargis forged a friendship
with an extremist Army general, Edwin 'Ted' Walker, a new brand
of politics emerged from the middle of America, establishing
Oklahoma as the birthplace of the religious right. Both men weren't
just politically minded, however. Recently revealed documents
indicate that the FBI regarded them as national threats.

By *Lee Roy Chapman and Michael Mason*

LITTLE ROCK WAS SHELL-SHOCKED. It was July of 1960, and in
the past year, five bombings had terrorized the city's public school system.
The state legislature of Arkansas attempted to thwart desegregation by
shutting down Little Rock's public high schools, but the bombings sent
a far more violent message to the city's pioneering civil rights community. Similar incidents throughout the South grabbed the country's attention, forcing the federal government to intervene. In Arkansas, the
government put a zealous Army general in command of the military
district to ensure safety and integration.

Federal Bureau of Investigation agents combed Arkansas for suspects
in the bombings, and they were looking for one man in particular: a
high-profile segregationist preacher from Oklahoma named Billy
James Hargis. According to FBI special agent Joe Casper, Hargis was
planning to bomb the Philander Smith College in Little Rock soon.
The preacher had recently met with two other bombing suspects at a
Memphis restaurant.

"We ought to get a permissive search warrant from him [Hargis] to search his home, car, and any outbuildings at his residence," Casper suggested. "We have evidence that these people we have arrested in Little Rock have been in contact with him."

The FBI had cause to be concerned. Hargis' tirades mirrored those from any number of early 20th century Ku Klux Klan pamphlets. He was anti-communist, anti-union, pro-segregation, and he preached those values on a 15-minute daily radio show that aired on stations throughout North America. Based in Tulsa, The Christian Crusade was the public name of Hargis' media empire, one that included a magazine, the daily radio program, Christian Crusade Publications, and a pioneering direct-mail operation that expertly distributed Hargis' propaganda throughout the world. By 1960, Hargis had the ability to martial sizeable crowds and stir them with his incendiary speeches. In the eyes of the FBI, he was a serious threat; in the minds of many Cold War Americans, though, Hargis was a new kind of patriot.

CRUSADING FOR PURITY AND ESSENCE

Before anyone heard Rush Limbaugh infiltrating AM radio, before televangelists like Pat Robertson and James Dobson organized the Christian Right, before Tea Party favorites Rand Paul and Paul Ryan began their campaigns, there was Billy James Hargis. Born in Texarkana, Texas, in 1925, Hargis was raised in poverty during the Great Depression and at an early age decided to commit his life to Christianity. Clean-cut, chubby, and baby-faced, he looked like a Kip's Big Boy statue come to life. By the age of 22, Hargis had become a religious renegade. After a brief stint as a pastor in Sapulpa, Oklahoma, he married a woman named Betty Jane and in 1948 started his own religious non-profit, Christian Echoes Ministry, where he began preaching against communism. Anti-communism wasn't a new message in Oklahoma; as early as 1917, with the start of the Bolshevik Revolution, civic organizations like the Tulsa Councils of Defense,[1] in conjunction with local publications like the *Tulsa World* and *Tulsa Tribune*, contributed to an atmosphere of repression and paranoia, now known as the Red Scare. But it was the strong presence of the Invisible Knights of the Ku Klux Klan in Oklahoma that made anti-communism an integral part of the Protestant faith—the Klan opposed Catholicism and Judaism as much as it railed against communism.[2]

The KKK took their symbolic cues from the Christian crusades of medieval Europe—knights, white robes, and fiery crosses—and they borrowed the terminology of the period. They called themselves the Invisible Empire, Knights, Dragons, and Wizards. By the time Hargis was a young man in the late 1940s, the Klan was in its decline in Oklahoma—but its potent mix of segregationist ideology, evangelical Protestantism, and anti-communism found a champion in the gifted young evangelist.

During the early part of the 1950s, Hargis traveled the country, lecturing on the many conspiracies facing Americans, like communist infiltration and fluoridated water. Hargis' Christian Crusade floundered at first, until Hargis came up with a flamboyant plan in 1953: He would take Bible verses, tie them to tens of thousands of hydrogen-filled balloons, and

---

1 In 1917, the National Council of Defense organized a national propaganda system in each state. In Oklahoma, the councils functioned primarily to identify anyone who did not approve of America and its presence in the war. The Tulsa County Council of Defense was organized through the Tulsa Chamber of Commerce and was a particularly enthusiastic participant in extralegal vigilante activities.

2 Following the Tulsa Race Riot of 1921, the Ku Klux Klan in Tulsa owned a large temple or "klavern" called Beno Hall: "The Tulsa Benevolent Association [KKK] sold the storied building to the Temple Baptist Church in 1930. During the Depression, the building housed a speak-easy, then a skating rink, then a lumberyard, and finally a dance hall before radio evangelist Steve Pringle turned it into the Evangelistic Temple of the First Pentecostal Church. In his first revival meeting, Pringle introduced a little-known Enid preacher by the name of Oral Roberts, who worked his animated, faith-healing magic on the bare lot next door. Roberts impressed in the tent atmosphere and preached with his cohort inside the vast auditorium." Excerpted from "Beno Hall: Tulsa's Den of Terror," by Steve Gerkin, published in *This Land* Volume 2, Issue 11, September 15, 2011.

launch them from Chalms, Germany, with hopes that the balloons would land over the Iron Curtain. His idea managed to attract the support of the International Council of Christian Churches,[3] which helped fund and realize the project. The ICCC's support of Hargis brought him onto the world stage of an emerging post-war phenomenon, right-wing evangelism. Hargis was now poised to become the spokesman for a new movement that fused American politics with fundamentalist Christianity.

NO FIGHTING IN THE WAR ROOM

Hargis' crusade found many allies, but it was his collaboration with one man that proved to be a catalyst for the formation of America's religious right. A West Point graduate, Major General Edwin "Ted" Walker was a WWII Army hero and leader in the Korean War. In 1957, Walker found himself in command of the Arkansas Military District in Little Rock, just as the city's civil rights tensions were escalating.

As President Eisenhower prepared to use federal troops to enforce the desegregation of Little Rock's public schools, Walker was protesting the matter directly to Eisenhower; he opposed racial integration. Nevertheless, Walker followed Ike's orders and ended up receiving national praise for helping to integrate Little Rock; a 1957 cover of *Time* magazine portrayed him as a hero. Walker would later state that he led forces for the wrong side in Little Rock—he believed black students had no business attending white schools.

Before the integration of Little Rock, Walker was a garden-variety anti-communist, but when the incident at Little Rock propelled him into the political spotlight, he became radicalized. The same year, both Billy James Hargis and Texas oil tycoon H.L. Hunt were bombarding Arkansas radio waves with their rightist sermons—programs that aligned completely with the position of Senator Joseph McCarthy, who believed communists had infiltrated the U.S. government.[4] Hargis, however,

---

3 The International Council of Christian Churches was founded by Carl McIntire, a fundamentalist radio broadcaster from Durant, Oklahoma.

4 Hargis claimed that he had ghostwritten a number of speeches for Senator McCarthy.

advanced McCarthy's views even further, and preached that the civil rights movement was itself a godless communist plot.

In 1959, when Walker was still in command in Little Rock, he met with a conservative publisher named Robert Welch, who had recently founded the John Birch Society on the premise that Eisenhower was in reality a communist.[5] Walker, primed for years by Hargis' radio rants, joined the society and turned against the government. He attempted to resign from the Army citing concerns over communist encroachment in the U.S., but Eisenhower refused Walker's resignation and instead promoted him to the position of Commanding General of the 24th Infantry Division.

Convinced that his commander-in-chief was a dreaded communist, Walker nevertheless agreed to accept Eisenhower's offer. In October of 1959, Walker took command of 10,000 troops in Augsburg, Germany. Now at the height of his military career, Walker devised a plan to propagate his views to U.S. servicemen who trusted his leadership—views that came directly from the teachings of the John Birch Society and the Christian Crusade.

While Walker was commanding his troops in Europe, the political landscape in America was changing drastically. John F. Kennedy was the embodiment of everything Walker hated and feared: he was Catholic, he was liberal, and he was sympathetic to the United Nations. Camelot—as Kennedy's presidency came to be known—was, in Walker's eyes, evidence that the U.S government had succumbed to communism. Kennedy was sworn into the office of the presidency on January 20, 1961, just as Walker was establishing the guidelines for the strict regime that would govern his troops.

"Within my authority and within the requirements of training necessity, I devised an anti-communist training program second to none—called 'Pro Blue,'" Walker wrote in a memoir. "Equally important—I

---

5 The John Birch Society is a conservative political advocacy organization. One of its founders was Fred Koch, who also founded Koch Industries. Koch advised JBS President Robert Welch on numerous issues. He believed many U.S. companies had been infiltrated by communism, as evidenced by the presence of labor unions. Today, two of Koch's sons, David and Charles, are among the largest contributors to conservative political campaigns and causes in America.

organized a Psychological Warfare section with the Division to extend the Pro Blue Program through six echelons, to include every officer and soldier—chaplain, medic and rifleman."

Established as an official U.S. Army project in January of 1961, the Pro Blue Program was the result of Walker's fear and paranoia about communism; the official plan was turgid with reprogramming techniques. Under the Pro Blue Program, troops of the 24th Division were required to participate in a series of indoctrination methods that included publications from the John Birch Society and supplied by Hargis. Service members and their families were required to participate in 11 different special activities, including a six-hour training session involving "communist techniques," the Freedom vs. Communism program, the Freedom Speaks program, which offered lectures from Pro Blue writings, and the Ladies Club and NCO Wives Club, which were discussion groups featuring guest lectures on anti-communism.

In 1961, the threat of communism came within 90 miles of America. Publicly, the Cuban revolutionary Fidel Castro insisted that he was not a communist, but Cubans themselves began revolting against his socialist reforms. That spring, communist countries came to Cuba's aid and squelched a U.S.-backed attempt to overthrow Castro's regime. The incident, known as the Bay of Pigs, cemented America's fear of Soviet encroachment, and that fear was promulgated through the upper echelons of the Department of Defense. Walker's Pro-Blue program confronted the threat of communism directly and aimed to "produce tough, aggressive, disciplined and spiritually motivated fighters for freedom."

The Pentagon admired Walker's program and planned to promote him to Lieutenant General in command of the 8th Corp in Texas.

"Dear Ted," wrote the Pentagon's Major General William Quinn, "One of our basic philosophies is that Commanders should tailor their troop information to their own ideas and needs. That is why we have followed the progress of your Pro-Blue with interest and with pleasure."

The intended promotion, however, never arrived. In April of 1961, a military-themed magazine *The Overseas Weekly* published an investigative report that detailed Walker's distribution of John Birch Society literature to the troops—readings that contained inflammatory material questioning the presidency and U.S. government policies.

A media controversy ensued.[6] Some outlets criticized Walker for his extreme views and suggested that military commanders had no business plying their troops with political propaganda; conservative outlets balked that politicians were muzzling the military. Finally, President John F. Kennedy himself weighed in on the matter:

> The discordant voices of extremism are heard once again in the land—men who are unwilling to face up to the danger from without are convinced that the real danger comes from within. They look suspiciously at their neighbors and their leaders. They call for a "man on horseback" because they do not trust the people.[7] They find treason in our finest churches, in our highest court, and even in the treatment of our water.[8] They equate the Democratic Party with the welfare state, the welfare state with socialism, and socialism with communism. They object quite rightly to

---

6 Hargis would later claim that a plot to smear Walker was hatched by the Kremlin because they feared what might happen if Walker gained more power in the military.

7 The Texas Minutemen were an extreme right-wing paramilitary group that supplied weapons to Cuban exile groups in Dallas and New Orleans. Walker has been often cited as its leader, though he denied being involved before the Warren Commission.

8 General Jack Ripper in the film *Dr. Strangelove* cites the fluoridation of America's water supply as evidence that communists had infiltrated the highest powers of government and were trying to destroy America's "precious bodily fluids." The character Ripper was based on General Curtis LeMay and Major General Edwin Walker. On November 22, 1963, *Dr. Strangelove* was set for its first screening. When news of President Kennedy's assassination reached Kubrick in California, he canceled the screenings and rescheduled the screenings for the following January. While waiting for the shock of the assassination to pass, Kubrick edited out a reference to "Dallas" in the film and changed it to "Vegas." The John Birch Society opposed the fluoridation of water, arguing that it was part of a communist plot to poison Americans. By 1960, about 50 million Americans were drinking fluoridated water, resulting in an estimate reduction of tooth cavities by 40%. Today, about 66% of the U.S. population drinks fluoridated water through their public water system. Hargis kept a file on fluoridation.

politics' intruding on the military—but they are anxious for
the military to engage in politics.

The Pentagon responded to political pressure by relieving Walker
of his command and transferring him to Germany. It would not be the
last time a Kennedy angered General Walker.

"When the administrators of federal government serve a higher
world government or a doctrine not provided by the people and the
Congress, there is no Constitutional President," Walker later reflected
in a small booklet. "With no President, there is no Commander in Chief
of the U.S. Armed Forces. I resigned."[9]

Walker left the Army on November 4, 1961. Instead of seeing it as
the end of his career, he sensed America was ripe for a political insur-
gency, and that he could help bring about a revolution of his own, one
that did not include communists or atheists. While in the military, Walker
enjoyed the support of countless personnel to help disseminate his ideas.
Now, with political aspirations in mind, he sought the support of an
organization that aligned with his sense of Americanism and anti-
communism. He needed the Christian Crusade.

THE CHRISTIAN CRUSADE GETS ON THE HUMP

In 1951, the *Harvard Business Review* published a quiet yet peculiar
essay by a business executive for James Grey Incorporated. In "Direct
Mail Advertising," Edward Mayer outlined a persuasive argument for
bombarding the American public with mail solicitations—a predecessor
of email spam techniques. It was an early-day manifesto that would
eventually become a cornerstone of the Billy James Hargis empire. Using
direct-mail marketing, Hargis began asking for small donations to be
sent to his ministry in Tulsa.

Throughout 1950s and early 1960s, Hargis' Christian Crusade built
momentum. During that period, Hargis hired a promising young Texan

---

9 Since Walker resigned instead of retired from the military, he relinquished
   his pension and military benefits. In 1982, President Ronald Reagan
   returned Walker to an active role status in the Army, allowing Walker to
   enjoy full benefits.

named Richard Viguerie. Armed with a keen understanding of databases, Viguerie devised mass mailings targeting donors who were likely to be fundamentalist separatists—the kind of people who would respond to antics like Hargis' balloon drops. With Viguerie's genius, Hargis reached a widening audience, but the Christian Crusade still needed an overall strategy that would propel it toward success. It was around this same time that Hargis met a publicist named Pete White, who had once helped the televangelist Oral Roberts build a successful ministry through the manipulation of mass media. By using the same strategies used by Roberts, combined with Viguerie's direct-mail ingenuity, Hargis' Christian Crusade rocketed from a small operation to a ministry that had "billings from $400 to $500K a year in 1963."[10] During this time period, Christian Echoes Ministry mailed an average of two thousand letters every day—many of those letters returning with a dollar or two stuffed in the envelope.

"Ours is purely an educational program," Hargis told the *Tulsa Tribune* from his Boston Avenue office decorated with gold-sprayed Joan of Arc statues. "We have the most extensive files anywhere on this matter of communism and we are trying to get that word to the people."

Hargis became more adept in rightist political rhetoric, which began earning him a national reputation as a conservative leader. In 1959, a Chicago-based organization called We, the People designated Billy James Hargis as its president. Founded by Henry T. Everingham to support conservative politicians, We, the People produced pamphlets promoting anti-communism and criticizing integration. In 1962, the organization held its first "T-Party" rally which aimed to end the "taxes, treason, and tyranny" of the political left. At that time, Hargis stepped down as president, ceding the position to Mormon leader Ezra Taft Benson, who referred to America's South as a "Negro Soviet Republic." Benson later served as president of The Church of Jesus Christ of Latter

---

10 Hendershot, Heather. *What's Fair on the Air: Cold War Right Wing Broadcasting and the Public Interest.* Pg 183.

Day Saints.[11] Today, We, the People stands as one of the earliest collusions in conservative politics between Christians and Mormons.

As the Christian Crusade ministry increasingly reached into mail-boxes and across airwaves, its message became more threatening to the civil rights movement. The FBI questioned Hargis over his involvement in the Arkansas school bombing plot and continued to monitor his activities. Hargis told his followers that the National Association for the Advancement of Colored People (NAACP) was a communist plot; he published a book called *The Negro Question: Communist Civil War Policy*, in which the author warned that "communists are deliberately maneuvering among the American Negroes to create a situation for the outbreak of racial violence;" he believed segregation was "one of God's natural laws;" he called Martin Luther King Jr. a communist-educated traitor and an "Uncle Tom for special interests." Despite the patronizing attitudes that Hargis held against African-Americans, he publicly asserted he was not a racist. It wasn't until Hargis joined forces with former Major General Edwin Walker, however, that racial bigotry became a common characteristic of the religious right.

OPERATION MIDNIGHT RIDE: TOO IMPORTANT TO BE LEFT TO THE GENERALS

Shortly after his resignation from the military, Edwin Walker began forging a friendship with fellow John Birch Society member Billy James Hargis. They agreed to go on a speaking tour of the U.S. together; Hargis would sermonize on the perils of communism at the national level and Walker would expound on the international threat. Walker parlayed these early lectures into political gain. He soon decided to run for governor of Texas and enjoyed the support of Dallas oilman H.L. Hunt. Walker ran under the Southern Democratic (Dixiecrat) ticket, though, and ended up in last place in the Democratic primary of February 1962.

Later that year, in September, Walker caught wind that the federal government planned to force the integration of an African-American

---

11 Marion Romney, a cousin to the father of politician Mitt Romney, was supposed to succeed Benson as president of the Church of Latter Day Saints but his health prevented him from doing so.

man, James Meredith, into the University of Mississippi. This was Walker's chance to retaliate against the government that had forced him to integrate Little Rock back in 1959. Walker took to the airwaves to instigate an insurrection against governmental control.

"I call for a national protest against the conspiracy from within," Walker declared. "Rally to the cause of freedom in righteous indignation, violent vocal protest, and bitter silence under the flag of Mississippi at the use of federal troops."

The next day, September 30, 1962, riots broke out on the university campus, resulting in hundreds being injured and two dead. Six federal marshals had been shot. Walker was immediately arrested and charged with sedition and insurrection against the United States.

Behind the closed doors of the FBI, however, government officials worried about Walker's mental health. Informants whispered that he appeared irrational during his public talks. The rumors were enough to compel U.S. Attorney General Robert F. Kennedy to order Walker placed under a 90-day psychiatric evaluation at a forensic center in Springfield, Missouri. Both the American Civil Liberties Union and prominent psychiatrist Thomas Szasz protested the hospitalization. Walker's attorney in Oklahoma City, Clyde Watts, fought the order of detention and was able to get Walker freed after only five days.

The detention radicalized Walker even further, but by siding with the racists during the Ole Miss riot, he began to cause concern amongst his allies.

"Walker has also been listening to advice from another source and refusing to pay attention to those who have tried to caution him," wrote Robert Welch, founder of the John Birch Society, adding that Walker could cause "very serious embarrassment to conservatives and the conservative cause in general."

In November of 1962, Walker stood before a grand jury regarding his role in the Ole Miss riot. His mental health was called into question and his role in the riot scrutinized, yet one of the most important black witness, Reverend Duncan Grey Jr., was never called to testify. The all-white Mississippi grand jury chose not to indict Walker.

Energized by the perceived escape from governmental injustice, Walker teamed up once again with Billy James Hargis. This time, they planned a 12-week, 29-city speaking tour starting in Memphis,

Tennessee, in late February of 1963. They called their series "Operation Midnight Ride," and planned to use the talks to create a larger support base. At this point, Hargis' Christian Crusade had grown to a monthly budget of $75,000—but that money wasn't necessarily representative of a large audience. Hargis told the *New York Times* that most of his funding came from oil companies.[12]

While Hargis and Walker were trying to push the general population to the right, they were also galvanizing the extreme fringes of conservatism with their neo-confederate message. According to Walker's FBI files, the Ku Klux Klan sponsored Operation Midnight Ride in both South Carolina and Arkansas.[13] Throughout America, Hargis and Walker preached against the evils of communism and invited popular right-wing speakers like Benjamin Gitlow, former Army chief of intelligence General Charles Willoughby, and Congressman John Rousselot to join them. The FBI reported that in Washington, D.C., there were about 100 attendees of Operation Midnight Ride and all of them were white.[14] While many inflammatory statements were made at the meetings, the FBI seemed most alarmed by Walker's rhetoric. In their files, the FBI deemed Walker a presidential threat probably due to Walker's proclivity to charge presidents as communist leaders and deny them allegiance; there may have been more serious reasons.[15]

---

12 It should be noted that at the Washington, D.C., stop for Operation Midnight Ride Hargis stated he had never received a penny from Texas oilman H.L. Hunt.

13 Walker's ties to the Klan ran deep. In 1964, he was the main speaker for Americans for the Preservation of the White Race in Brookhaven, Mississippi. A year later, in 1965, the Imperial Wizard of the United Klans of America offered Walker the position of Grand Dragon of the UKA of Texas. Walker turned the offer down.

14 According to Hargis' recollection 30 years later, 2,000 people attended the first evening of Operation Midnight Ride in Washington, D.C. He also stated that he and Walker had toured 100 cities and that their rallies were attended by over 100,000 people.

15 The FBI kept Walker under regular surveillance following his resignation from the Army. Please refer to footnote 17 & 20 for additional motives the FBI had to monitor Walker's activities.

More than 4,000 people attended the last stop of Operation Midnight Ride in Los Angeles in early April of 1963.[16] Members of the John Birch Society, which had taken over the Young Republicans organization, welcomed the speakers. They presented Walker with a plaque calling him the "greatest living American," and they listened patiently while Hargis delivered an almost two-hour-long talk. The entire operation was a smashing success, or in the recent words of conservative talk show host Bill O'Reilly, "a Paul Revere-like barnstorming tour."

As Hargis and Walker fomented fears of communism, they could not have anticipated their agitation of one particularly troubled man in Dallas. Lee Harvey Oswald, a former Marine, had recently purchased a 6.5mm Carcano Model 91/38 rifle by mail order. Oswald had been following Walker closely enough to formulate an opinion that Walker was a fascist. He had also cased Walker's Dallas residence at 4011 East Turtle Creek Boulevard and took photos of the house. According to the FBI's questioning of Oswald's wife, Marina, Oswald took a bus to Walker's house on April 10, 1963, just days after the first leg of Operation Midnight Ride ended. Hidden in bushes about 100 feet away, Oswald waited until the moment was right and fired a shot through Walker's window, barely missing his head. Walker glanced around, thinking at first that a firecracker had been tossed into the room. Oswald claimed to Marina that

---

16 One week prior to the finale of Operation Midnight Ride in Los Angeles, a bombing destroyed the offices of the American Association for the United Nations in nearby Encino. The executive director blamed the bombing on the incitement of UN fearmongering by extremists; it was no secret that Walker and Hargis vehemently opposed the UN.

he fled the scene on foot and took a bus home, but other records suggest that he may have acted with two other accomplices.[17][18]

"Nothing in my 50-year career of standing up for Christ and fighting Satanic communism equals the success of that undertaking," Hargis would later reminisce about the tour.

With Operation Midnight Ride behind them, Walker and Hargis turned their aspirations to the national political races, making it clear that their choice for president was the libertarian senator Barry Goldwater. In August of 1963, Martin Luther King Jr. delivered his momentous "I Have a Dream" speech in Washington, D.C.; its hopeful message of peace and unity was in direct opposition to Walker and Hargis' aggressive calls for civil uprising. Two months later, in October of 1963, Walker attended a conference in Dallas in which he once again bashed President Kennedy and his policies. He was probably unaware that Lee Harvey Oswald was in the audience listening.

Hargis and Walker reunited for another tour of Operation Midnight Ride, this time throughout Texas during the month of November. On November 17th in Dallas, they were joined by Alabama's segregationist governor, George Wallace, who opposed Kennedy's plan to run on a Democratic ticket. It was well known to many that Kennedy would soon be in Texas campaigning for the '64 election.

"There were concerns among people close to Kennedy about his traveling to Dallas," says historian Robert Dallek, "because the city had a reputation for being the bastion of the right wing."

---

17 Walker's conflicting testimonies, actions, and activities surrounding the Kennedy assassination have created a number of challenges for researchers and historians. Here's what we do know: According to FBI records, Walker was informed shortly after his assassination attempt that the shooter was Lee Harvey Oswald, and that Oswald was likely not alone—yet before the Warren Commission, Walker denied knowing any of this prior to the Kennedy assassination. Not long after the attempt on his life, Walker hired two detectives from Oklahoma City to pose as men seeking to kill Walker. The detectives attempted to entrap a man named William Duff, a former live-in friend of Walker's (there were several). Duff accepted the hit, but then turned around and called the FBI. Duff also passed a polygraph test denying that he tried to shoot Walker, and the case against Duff was dropped.

18 Hargis believed that Fidel Castro ordered Lee Harvey Oswald to shoot Walker.

With the bulk of their energies devoted to vitriolic political speeches and publications, both Hargis and Walker fostered an environment where an assassination could occur.

According to Warren Commission reports, Walker was involved in two controversial printings criticizing Kennedy in November of 1963: an advertisement in *Dallas Morning News*, which stated "Welcome Mr. Kennedy," that accused Kennedy of communist sympathies, and "Wanted for Treason," a handbill that mimicked FBI wanted posters, with front and profile views of Kennedy. Prior to Kennedy's arrival in Dallas, Walker made the extravagant gesture of flying three flags upside down in front of his house—the international distress signal.

On November 22, 1963, Kennedy was assassinated at 12:30 p.m.[19] Following 10 months of investigation, the Warren Commission concluded that Lee Harvey Oswald, acting alone, shot and killed the president.[20]

"Our hearts, as a Christian people, go out to Mrs. Kennedy and her family, as well as to our new president," Hargis wrote in December of '63. "We stand as one man in disbelief that an enemy of our country could be so brazen in our midst."

Soon after Kennedy's assassination, Walker flew his flags right side up and at full mast, in defiance of the traditional half-mast position declared during times of national mourning.

BEFORE ALL THE FACTS ARE IN

Throughout the 1960s, Hargis' Christian Crusade enjoyed tremendous success, but not without its challenges. The Internal Revenue Service began its battle with Hargis, alleging that the Christian Crusade over-

---

19 At the exact time of Kennedy's assassination, both Hargis and Walker were passengers in different airplanes. Hargis was en route from Los Angeles to San Diego; Walker was between New Orleans and Shreveport.

20 In 1962, a former Castro sympathizer turned CIA informant named Harry Dean infiltrated the John Birch Society. He claimed that society members Walker and John Rousselot hired two gunmen to kill John F. Kennedy, and that they planned to frame Lee Harvey Oswald. Dean, however, could not produce any evidence to substantiate his claim.

stepped the political boundaries of a religious organization.[21] Undeterred, Hargis continued building his empire and publishing tracts, pamphlets and books. He started a foundation for missionaries, and created an anti-abortion organization.

In 1971, Hargis founded American Christian College and changed the mission of the Christian Crusade. No longer would it focus on external problems (anti-communism), but instead "internal moral problems" like drug use, the sexual revolution, and "Satan worship." He remained incredibly productive and financially successful, and rightfully referred to Tulsa as the Christian "Fundamentalist Capital of the World."

That world met its Doomsday when, in 1974, *Time* magazine accused Hargis of sexual misconduct with several of his Bible college students, both female and male. The incident forced Hargis' resignation from the college.

"It was a really challenging time for our family," recalls Hargis' daughter, Becky Frank, who now serves as the president of the Tulsa Chamber of Commerce. "I think Mom and Dad did a really beautiful job working through all of those things." As an owner of a Tulsa-based public relations firm, Frank helps religious organizations manage crises through their faith-based consulting services. Among the firm's more conservative clients are Oral Roberts University, which faced a major financial scandal, and Victory Christian Center, a Tulsa megachurch currently embroiled in a child-rape investigation.

"Several of our team members have first-hand experience in working for faith-based universities and organizations, both inside and as a consultant," boasts the firm's website. "The team understands the culture and knows the challenges. Not only do they understand where you are—chances are, they've been in your shoes."

Not long after Hargis' scandal, General Walker fondled an undercover policeman in the restroom of a public park in Dallas and was arrested for public lewdness. Twice. Walker pleaded no contest and paid

---

21 The tenth circuit court of appeals eventually upheld a ruling in 1972 that caused Hargis' Christian Crusade to lose its tax exempt status. Other churches have since lost their tax exempt status for participating in political campaigns.

a fine; Hargis denied the allegations of sexual misconduct yet told a reporter that he was "guilty of a sin but not the sin I was accused of."[22]

The American Christian College closed its doors in 1977.

The allegations of Walker's attempted assassination by Oswald remains one of the most fascinating and obfuscated subplots related to the Kennedy assassination. That connection haunted Walker his entire life; his personal papers are replete with Freedom of Information Act requests that petition for the release of government files surrounding the assassination. Walker died of lung cancer on Halloween day, 1993.

"My heart is sad today. I lost one of my best friends Sunday," Hargis said in a televised tribute, adding "I never had a greater friend than General Edwin A. Walker; I never knew a greater patriot."

The many political and religious figures who associated with Hargis continue to shape America's conservative landscape today. Hargis' mail-order apprentice Richard Viguerie helped establish the Young Americans for Freedom, a conservative activism program for youth. Viguerie later became a pioneer of direct-mail politics and one of the GOP's most successful fundraisers.[23] Conservative talk radio hosts like Rush Limbaugh, Bill O'Reilly, Sean Hannity, and Glenn Beck all borrow—knowingly or not—from Hargis' pioneering speaking style and Old South ideology. Former American Christian College president David Noebel, a fellow "Bircher," authored numerous books that argued against perceived evils such as rock music, homosexuality, and most recently, communism.

Hargis continued his ministry until his death from complications related to Alzheimer's disease in 2004. His son, Billy James Hargis II,

---

22 During much of the Red Scare, homosexuality was often conflated with communism. David Johnson, author of *The Lavender Scare: The Cold War Persecutions of Gays and Lesbians in the Federal Government*, says "The politicians behind the Lavender Scare asserted that homosexuals were susceptible to blackmail by enemy agents and so could be coerced into revealing government secrets. In other words, the official rationale wasn't that homosexuals *were* communists but that they could be *used* by communists."

23 In 2004, Viguerie commented to the *New York Times* that Karl Rove was one of his direct-mail marketing competitors in Austin. Rove employed the same strategies that Viguerie pioneered in order to help mobilize the religious right in George W. Bush's favor.

continues the Christian Crusade online, though publications are some-what irregular.

NOTE: *Research for this article was conducted with the help of Special Collections at the University of Arkansas Libraries in Fayetteville, the Dolph Briscoe Center for American History, University of Texas at Austin, and the Eagle Forum Archives and Library in St. Louis, Missouri. Special thanks to independent researchers Ernie Lazar and Paul Trejo for their assistance.*

TWO

CONVICTION AND TRANSFORMATION

DEATH'S YELLOW DOOR

A former Associated Press reporter, who's witnessed 16
executions, writes about life inside the death chamber

By *Kelly Kurt*

We may be indifferent to the death penalty and not declare
ourselves either way so long as we have not seen a
guillotine with our own eyes. But when we do, the shock
is violent, and we are compelled to choose sides, for
or against.

—Victor Hugo, *Les Miserables*

Within the maze of oppressive gray halls of the Oklahoma State Penitentiary's H unit, the door that leads to the death chamber
seems as out of place as a birthday balloon. It is yellow. Bright, daisy
yellow. The color is unnerving.

It's almost 6 p.m. when I cross the threshold with six other media
witnesses. Gary Roland Welch already lies strapped to a gurney a few
feet away behind the window of the adjoining room. He's hidden from
view by a closed shade. We take our seats on a row of metal folding
chairs and listen for lingering signs of death row's sendoff. The sound
began 10 minutes earlier, a forceful clanging and rhythmic tapping that
echoed through the concrete corridors. CLANG. CLANG. Ping. CLANG.

CLANG. Ping. This is how other condemned men pay their respects—by slamming their cell doors with their feet or tapping their commodes. Death row's goodbye sounds like someone trying to break out.

Six stone-faced men—prosecutors, law officers, and a state official—take seats in front of us. Behind us, behind one-way glass, sit three family members of the man Welch killed. No one is here on Welch's behalf. My stomach churns as we sit in silence, waiting for the mini blind to rise.

When the shade finally goes up, Welch is looking at us. His thick body is bound to the gurney—legs, arms, chest, shoulders. Tubes run from his arms and disappear into the wall behind him. I glimpse a colorful tattoo on a forearm. A graying ginger beard covers his jaw and chin. He turns his head and his eyes meet mine.

In a matter of minutes, the 49-year-old will choke on his last word and die, marking the nation's first execution of 2012. For now, he lifts his head, straining to see each witness through the glass. His eyes reach the row's end, and something unexpected happens.

The condemned man suddenly smiles.

And then, he winks.

I am here to witness a homicide. Not a murder, which is a crime. Even the governor is in on this death.

I've been here before and this is what I've seen every time: A brightly lit room. A clock on the wall. A warden standing with clasped hands. A prison official on a black wall phone with a long coiling cord, ready in case the governor hands down a last-second reprieve. What I've never seen: a reprieve. Or the three executioners hidden behind the wall. No one sees them. They arrive wearing hoods on their heads and faces to cloak their identities.

I am told that some people see the face of Jesus in the pattern of the concrete wall next to the yellow door, but I've never seen that either.

Sometime before Welch's January 5 execution date, I realize that I have lost track of how many men I've seen die here. Since 1915, Oklahoma has executed 177 men and three women. The oldest was 74. The youngest, 18. Ninety-seven died by lethal injection, 82 by electrocution, and one by hanging. Most of the executions I witnessed took place in the late 1990s and early 2000s, a time when Oklahoma's death chamber was one of the nation's busiest. Welch's execution, I later learn, is my 16th.

More than 60 percent of Americans favor the death penalty. But very few people actually have witnessed a modern execution.

At one time, executions in Oklahoma were public. A crowd of 30 or 40 onlookers crammed into the penitentiary known as Big Mac to watch the warden flip the switch on Old Sparky, the heavy wooden electric chair with its leather straps and helmet. Newsmen and sightseers, even children, were there, says Dale Cantrell, a 28-year Big Mac veteran who serves as the prison's de facto historian. A 1934 story by the Associated Press described what they heard and saw—"a sudden hum of a motor, a violent stiffening of the body." A crackdown on the circus-like atmosphere ultimately brought a section of law entitled "Persons Who May Witness," which largely slammed the door on public access. It did provide that "reporters from recognized members of the news media will be admitted upon proper identification, application, and approval of the warden."

Sister Helen Prejean, the death penalty abolitionist whose book *Dead Man Walking* spawned an Oscar-winning film and an opera that will open in Tulsa this month, predicts more Americans would turn against the death penalty if executions were more open. Responding to arguments that public executions could "coarsen" society, she wrote:

> An execution is ugly because the premeditated killing of a human being is ugly. Torture is ugly. Gassing, hanging, shooting, electrocuting or lethally injecting a person whose hands and feet are tied is ugly. And hiding the ugliness from view and rationalizing it numbs our minds to the horror of what is happening. This is what truly 'coarsens' us.

Witnessing executions did start to feel like ugly business to me—but not at first.

It was part of my job as a reporter for the Associated Press, the one organization Corrections Department policy guarantees by name to claim one of the 12 seats reserved for the media. I was surprised to discover that I could witness a man's dying breath, write about it in detail, and later drive home, with my eyes on the road and my mind on dinner. Only once did a dead man haunt my sleep. I opened my eyes and saw him hanging by a meat hook above my bed. When I awoke fully, I was sitting up, staring at the ceiling fan.

With every execution, however, came a family's story of deep and lasting loss. The victim's survivors told me again and again how their lives had been shattered by a single act of violence. Dusty Miller, who was left to raise three children alone, marveled that a killer "could meet somebody like Gwen [his wife] and still make a decision that the world didn't need her anymore." The parents of Michael Houghton and Laura Lee Sanders, who were burned alive in the trunk of a car, endured more than 15 years of court proceedings before witnessing the lethal injection of one of the killers. The niece of Muskogee grocer Claude Wiley described his smile and kindness. He often delivered food to the poor and home-bound, until the day he made a delivery to a home where a man was waiting for him behind the door with a baseball bat.

Sometimes an elderly woman, the mother of the condemned, sat in front me, clutching a tissue and weeping with loss, too. Jim Fowler, himself the son of a murder victim, saw his son executed for killing three people in a botched robbery, saying afterward in a shaking voice, "It makes your gut sick to see your boy die."

Some people call capital punishment justice. Others call it barbaric. In the death chamber, I feel a pervasive sadness and sense of futility. When people ask me what I've learned about the death penalty, I tell them the only thing I know conclusively: It doesn't take away the sadness or bring anyone back. But it does shut a person up.

What I have heard:

A cop's killer begging his victim's family, "Forgive me as the Lord has forgiven me."

A woman's weeping for her condemned son, whose crimes included the murder of his sister.

The warden announcing, "Let the execution begin."

Victims' families clapping after a five-time killer is declared dead.

What I have never heard: a condemned man cry.

———————

Welch turns his scraggly bearded face toward the ceiling and speaks.

"I was just going to ask everybody if they could hear my brothers out there," he says, referring to death row's clanging. "I know it's kind of quiet now, but I want to acknowledge that my brothers are here for me to send me off on my journey. They are here on my behalf."

Welch claimed he killed Robert Hardcastle in self-defense on the evening of August 25, 1994. He said he went to the 35-year-old's Miami home in pursuit of drugs and ended up fighting for his life after Hardcastle came at him with a knife.

"My intentions were never to kill him," he told a *McAlester News-Capital* reporter during his clemency hearing in December. "But I also didn't intend for him to kill me either."

The jury believed the prosecution's story—that Welch assaulted Hardcastle in his home and then he and a co-conspirator, Claudie Conover, chased him into a ditch. There were multiple witnesses, including a family taking their 11-year-old to football practice, who saw Welch stab Hardcastle repeatedly with a knife and, when it broke, slash him with a broken beer bottle.

The first police officer on the scene, Officer Jim Gambill, found Hardcastle covered in blood sitting up in the ditch with his clothes in shreds. The officer recognized him. He and Hardcastle had grown up playing Little League ball together.

"Jim," Hardcastle said, "Gary Welch did this shit to me. Get that motherfucker."

Hardcastle then asked for some water and soon after fell on his back and died. He left behind 2-year-old twin sons.

"A big hole remains in our hearts that will never go away," Hardcastle's parents wrote to the Pardon and Parole Board, which rejected clemency by a vote of 3-2. "To know justice has been served gives us some closure to the agony we have had to endure."

"Closure" is a word that means different things to people whose lives have been turned upside down by crime. Grieving families after the Oklahoma City bombing described it as justice or, in some cases, vengeance. For some, it meant the end of round after round of court appeals or at least the silencing of the killer. Some described closure as relief from intense grief. Brooks Douglass, the man who authored Oklahoma's law allowing victims' families to watch executions, told me for an AP story that he did not find immediate solace after watching one of the men who killed his parents die for the crime. But, he said, the execution did restore his faith in the justice system.

The Supreme Court struck down the death penalty in 1972, finding that the power of juries to decide whether a defendant should live or die for a crime resulted in arbitrary and capricious sentencing. States brought capital punishment back, rewriting their statutes and giving judges and juries new sentencing guidelines.

But Lyn Entzeroth, who teaches a course on capital punishment at the University of Tulsa's law school, believes the system remains flawed.

"To me there is no way of discerning what murder case gets death and what murder case doesn't," she says. She notes a report by the Death Penalty Information Center that shows county-by-county discrepancies in how often the death penalty is sought.

Fifteen counties, including Oklahoma County, were responsible for 30 percent of the nation's total executions since 1976. Exclude Texas (with nine counties on that list), and Oklahoma County tops the list with prosecutions resulting in 36 executions since 1976. Tulsa County was 14th with eight executions.

"The discretion of that prosecutor in that county can have a huge effect," says Entzeroth, who also co-authored a death penalty casebook used in law schools. "When Bob Macy was the DA in Oklahoma County, there were a large number of death sentences sought. That's changed since then."

Support for the death penalty remains high—61 percent, according to a 2011 Gallup poll. But that number represents the lowest level of support since 1972 and a significant decline from an all-time high of 80 percent in 1994.

A spate of exonerations tied to DNA evidence may account in part for the decline. Evidence of innocence has brought the exonerations of 140 people on death row since 1973, with 66 of those occurring since 1999, according to the DPIC. Four states in four years—New Mexico, New York, New Jersey, and Illinois—have effectively abolished the death penalty. And late last year, Oregon Governor John Kitzhaber declared a moratorium on the death penalty, saying he refused "to be a part of this compromised and inequitable system."

Along with concerns about wrongful convictions, the option of life without parole sentencing is changing the debate, Entzeroth says.

"Because someone has committed a horrible murder, we as a society would like that person incapacitated, not back out on the street some day," she says. "The option of life parole gives that option, that security."

———————

What no one saw (other than the robbers): Who pulled the trigger that fired the bullets into my friend, Michael Fifer.

Mike left college to stay home with his terminally ill mother. Years later, he ended up working the graveyard shift at a Circle K in Tulsa to pay the bills. He didn't get to choose his final words on November 30, 1991, the night the gunman pulled open the convenience store door. He died facedown on the floor, shot in the neck and back. Two teens, Johnny Davis and Eric Johnson, each accused the other of being the shooter. Both received no-parole life terms for the killing, though Johnson's was later reduced by an appeals court. A prosecutor said the jury gave then 17-year-old Davis the no-parole term to ensure he "didn't get out."

But he found a way out.

In 1996, Davis slid through 6-inch bars and climbed four stories down a homemade rope to escape the maximum-security floor of a private prison in Texas. He was on the run for four days.

Davis is now 37 years old. Mike died at age 25.

A murder that touches your life changes you forever. I still carry the weight of it. At some point, I stopped using the word "closure" in news stories.

———————

Hours before I'm in the death chamber, I stand in the threshold of my closet. It sounds frivolous, but deciding what to wear to an execution is worse than deciding what to wear to a funeral. I reject the new black-and-white striped shirt that my kids dubbed "the burglar shirt." The sweater I got for Christmas seems too bright. I end up in a white shirt and black pants. When I stop for a soda to carry me to McAlester, the store clerk comments, "Black and white? You must be a waitress." I shake my head. He tries again. "Band leader?" I leave him squirming. How do you tell someone you dressed like this to watch a man be put to death?

Freedom meets its end on a long, winding road at McAlester's edge before I even get to the Oklahoma State Penitentiary. If there's a road to perdition, it's this one.

I pass a minimum-security prison, the county jail, a juvenile detention center, an animal shelter, and a street named Electric Avenue on the way to the prison gate. Built in 1904, Big Mac rises like a medieval fortress behind 30-foot, whitewashed walls topped with coils of razor-tipped wire. I glimpse armed guards watching from a prison tower as I drive through the gate, past the warden's house where Christmas lights twinkled one December when I came here for two executions in seven days.

Executions used to take place at midnight. That meant that after the U.S. Supreme Court rejected an inmate's final appeal, we had time to eat dinner. While the condemned ate his last meal, journalists, photographers, prosecutors, and visiting law officers rushed to Pete's Place or some other Italian eatery in Krebs for heaping plates of pasta and lamb fries. In the late-night darkness, I scurried back to the lockup, burdened by too many carbs and the dread of what was to come.

I was at the prison as a student journalist on September 10, 1990, when Charles Troy Coleman became the first man executed in Oklahoma following the reinstatement of the death penalty. It was the inauguration of lethal injection, too. Reporters, TV crews, and photographers jammed the prison's visitation center—a one-room building that converts to a media center on execution nights. These days, often only two or three reporters come to witness. TV crews make rare appearances.

This time, when I pull open the door to the media center, more than six years have passed since I last saw an execution. Jerry Massie, the Corrections Department's public information officer, is inside waiting like always. He's been the media wrangler at every execution I've witnessed, and there's something comforting about finding him here, sitting in front of a tray of chocolate chip cookies and bottled waters. More than once after an execution, I've heard him quietly ask some reporter, "You doing okay?" But Massie is also the gatekeeper to getting inside and tends to give the impression that causing him trouble is a bad idea.

Tonight, there are seven media witnesses, four of whom have never seen an execution. Massie goes over the rules. We can't take anything in. No recorders. No notebooks. No pens. No cell phones. (The phones, we're later told by prison spokesman Terry Crenshaw, can sell for $1,000 inside the lockup.) And if we need to go to the bathroom, we better do it now "because once you get to the H unit, it's almost impossible to use a facility," Crenshaw says. We pile into two vans that drive to the back of the prison where the modern H unit crouches in the earth like a bunker. Inside, a female guard tells me to take off my shoes, turn around, spread my arms and turn my palms up. She pats me down, first from the back. "Coming around," she says, as her hands glide over me searching for contraband.

We put on our shoes and enter a barred holding area. The heavy cell door behind us slowly rolls shut and locks with a reverberating KUH-CHUNG. In a prison, you wait for doors to open, and slowly the one in front of us does. We are led to the law library, a rectangular room where inmates can work on their cases enclosed in small cells with desks.

"Do you have the notebooks?" I ask Crenshaw.

The prison usually provides us with notebooks and pencils, but this time they're missing. He sends an officer in pursuit of them. The clanging from death row begins, and Crenshaw notes it is louder than usual. The notebooks arrive. There's a knock at the library door. It's time.

———————————

What we report: No one says much of anything on the ride back to the media center after Welch is dead. I look out the window and notice the moon, a five-eighths moon, shining on prison buildings. The seven of us reassemble in the media center to piece together what we saw and heard.

Who did he wink at? "Was he winking at the DA?" I ask, thinking of the case's prosecutor who was sitting at the end of the row where Welch directed his smile.

"No," says the reporter from the McAlester paper, who had previously had a lengthy interview with Welch. "I smiled at him."

Massie, overhearing, puts his head in his hands.

"Should I not have done that?" she asks.

"Probably not," Massie sighs.

Over the next few minutes we scan our scribbled notes and contribute bits and pieces of Welch's last statement. None of us got it down in its entirety.

The reconstruction goes like this:

Me: "I had, 'I want to acknowledge ... ' Um."

Second reporter: "' ... that my brothers are here with me ... ' "

Third reporter: "'here with me to send me off on my journey. They've already given me my sendoff ... ' "

Me: "I heard 'my little sendoff.' "

A fourth reporter questions the order of sentences. We re-examine our notes. We move a sentence.

Everyone works to get it just right, although it's doubtful anyone will ever question those final words. You can't libel a dead man.

The clock on the death chamber wall reads 6:04 p.m. Welch finishes his last statement saying, "They've already given me my little sendoff. So let's get it on because that's what we're here for."

Each of the three executioners injects a different drug. The first, phenobarbital, is the same sedative used to euthanize pets. It causes unconsciousness. The second, vecuronium bromide, a paralyzing agent, halts respiration. The third, potassium chloride, stops the heart.

"Let the execution begin," says the warden, setting off the process.

Immediately, Welch launches into a chant, his chest heaving against the straps:

"Valhalla. Odin. Slay the beast!" he says rapidly, almost shouting. In Norse mythology, Valhalla is the great hall in which the one-eyed god Odin receives the souls of slain warriors. The hall has 540 doors. "Valhalla. Odin. Slay the beast! Valhalla. Odin. Slay ... the ... beast. Valhalla." He slurs and chokes. "O...."

The next several minutes are awkwardly silent as we stare into the sterile room. My thoughts turn to the details of the crime that was so heinous jurors thought a man should die for it. I picture Robert Hardcastle lying slashed along a road, bleeding from nine stab wounds and a dozen other serious cuts. He died eyes open, his head on green grass, no chance to say goodbye to his sons. I see Welch, his eyes closed, releasing a slight snore and then going still. His face slowly changes from pink to purple to gray. There is no terror in this quiet scene, except for the fact I know this man is tied to the bed and his life has just been taken.

The physician steps forward, checks for a pulse and finding none, looks at the clock. "Time of death," he pronounces, "6:10 p.m."

The mini blind goes down. The door opens. We file out into the darkness.

I've walked through death's yellow door 16 times to see 16 men die. They were Benjamin Brewer, Michael Edward Long, Stephen Edward Wood, Scotty Lee Moore, Bobby Ross, Gary Alan Walker, Charles Adrian Foster, Gregg Francis Braun, Mark Andrew Fowler, Vincent Allen Johnson, Alvie James Hale, Daniel Juan Revilla, Scott Allen Hain, Robert Don Duckett, Kenneth Eugene Turrentine, and Gary Roland Welch. The crimes that brought them here claimed 30 innocent men, women, and children. Every story has two sides and, in the death chamber, I've sat sandwiched between them.

Here's what else I have seen: When the execution is over and the mini blind goes down, you still see a face looking at you from the window of the death chamber: the other part of the story.

That face is your own.

BLIND SPOT

How the murder of a Fortune 500 CEO led to the downfall of America's most notorious mob boss, Whitey Bulger

By *Laurence J. Yadon*

"I'VE BEEN ARRESTED!" Gasko croaked over the cell phone as the FBI agents watched his every move. Seconds earlier, a neighbor had scolded the officers for the way they surprised and roughed up the old man in the storage area of his seedy Santa Monica apartment complex. She noticed that Gasko seemed ashamed as he looked down at the grimy floor. Soon, Gasko's "wife," Carol, would also be sporting silver bracelets.

When Osama Bin Laden was killed in May 2011, bald, bearded 80-something Charles Gasko knew he was in trouble. With Bin Laden gone, Gasko became the most hunted man on America's fugitive list thanks, he thought, to those rich cake-eaters in Tulsa.

It wasn't much of a life anyway, if one of the Gasko neighbors could be believed. He couldn't even lift a laundry basket or keep up with Carol on the Santa Monica boardwalk nearby. Charles and Carol lived like lower-middle class pensioners getting by on next to nothing, trapped in four small rooms with bare, bashed-in walls that hadn't been painted in years. They walked around on dirty gray carpet installed in the '80s.

At least the price was right, thanks to rent control. The Gaskos paid only about $900 a month, a bargain in pricey Santa Monica. The place was dark most of the time, thanks to the black curtains covering the windows facing a nearby luxury hotel, when Gasko wasn't window peeping. But unlike most pensioners, the Gaskos had nearly a million dollars in cash hidden away in their apartment at the Princess Eugenia.

They came for him on June 22, 2011, two days after the FBI rolled out a $2 million reward for the old man's arrest. Gasko had been ratted out by Miss Iceland 1974, a neighbor who noticed how well he had cared for an abandoned cat named Tiger. She'd called the authorities the day earlier from her summer home in Reykjavik the minute she recognized the Gaskos on television. But the tired old man who pretended to be losing a battle against Alzheimer's wasn't Charles Gasko after all. His real name was Bulger, which sounded vaguely German or Polish, but was really Gaelic. It meant "yellow belly."

Back in South Boston, they called him Whitey.

James Joseph "Whitey" Bulger grew up "in the shadow of Yankee Babylon," gazing at pale, distant towers that marked the boundaries of an ebbing Protestant ascendancy. Downtown Boston was bordered by mostly Catholic Poles, Lithuanians, Italians, and his own troublesome Irish. Close friends in "Southie" called him Jim. "We were in a *neighborhood,* an enclave, [from] which a trip downtown was considered 'going to Boston,'" Whitey's younger brother William B. "Billy" Bulger, remembered later.

Whitey was born in September 1929, the month before the Great Depression began. Billy came along less than five years later. Their old man worked as a railroader until two freight cars collided in a train yard with him in between. One arm was so badly mangled that a doctor barely looked at it before he started cutting. In those days before workers were compensated for on-the-job-injury, the Bulger family of eight was now condemned to poverty.

Young Billy loved books and politics. He became a university president, but his white-haired older brother preferred bookies and larceny. At first, Whitey worked alone. He eventually joined a minor street corner gang called the Shamrocks. After some time in a reformatory and the Air Force—from which he was honorably discharged in 1952, despite a spotty conduct record—Whitey took a federal fall for hijacking and armed robbery. During a nine-year sojourn through three federal prisons, he became a life-long friend of "The Choctaw Kid," Clarence Carnes—the pride of Daisy, Oklahoma, and youngest inmate ever sent to Alcatraz. Whitey was released in 1965.

He returned home and became an enforcer for the Killeens, the premier Irish mob in South Boston. Six years later, in 1971, the Killeens tangled with their rivals, the Mullens, in a deadly conflict prompted by a random, drunken brawl in which Donald Killeen bit off the nose of Mullen factionist Michael "Mickey" Dwyer. Although Killeen had the nose scooped out of a gutter, packed in ice and rushed to the Boston City Hospital where Dwyer lay moaning, the Second Irish War was on.

Whitey's first assignment during the second war was a disaster. He killed Mullen enforcer Paulie McGonagle; only it wasn't Paulie who ended up on ice. By mistake, Whitey (or his designated hitter) drilled Paulie's look-alike brother Donald, who some say wasn't even in the rackets. This got Whitey's boss, Billy O'Sullivan, killed in late March, 1971, prompting Whitey to make his move.

According to most accounts, Whitey approached Howie Winter to make a deal. Winter was the leader of the mostly Irish yet commendably diverse Winter Hill gang, named for a section of Somerville, a blue collar Boston suburb with the ambiance of Sand Springs. Winter (his name is pure coincidence) became leader of the Winter Hill gang in 1965, during the First Irish War, when gang founder James "Buddy" McLean was killed. That conflict began on Labor Day 1961, when McLaughlin gang luminary Georgie McLaughlin made a subtle pass at a girlfriend of Winter Hill gang associate Alex Rocco by pinching her breast. The casualties resulting from that flirtation included 60 dead mobsters and hangers-on.

But in mid-May 1971, the traditional tale relates, Whitey killed his own boss, Don Killeen, to end the second war, survive, and move up. Other sources insist that Killeen was done in by the Mullens. Whoever pulled the trigger, Howie Winter and the Mafia, represented by the Partriarca crime family, soon mediated a merger of the Mullens and the Killeens into the Winter Hill gang.

Beginning in 1973, despite a declared moratorium on violence, Whitey and his associates killed a number of old Mullen rivals now operating within the newly merged Winter Hill gang, notably including Paulie McGonagle, the rival Whitey had tried to kill two years earlier.

The next year, Whitey began regularly teaming up with Stephen Flemmi, another associate of the Winter Hill gang. Five years later, in 1979, Flemmi and Whitey ascended to Winter Hill leadership when Howie Winter and his entire management cadre were rolled up and jailed for fixing horse races, with charges against Whitey and Flemmi quietly dropped. This was no coincidence, since Flemmi and Bulger were FBI informants.

Whitey may have been a lucky charm, but a problem was brewing 1,600 miles away in Tulsa that required his attention. And that problem was another hard-charging Boston native three years older than Whitey who ran the Telex Corporation. His name was Roger Wheeler.

Even today, litigation-prone Roger Milton Wheeler is remembered in Tulsa as a brash, bold innovator. Stories of his rise from salesman to top-shelf executive—accounts of hallway firings, urban legends of altered contracts, and recollections of bluffs Wheeler ran against the Securities and Exchange Commission—are still told in midtown places where Tulsans of a certain age gather for morning coffee or evening grape.

Yet there is also his compassion for the most obscure Telex employees, and the quiet generosity that prompted him to rehabilitate a camp enjoyed by generations of Tulsa children once his fortune was made. Wheeler and his employees transformed Telex from a hearing aid and stereo equipment manufacturer into a computer peripheral powerhouse. The trim, volatile tycoon even challenged IBM in court and won $353 million at trial (although IBM won an $18 million counterclaim for industrial espionage). Eventually, the award to Telex was reversed and the case was settled with no cash changing hands in mid-October 1975, 72 hours before the Supreme Court in Washington was scheduled to announce whether or not it would hear a Telex appeal.

Since Telex admitted four months earlier that it did not have the cash to pay IBM the $18 million, some in the business press speculated that Telex had been on the verge of bankruptcy. Later, Wheeler had to be ordered to pay his own attorney about $1.3 million for litigating the losing case. But within months of the IBM deal, prospects for Telex began to improve.

Now a Fortune 500 CEO, Wheeler began buying and selling other successful businesses on the side. In the market for cash-generating gaming operations, in 1979 he purchased World Jai Alai Inc., a privately owned corporation founded by Bostonians in the '20s, with operations in Connecticut and Florida. Jai Alai resembles racquetball, with players wielding a long, funnel like scoop to catch and then release a ball into play. The teams are professionals paid out of the betting proceeds, making the sport perpetually ripe for "the fix." The Jai Alai ball travels with such dizzying speed that career-ending injuries are not unusual. At least four players have been killed playing Jai Alai since the 1920s.

First National Bank of Boston had recruited Wheeler for the deal. The descendants of the World Jai Alai founders were looking for a buyer just at the time Wheeler was in the market for businesses that threw off cash and lots of it. World Jai Alai was all of that, spewing out about six million dollars ($14 million today) over operating expenses every year.

In theory, once the loan was paid off in little more than eight years, the six million dollar annual cash boodle would all belong to Wheeler. The Boston bankers even offered to finance the whole $50 million deal themselves, with one catch. Current management, including Richard Donovan, and John Callahan, a former banker at First National, had to remain in place. Callahan was a certified public accountant with Winter Hill connections.

Acquaintances and family members opined years later that Wheeler may have known about the connections between organized crime and World Jai Alai before he made the deal. After all, it was unlikely that an astute businessman like Roger Wheeler could somehow miss or ignore how close his Connecticut Jai Alai operation was to several organized crime centers—places like Boston, New York, and Philadelphia, all less than 250 miles away. Newspaper and magazine accounts published years later would conclude that Wheeler did not understand or appreciate the risk of mob interference in World Jai Alai until it was too late and he was on the hook for the $50 million. And, according to these accounts, it was only then that he discovered that his profits were being skimmed daily.

However early Wheeler learned the full extent of mob involvement in World Jai Alai, by late 1980 he had discovered the size of the skim and began taking actions to protect his investment. According to one account, in February 1981, John Callahan called in Winter Hill assassin Johnny Martorano to deal with Wheeler.

There are several underworld versions of how the Wheeler assassination was arranged. If Martorano is to be believed, it all began over dinner with Callahan at Yesterday's Restaurant in Fort Lauderdale. Callahan complained he had a problem in Tulsa and needed help from Martorano, who owed him for favors done years before, although Whitey Bulger had to approve the action.

Martorano claimed in his memoirs that he hadn't been offered any money for the job, although he eventually received $50,000, which he split with Winter Hill associates. According to Martorano, Wheeler was killed because he would not sell World Jai Alai to Callahan. Eventually, Martorano claimed, Callahan offered Bulger and Flemmi a bonus skim of $10,000 a week to get rid of Wheeler.

A Winter Hill veteran named Joe McDonald agreed to drive the getaway car as a return favor to retired FBI agent H. Paul Rico, a World Jai Alai security man who was also allegedly part of the skim. According to Martorano, Rico provided the background information necessary to track and kill Wheeler.

Northeastern Oklahoma was not the hot, dry desert full of cowboys or hostile Indians Martorano or McDonald might have imagined back in South Boston. And, in late May 1981, Tulsa was flush with money. New power couples, some in their 30s or even younger, spent, dressed, bought, and built with lavish abandon. Tulsey Town was jumping all over again. The latest oil boom, then barely five years in the making, would never end — or so it seemed. And one big prize was membership at "the Hill."

Of course, you couldn't simply buy your way into Southern Hills Country Club, not without the necessary connections, manners, and social graces. At one time, you had to be white and Christian, although race and religion restrictions were eventually eliminated. Southern Hills, then scarcely 40 years old, was and is considered a monument to old Tulsa money. Although he came from "nothing," Roger Wheeler—by then a 20-year member—easily qualified as old money, having made his first big business deal in Tulsa 30 years earlier.

The assassins drove past the white 61st Street gatehouse as if they owned the place, meandering up the oak-lined road which climbed gently leftward past the championship golf course that Tiger Woods would praise years later, as had Jack Nicklaus and Arnold Palmer as young men.

Martorano and McDonald probably didn't notice the polo fields, skeet shooting range, or the bare grass where first-class stables and a riding arena had been before a tragic fire five years earlier. They were far too preoccupied with the assignment to appreciate the tidy gardens or the children at the pool basking in the sunlit spring afternoon.

Martorano had killed at least 18 people by then, many of them with a quick pistol shot to the back of the head in cars, trucks, bars and alleys, often in the company of the victim's friends. Most of the men Martorano killed never knew it was coming, but Roger Wheeler would be different.

A few days before, Martorano and McDonald had flown into Oklahoma City as "Richard Aucoin" and "John Kelly." They rented a car, drove the 120 miles or so to Tulsa, and stayed in a series of mediocre Tulsa motels. Their last stop was the aging and neglected Trade Winds West, which had once hosted presidential candidates. While they waited for the "hit kit" containing weapons, bullet proof vests, and assorted goodies to arrive from Southie, they used detailed information provided by former FBI agent H. Paul Rico to determine where best to assassinate the target.

They also looked for a good fast car to steal. The ideal "boiler" could be quickly driven away from the hit and dumped elsewhere to distract authorities while Martorano and McDonald highballed to Oklahoma City in their nondescript rental car. And when the bulky hit kit arrived at the downtown Tulsa bus station, the killers moved their plan forward. It had been shipped to "Joe Russo"—another prolific assassin then working in Boston, perhaps to deflect attention to the Mafia later.

Martorano had already decided they could not kill Wheeler at his mansion. The house, located at 1957 East 41st Street, is now hidden by a development, but was then fronted by a largely open, seven-acre estate that would have revealed the direction of their escape to witnesses. Nor was it practical to take him out at the Telex headquarters, high atop a hill surrounded by acres of bare ground some three miles east of the

Wheeler manse. So they decided to kill him where Wheeler likely would be most relaxed and least on his guard—after his regular Wednesday afternoon golf game at Southern Hills.

Ordinarily, Wheeler played with a foursome and capped the game with a Scotch and milkshake in the clubhouse. But today, he quickly showered and joked with golf shop manager George Matson about his score on the way out. He shot an 88 and lost five bucks. "These boys are killing me," Wheeler carped in jest, according to one news article.

Earlier, that Wednesday afternoon, May 27, Martorano and McDonald acquired a stolen Pontiac left for them at a large apartment complex near the country club and doffed disguises purchased at a Tulsa theatrical shop. They scouted the parking lot just behind the swimming pool, found the Cadillac they were looking for, and waited for Wheeler to appear so they could finish the job and fly back to Florida. That day, Wheeler had parked on the far southern edge of the asphalt next to a light pole, facing a small, placid pond surrounded by willows. They didn't have to wait long. Soon, the trim figure in a pin-striped business suit walked briskly out of the clubhouse past them towards the Caddy, already late for a meeting back at Telex.

Wheeler opened the door and climbed in, oblivious to Martorano rushing from behind on his left. Martorano testified a quarter century later that he grabbed the door to keep Wheeler from closing it and shot him between the eyes with a .38 snub-nosed pistol just as Wheeler jumped or fell backward into the seat. The pistol fell apart as it fired, dropping four bullets, but Martorano didn't stop to pick them up, although he managed to retrieve the cylinder. Or perhaps he left the bullets on or near Wheeler as a stark warning to others—a not uncommon occurrence in such a hit.

Once Martorano was back in the Pontiac, McDonald careened eastward out of the parking lot in a counterclockwise semicircle, passing the party barn called Snug Harbor and the tennis courts. Finally, after a sharp right turn, they sped beyond the eleventh hole of the golf course on their left and slipped out the country club gate into Harvard Avenue traffic. Although newspapers reported the pair promptly disappeared, within a few days an anonymous caller told police that they stopped long enough to pick up a second car on the residential road paralleling the winding contours of 61st Street to the north a few minutes after the killing.

Of course, Wheeler never knew he'd been taken out on the orders of Whitey Bulger, a thug for all seasons who came of age less than 14 miles from where Wheeler began his wheeling and dealing on the streets of Reading, Massachusetts. Nor would he know of his own grieving daughter, standing watch alone in the dusk at Southern Hills as detectives investigated her father's murder.

Wheeler braved through those last seconds of consciousness comforted by club manager Dean Matthews but surrounded by curious kids in swimming suits, his head leaning against an old gym bag. He may have wondered how he ever thought he could buy a cash-business ready-made for mobsters, say no to the skim, and live to tell the tale.

Yet, the fate he unwittingly fashioned for himself had been there all along, obscured by the brightness of a late spring afternoon, but mostly hidden by his own unbridled confidence: the specter of violent, lonely death and destiny in a cheap fake beard, with sunglasses hiding lifeless eyes, rushing into his face from out of nowhere, from behind his own blind spot.

SERVING KAGAME

While Paul Kagame, Rwanda's president, delivered a commencement speech to the graduates of Oklahoma Christian University, 10 of whom were Rwandan, officials were waiting in the wings to serve him notice of a civil lawsuit claiming he'd purposely initiated a genocide in his own country

By *Collin Hinds*

ON APRIL 30, 2010, a team of lawyers and process servers arrived at the campus of Oklahoma Christian University (OCU) in Edmond to serve notice of a civil lawsuit that had been filed the day before in federal court in Oklahoma City. The defendant being served was His Excellency Paul Kagame, president of the long-troubled African Republic of Rwanda, a country famously drenched in the blood of genocide. While lawyers pleaded with American Secret Service agents and Kagame's body guards to allow them to deliver summons and the hundred-plus-page-long petition, Kagame was giving the commencement speech to OCU's graduating class, 10 of whom were Rwandan citizens.

The lawsuit was filed, in part, on behalf of Madame Agathe Habyarimana, the widow of Juvénal Habyarimana, the former president of Rwanda. It alleged that in 1994, Kagame, a Tutsi, assassinated former President Habyarimana, a Hutu, by ordering his jet shot down as it approached the runway in Kigali, Rwanda's capital. The suit claimed it was Kagame's intention to spark an outbreak of widespread violence, which ultimately resulted in genocide, by ordering the shooting of the Falcon 50 that carried Habyarimana and the president of Burundi, Cyprien Ntaryamira, whose widow is also a plaintiff in the suit.

The two presidents were flying back to Kigali from neighboring Tanzania after signing a peace accord between exiled Tutsi forces and the Hutu-led government of Rwanda. The jet was struck by two surface-to-air missiles fired from close range. All aboard were killed. In retaliation, Rwandan Hutu extremists unleashed one of the deadliest acts of genocide the world has ever seen, systematically killing Tutsis and anyone sympathetic to them.

The lawsuit states, "General Paul Kagame deliberately chose a *modus operandi* that, in the context of the particular tension pervading both in Rwanda and Burundi between the Hutu and Tutsi communities, could only bring about bloody reprisals against the Tutsi community, and which offered [Kagame] a veneer of legitimacy for his renewal of hostilities and his seizing of State power in Rwanda by criminally violent means." In the lawsuit, the widows of the dead presidents accused Kagame of wrongful death and murder, crimes against humanity, violations of the rights of life, liberty and security, and torture, among other things, and requested damages against him in the total amount of $350 million.

The plaintiffs had to clear two procedural hurdles before the lawsuit could even begin in earnest. The most daunting issue was the question of service and notice to Kagame. Before a judge can make any order affecting the rights of a particular defendant, a defendant must be given notice. It is usually accomplished by a process server physically handing a copy of a filed lawsuit and other legal documents to the person being sued.

The other hurdle was jurisdictional. American law dictates that there must be a substantial connection between the person being sued and the place they are sued. In the case of *Habyarimana v. Kagame,* attorneys for Habyarimana would have to show that Kagame had substantial connections and contacts with the federal jurisdiction of the Western District of Oklahoma in order to maintain the suit there. It was the OCU-Kagame connection that the lawyers were counting on to fulfill the jurisdictional requirement.

In accordance with the Rwandan Presidential Scholars Program, scholarships funded by the Rwandan government are awarded to 10 Rwandans each year to attend OCU. Upon graduation with either bachelor's or master's degrees, the graduates are required to return to Rwanda to "help develop their country," according to OCU's website.

While lawyers negotiated with the Secret Service and Kagame's entourage, Kagame addressed the assembled graduates: "I am sure you know that among the distinguished [graduates] today are the first cohort of Rwandan scholars at OCU. Their graduation marks an important milestone in the partnership, and indeed, friendship between OCU and Rwanda." Extolling the necessity of an educated citizenry, Kagame said, "You need no reminding that in Rwanda, one of the long-lasting consequences of genocide was the decimation of the educated class."

Of the "decimation" of 1994, Philip Gourevitch, author of the book *We Wish to Inform You That Tomorrow We Will Be Killed With Our Families,* wrote:

Decimation means the killing of every tenth person in a population, and in the spring and early summer of 1994 a program of massacres decimated the Republic of Rwanda. Although the killing was low-tech—performed largely by machete—it was carried out at dazzling speed: of an original population of about seven and a half million, at least eight hundred thousand people were killed in just a hundred days. Rwandans often speak of a million deaths, and they may be right. The dead of Rwanda accumulated at nearly three times the rate of Jewish dead during the Holocaust. It was the most efficient mass killing since the atomic bombings of Hiroshima and Nagasaki.

Ron Frost, Vice President of Communications at OCU, said that some of the first Rwandese students to attend the university were orphaned by the genocide. Some were old enough in '94 to have visible memories of family, friends, and neighbors being murdered by machete.

———————

Rwanda's inter-tribal animosities began with their colonial occupiers, the Belgians, as early as 1919. Through a mixture of biblical myth and Nazi-style eugenics, the Belgians decreed the Tutsis to be one of the lost tribes of Israel, and inherently superior to their countrymen, the

Hutus. Tutsis took the flattery to heart. The Belgians placed Tutsis in middle-management roles overseeing and directing the hard and forced labors of their designated inferiors, the Hutus. The Belgians even went so far as to issue identification cards labeling a person either Hutu or Tutsi. Though there exists so much inter-marriage between Hutus and Tutsis to blur any genealogical difference between the two, it was considered a high distinction and prize to have the word "Tutsi" printed on your identification card.

Rwandan history after the withdrawal of Belgium is pocked by a series of uprisings and clashes between the two tribes. In 1961, when Paul Kagame was four, he and his family fled for Uganda during a revolt that left as many as 150,000 Rwandans dead, with Tutsis taking the largest number of casualties. Kagame was raised and schooled in exile. As a young man, he became involved in military operations as a guerrilla fighter in the Ugandan National Resistance Army that eventually overthrew the Ugandan government in 1985.

Shortly thereafter, Kagame helped to form the Rwandese Patriotic Front (RPF), which was comprised of both exiled Hutus and Tutsis in Uganda. From the start, their aim was to seek re-entry to Rwanda for its exiled population and to gain involvement in Rwandese governance.

In 1990, Kagame was the second in command of the RPF while he was undergoing special military training at Fort Leavenworth, Kansas, in the U.S. Army Command and Staff College. The training was offered to Kagame by the president of Uganda, who had the backing of the U.S. government after having overthrown the brutal regime of Obote Milton. Kagame quit his training early to return to Uganda when news reached him that the leader of the RPF had been killed in combat by Rwandese forces.

At about the same time, peace talks began between the RPF, with Kagame at the helm, and the Rwandan government, headed by then President Habyarimana. By all accounts, Habyarimana was less than enthusiastic about the proposals being generated in the peace talks. The talks revolved around proposals that would substantially diminish Habyarimana's influence as head of state.

Peace talks notwithstanding, a vicious propaganda machine was busy cranking up Hutu hostility towards Tutsis within Rwanda, and with the apparent blessings of Habyarimana and his wife. A widely read newspaper called *Kangura*, founded in part by her in reaction to a moderate periodical critical of her husband, became the daily digest for the "Hutu Power" movement that was picking up steam. One edition ran with an article entitled "The Hutu Ten Commandments." The eighth commandment stated, "Hutus must stop having mercy on the Tutsis."

The commentators at radio station RTLM, based in Kigali, and whose signal reached across Rwanda, began to refer to Tutsis as "cockroaches" and warned them to watch their backs.

The dreaded *interahamwe* was formed. *Interahamwe* means "those who fight/attack together" in the Rwandese African tongue. The *interahamwe* consisted of groups of young machete-wielding Hutu men who would be responsible for most of the 800,000 Tutsi dead by the end of the summer of 1994.

Interahamwe groups would regularly have rallies "where alcohol would flow freely, giant banners splashed with hagiographic portraits of Habyarimana flapped in the breeze, and paramilitary drills were conducted like the latest hot dance moves," writes Philip Gourevitch. "The president and his wife often turned out to be cheered at these spectacles, while in private the members of the *interahamwe* were organized into small neighborhood bands, drew up lists of Tutsis, and went on retreats to practice burning houses, tossing grenades, and hacking dummies up with machetes."

"Hutu Power" Radio RTLM reported to Rwanda that Juvénal Habyarimana was dead. Its commentators encouraged that "the tall trees be chopped down," code for "kill the Tutsis," and began almost exclusively referring to Tutsis as "cockroaches." According to multiple sources, commentators at RTLM would read out names of Tutsis and Hutus sympathetic to Tutsis, and give directions as to how to find them. In turn, RTLM would announce the news after someone on their list had been killed by the Hutu *interahamwe*.

At the outset of the genocide, Agathe Habyarimana flew to Paris, where she lives in exile to this day.

Some have speculated that Hutu extremists were responsible for shooting down Habyarimana's plane in retaliation for signing the peace accord with the RPF, and as a pretext for sparking the genocide that resulted. Others believe that the orders to shoot down the plane were given by the RPF, and specifically by Kagame himself, also as a pretext to spark the genocide and justify an invasion into Rwanda from the northeast in Uganda, which is exactly what happened. Kagame steadfastly denies the accusation that the RPF, and he, had anything to do with the shooting down of Habyarimana's jet.

Lt. Col. Charles Vuckovic, a U.S. defense attaché for the Defense Intelligence Agency, was in Kigali when the president's plane was shot down. He told reporters for PBS' *Frontline*, "There are many theories as to who shot down the plane. I don't know if anybody has the answer to that. Was it Hutu extremists or was it Tutsi extremists? Was it done by the Tutsis as an excuse to begin the movement south by the RPF and take control of the country? Hard to say. Or was it used by the Hutu extremists to begin the genocide that took place? I don't know the answer to that."

After the RPF took over Rwanda and quashed the Hutu-led genocide, the French government produced a report that concluded the genocide was intentionally sparked by the RPF and Kagame. The plaintiffs' case in the Oklahoma lawsuit relies heavily on that investigation conducted by French authorities.

An investigation was also undertaken by the Kagame-led Rwandan government. Not surprisingly, the report concluded that President Habyarimana was assassinated by members of his own inner circle. Kagame's report concluded, "The attack was a deliberate attempt by Hutu extremists close to the president to scupper an imminent peace agreement with the Tutsi-led Rwandan Patriotic Front (RPF) rebels."

A new investigation by the French corroborates Kagame's version of what happened, and directly contradicts the previous French investigation championed by the plaintiffs in the Oklahoma case. On January 11, 2012, two French judges announced that based on their investigation into the matter it is their belief that the missiles were fired from a Hutu military base by Habyarimana's own soldiers. For the foreseeable future that is the narrative the French government and Kagame's Rwanda have settled on, thereby thawing what had been a contentious relationship between the two countries.

In the commencement speech given by Kagame at OCU, he also said, "The ills that have characterized our country... such as conflict, poverty, disease and corruption are in many ways a result of lack of value-based leadership. In Rwanda, we learnt that lesson the hard way … " He ended his speech by saying, "Congratulations again to you all, and may God bless you." Kagame left the OCU campus, surrounded by his bodyguards, without papers being served on him. University officials escorted the lawyers for Agathe Habyarimana off campus grounds.

Peter Erlinder, one of the lawyers for the plaintiffs in the case and an international law professor at the William Mitchell College of Law in Saint Paul, Minnesota, said, obviously disgruntled, "Rather than accept service, members of [Kagame's] staff refused to accept documents and the university ordered process servers and lawyers to leave campus … which is interference with service of process, a misdemeanor under Oklahoma law. … [B]ecause the university has now involved itself in the conspiracy to cover up Kagame's crimes, they have exposed themselves to liability."

According to university officials, there has been no legal retaliation on the part of the plaintiffs in the Oklahoma City case to date, and there is none expected.

Ron Frost of OCU said with a chuckle, "There was no way [process servers] were going to get within 20 feet of President Kagame." According to Frost, Kagame's bodyguards numbered close to 30 and were armed with automatic weapons.

———————

After months of legal wrangling between the plaintiffs' lawyers and Kagame's over the procedural issues of whether Kagame was properly given notice of the law suit, and whether the Western District of Oklahoma was the proper court to hear the case, the U.S. government stepped into the fight.

The Department of Justice (DOJ), at the behest of the Obama administration, filed a "suggestion of immunity" in September 2011. The DOJ's suggestion of immunity urged the court to dismiss the suit against Kagame citing international law, foreign policy, and precedent. In the history of American jurisprudence a suggestion of immunity filed by the DOJ on behalf of a sitting head of state has never been rejected.

The Oklahoma City federal judge, Lee West, dismissed the suit against Kagame on October 28 of last year. The lawyers for the widows are appealing the Oklahoma judge's ruling.

In September, a French court rejected a case filed by the Rwandan government against Habyarimana to have her extradited to Rwanda to stand trial for the planning and execution of the genocide, an accusation she has always denied. A Rwandan official said that the French ruling would be respected "for whatever it is worth."

Rwandan students enrolled at OCU declined to be interviewed for this article. When asked why, Ron Frost said, "We asked a few of our Rwandan students if they would like to be interviewed. They would just rather not talk about it."

Maybe their silence is rooted in a pragmatic wisdom. That the blame for the genocide that occurred over a decade ago in Rwanda, leaving close to one million men, women, and children dead, can finally and legally be assigned to one person or another, to the satisfaction of all, seems as improbable and as unhelpful as the case against Kagame moving forward in Oklahoma federal court.

TULSA: JUST A SHOT AWAY

A 'Vanity Fair' contributor offers his thoughts on the legacy
of Larry Clark's critically acclaimed book

By *Nick Tosches*

It was through *Tulsa* that I first became aware of Larry
Clark and his work. The book had only recently been published—yes,
it was that long ago—and I was of an age at which I was convinced
beyond all doubt that I would never live to see the age at which I now
set down these words.

This conviction had a lot to do with the way I had spent my
youth, or cast it to the winds that claimed it and me. Had I grown up in
Tulsa rather than in Newark and Jersey City and Manhattan, I could
easily have seen myself in the book I had discovered. In fact, I did *feel*
something like a blurred shadow of myself as I first made my rapt way
through its pages.

What I beheld was more than a bunch of pictures. They were, to
be sure, photographs—glimpses into what could be perceived as the
lives of those who were, in Blake's words, "form'd / To destruction from
the mother's womb"; or as glimpses of the dangerous course of fun pure
and simple—but they were so much more than what lens and shutter
seemed capable of capturing.

These deceptively simple pictures evoked and expressed things that
most writers could not evoke and express as effectively in words. The

adage that a picture is worth a thousand words is more well-worn than true. What I saw in *Tulsa* was the rare exception.

The title of the book, so fine and strong in its direct and simple brevity, is geographically specific. But the longer I lived with the book, the more I came to see that the Tulsa of *Tulsa* was not only Newark, Jersey City, and New York City as well. It was the world—or at least a certain world and all those who live, or lived, within it.

I've never met Larry Clark. I had the opportunity when my friend Chiemi Karasawa worked with him as the script supervisor of his moving picture *Kids*. Instead I gave her a copy of the first revised and expanded edition of his book *Teenage Lust*, along with a black Sharpie. The book was still fully and tautly shrink-wrapped. I told Chiemi to have him sign the shrink-wrapping. When she handed him the book and the Sharpie, he instinctively brought his thumbnail to the book to open and dispose of the tightly enclosing plastic, that he might sign the book properly. Chiemi caught his hand in time, explaining what I wanted. He was mystified for a moment, then, as if with complete and sudden comprehension, signed the shrink-wrapping and printed "New York City / 1994" beneath his signature. A unique collectors' item that would cease to be so the moment that the inaccessible became accessible. A perversely fitting physical anti-metaphor, I figured, for the work of a man who renders accessible, and more, that which is hidden and closed from many of us.

We may never have set foot in Oklahoma, but we all live in or near Tulsa: the Tulsa to which Larry Clark and his *Tulsa* have brought us.

GRACE IN BROKEN ARROW

How greed, corruption, and denial corroded an
Oklahoma megachurch in 2012

By *Kiera Feldman*

"Many are the afflictions of the righteous, but the Lord
delivereth him out of them all."

— Psalm 34

No MORE SLEEPOVERS. No more babysitting, or car rides home.
No more being alone with children or "lingering hugs given to students
(especially using your hands to stroke or fondle)." Aaron Thompson—
Coach Thompson to his PE students—sat in the principal's office at
Grace Fellowship Christian School as his bosses went through the
four-page Corrective Action Plan point by point. It was October of 2001,
the same month Aaron added "Teacher of the Week" to his resume.

Grace's leader, Bob Yandian—"Pastor Bob" as everyone calls him—
wasn't there: no need, he had people for this kind of thing. Pastor Bob's
time was better spent sequestered in his study, writing books and radio
broadcasts. His lieutenant, Associate Pastor Chip Olin, was a hardnosed
guy, "ornery as heck," people said. Olin brought a *USA Today* article on
the characteristics of child molesters to the meeting. At age twenty-four,
Olin explained, Aaron was acting immature and unprofessional, and
someone might get the wrong idea.

The first two recommendations of what became known as the "do not fondle" agreement were prayer and "building relationships with young men and women of your age group in Sunday School and singles group activities" at Grace Church, which ran the school. "Leaders in the kingdom are judged not so much by what they accomplish as by the character they reveal—who they are before what they do," the document continued. Aaron was to "live a lifestyle above reproach"—to act such that no one would question his character.

Associate Pastor Olin let head administrator John Dunlavey, Aaron's other boss, do much of the talking. Olin had only just read the Corrective Action Plan for the first time as he walked down the hall en route to the meeting. He was mostly there as an observer. It was Dunlavey's brainchild, after all.

Dunlavey didn't mean that kind of "fondle." He'd tacked it on, thinking it best described the overly affectionate hug-plus-hand-stroking he'd seen Aaron give a boy one day at lunch. With his big, square glasses and brow that furrowed in concentration, Dunlavey was more the earnest science teacher he once was than the administrator he'd become. He'd looked up "fondle" in the dictionary, and it seemed the most precise. Science guys love precision.

Dunlavey didn't think babysitting and all the rest were problems, just symptoms: Aaron had become too close to Grace families. Misplaced loyalties. That was the real issue.

Young boys were leaving Grace over the past few years, and no one knew why. One boy moved a full 1,200 miles away. He still skateboarded with friends and did normal kid stuff, but he was having horrible nightmares and failing classes, unable to contain his inexplicable fury at teachers. At one point, he told his mother he couldn't stand how he felt and no longer wished to live. But Grace's leaders would not know or would not admit such things about their flock until much later.

Grace Church sits atop a hill just south of Tulsa, off a two-lane country road with a speed limit of fifty. The boxy, tan bunker of a building has flagpoles at the entrance, making the church look like a fortified post office. Eighty acres of grassy fields spread out below. Houses in the area range from spacious to McMansion, and new developments get names like Ridgewood or Shannondale. In the incorporated suburb known as Broken Arrow, Oklahoma, the ratio of car dealerships to churches is about 1:1. The nearest strip mall to Grace has a drive-thru Starbucks, a Wal-Mart, and a fast food chicken restaurant that pipes soft Christian rock over speakers into the parking lot. Such is the way of Tulsa geography: blacks to the north, Latinos and Asians to the east, miscellany in midtown, and evangelicals and big box stores in the south.

Fall of 2001 was the grand opening for Grace's new children's building, a real beauty, the pride and joy of the whole church. "Grace is the place for kids" was the church's slogan back then. The new, 56,000-square-foot building had two stories of classrooms, plus amenities like a Chuck-E-Cheese-style room with tubing and a ball pit, "Bob and Loretta's Soda Shoppe" (an old-fashioned ice cream parlor named after Pastor Bob and his wife), and the crowning glory: an antique carousel beneath a vaulted glass pyramidal ceiling. Bejeweled with big amusement park light bulbs, the carousel's gold and aqua paneling positively glowed: $125,000 well spent. Grace took out a $7.5 million loan to finance construction of the children's building, and when all was said and done, the whole thing was worth nearly $10 million—over half the value of all their buildings combined. In time, a new auditorium would be built, too, which would connect the children's building to Grace's main wing. They'd begun a fundraising campaign back in 1998: "Investing in Eternity." That was the year Pastor Bob published his book *Righteousness: God's Gift to You.* "You don't need to crawl on your knees or do any 'good works' to try to earn God's approval," Pastor Bob promised.

Aaron Thompson was the teacher all the girls had crushes on and all the boys idolized. The younger kids mobbed him around campus and clamored for hugs. His smile was radiant, his Believer's pedigree sterling. Aaron had grown up at Grace Church. In high school, he was senior class president and a star basketball player, before heading to nearby Oral Roberts University. Parents frequently had Aaron over for dinner, asked him to babysit, or hoped he could stay with the kids for a week while they went on vacation. Aaron fielded invites for family outings big and small, from camping trips to ice cream at Braum's after church. Parents were delighted to have a young man like Aaron in their children's lives. He was the golden boy of Grace Church.

And yet, in August of 2001, prior to the signing of the "do not fondle" agreement, Grace received an unsigned letter. It read:

> This is a matter of life or death for a child or children. People have been known to commit suicide for this very reason ... Everything you need to know will be revealed if you will monitor the boy's locker room and private hallways or areas when no one is around, especially before and after the PE classes. Watch your staff when they are alone with young boys, even for two minutes. Ask yourself, "Why have certain boys left Grace?" and "Why are some boys tardy often?"

Olin didn't think the letter was about Aaron to begin with; Dunlavey came to agree as the meeting with Aaron wore on. Yet still, Dunlavey thought, perhaps Aaron's behavior was being misconstrued somehow, and so he read the letter aloud.

"Aaron, is this you?" Dunlavey asked. "Are you doing anything that might cause somebody to write this kind of a letter?" Aaron assured them he was doing no wrong. He was repentant, open to correction. Olin had high hopes for Aaron. Everyone did. For the remainder of the school year, Aaron was on probation. Violation of the agreement would mean termination. Olin, Dunlavey, and Pastor Bob would discuss Aaron's progress during their weekly meetings.

Aaron left Grace and headed to Cheddar's, a nearby restaurant, to meet with the teachers on his unit. They were the Specials Teachers, the "Special Ts," they called themselves, a tight-knit crew that taught subjects like PE, music, and Spanish—all women except for Aaron. Aaron plopped down in the booth, late and very upset. "What's wrong?" asked Laura Prochaska, the computers teacher. "We're your sisters. Talk to us."

Aaron swore them to secrecy, then confided that Grace had made him sign papers saying he could never take kids to the movies or babysit or hug them. "I can't be their big brother," he lamented.

"Just don't do anything questionable that they could get you for," Prochaska advised. "They must not think it's such a big deal, but they want to protect themselves by having you sign this contract."

"Maybe you should think about quitting," another teacher added, encouraging him to take the protest route.

"No, no. I'm not a quitter," Aaron told them. "I'm going to see this through."

The "Special Ts" didn't know he'd already been molesting children at Grace for years. From that day in October until his arrest on March 25, 2002, Aaron Thompson would sexually abuse four more boys. One of them was the son of a teacher sitting there in the restaurant booth.

This is a cautionary tale. It is about deference to authority, and denial, and the human cost of privileging an institution above people. According to Oklahoma law, anyone having "reason to believe" that a child is potentially being abused must make a report to the Department of Human Services or the police. Child abuse experts urge us to follow the law and not take it upon ourselves to evaluate or investigate allegations or suspicions of abuse. But that is exactly what Grace did. And they reaped what they sowed.

Grace Church was Oklahoma's Penn State of 2002. After such things come to light, we always wonder: how on earth did that ever happen?

Here is how it happened.

The public record is suspect when it comes to what was going on behind the scenes at Grace before Aaron's arrest. For starters, don't trust what I just told you about the signing of the "do not fondle" agreement on that day in October 2001. All that was reconstructed from the testimonies and depositions head administrator John Dunlavey, Associate Pastor Chip Olin, Principal DeeAnn McKay, and Pastor Bob later gave during the negligence lawsuits in which Grace became mired. The only problem is that what they said under oath doesn't square with the recollections of two teachers who were sitting in the restaurant booth with Aaron immediately after he signed the agreement.

During the lawsuits, everyone at Grace said the Corrective Action Plan was Dunlavey's idea—they simply followed his lead. (Pastor Bob said he green-lighted Dunlavey's idea in advance, got the executive summary of Dunlavey's text afterward from Olin verbally, and only read the actual document in the wake of Aaron's arrest.) And yet, Laura Prochaska and another Specials Teacher who spoke on condition of anonymity distinctly remembered Aaron telling the group, "Chip [Olin] made me sign this thing."

The second teacher had been a member of Grace Church for decades. "Knowing all the personalities as well as I do, John [Dunlavey] would not have come up with something like that. That was a Chip thing," she assured me. "If [Dunlavey] had had to write an agreement, it would've been dictated to him by Chip Olin," she added. "They liked puppets around there."

The Corrective Action Plan was just one plot point in the whole story. Who knows what else didn't quite happen as Grace said it happened? Conveniently, Grace's version of the story protects the man at the top.

Pastor Bob has long been a pillar of the national charismatic Pentecostal community. Colleagues describe him as "a pastor's pastor," a wingman for the mega-pastors. Decades ago, Pastor Bob was Dean of Instructors at RHEMA Bible Training Center while founder Kenneth Hagin Sr. pioneered the hugely influential Word of Faith movement, which teaches that the Lord blesses the faithful with healing and financial rewards (provided they tithe). Today Pastor Bob is a board member of Joyce Meyer Ministries, which brings in about $100 million in donations annually, affording Meyer the luxury of traveling by private jet.

At Grace, the stage is dark and bathed in soft pastel lights when the eleven-member worship band leads the congregation in the gentle murmuring called talking in tongues; but when Pastor Bob takes to the pulpit, on come the harsh fluorescents: it's business time. Pastor Bob, ruddy faced and paunchy, preaches the prosperity gospel of health and wealth. His eyes narrow as his nasally voice rises. He even incorporates his love of fancy cars into sermons. He has owned several over the years, including a pair of his-and-hers BMWs: Pastor Bob bought his wife's Beemer, and Grace bought his. Pastor Bob is known for his "practical wisdom."

The first lawsuit, *John Does 1–7 versus Grace*, went to trial in September 2004.

"I don't really make 'Chip' decisions," Associate Pastor Chip Olin testified. "I'm an extension of Pastor Bob."

Maybe it began with the tittytwisters. Or the tousled hair, the hugs, the body slams.

"Older brother-type stuff," Josh[1] remembers. "He would slowly desensitize you."

Josh was Aaron's first victim, although of course he didn't know it back in 1996. Aaron would ask him to stay after gym class to help put away PE equipment.

Josh and I are sitting in a Mexican restaurant in downtown Tulsa, next to a mock-up boxing ring that has been incorporated into the décor. His bicycle is locked up outside. Josh wears a jean shirt with pearl buttons and rolled sleeves. He is quick to smile and has a little stubble, a handsome twenty-something. An autodidact since high school, Josh just sent off a round of out-of-state college applications. We compare notes on the arduous application process before hunkering down to talk about what we came here to talk about.

It was the end of fifth grade, and Josh was 11 years old. A cute, happy kid with a toothy grin and a center part in his hair, the 1990s style that made little arches on either side above the forehead. Josh's father had died a few years earlier. Now Josh wonders if it made him vulnerable, eager to latch onto a male figure, someone to connect to, hoping to please the golden boy of Grace Church.

"We had played dodgeball, and he asked me to bring in all the stuff with him," Josh begins to tell me. "When I was in the closet putting things away, he came up behind me and grabbed me and slid his hand down and touched me."

Afterward, Aaron told Josh to go to the nurse and get an Advil, a cover for being late. He spent all of the next class staring silently into space, trying to process what had happened. From there, it escalated. During Josh's fifth- and sixth-grade years, this became just about a weekly occurrence. In the supply closet by the gym, in the gym itself, in the coach's office that locked from the inside, in the boy's locker room that

---

1 Names have been changed to protect the innocent.

connected straight into the coach's office. Aaron's hand down Josh's pants, Aaron's hand putting Josh's hand down his own. Josh started to get used to it.

Josh became withdrawn, jumpy, moody. His parents didn't know what to make of his drastic personality change but assumed it was just a phase. He couldn't concentrate. That was the year he got misdiagnosed with Attention Deficit Disorder.

Like most abusers, Aaron was very skilled at coercing his victims into cooperating with their abuse. Josh felt guilty: he'd gone along with it. And Josh knew God knew.

For evangelicals, God is a personal God, there with you in every moment. Josh worried and worried: what did He think of him? It was a gut anxiety, ever-present. He hoped, desperately, that God would help him or guide him somehow. Josh did what he had been taught to do when he didn't know what to do: he prayed. He prayed constantly. But deliverance never came. He was eleven, maybe twelve. Josh found his mom's handgun and placed the barrel into his mouth. This way, he thought, he'd get to be with his dad again. When he finally got up the nerve to pull the trigger, nothing happened. It wasn't loaded. Josh took it as a sign. He didn't try again until years later.

The escalation continued. Before long, Aaron was having Josh perform oral sex on him and doing likewise to Josh. If it came out that this was going on, Josh knew he would be the talk of the school. Children are cruel, and Christian children no different. He liked it, they'd taunt. Walking down the hall, it felt like kids were staring at him. Surely they could tell, surely they knew that Josh had brought this on himself. Aaron had convinced Josh that Aaron was keeping Josh's secret.

Throughout it all, of course, Josh was still being asked to help put things away after gym class: he was needed and wanted and chosen. Abuse binds the abused to their abuser, power and control the engine driving all.

"He made you feel—" Josh pauses to find the word for the memory. "Special." Aaron treated him like the adult that he was not.

Sometime in 7th grade, Josh's face, neck, and back became covered with horrible, painful acne—in all likelihood a product of stress. But also puberty: it was 1998, and Josh was thirteen. The abuse tapered off.

Time passed. Josh drew into himself. Eventually, he started noticing younger boys coming out of the gym, late for their next class. Boys who seemed to have special friendships with Aaron. And that's when it hit him: there were others.

––––––––––––––

Aaron went way back with Grace's youth pastor and basketball coach, Mike Goolsbay, a big teddy bear of a man with spiky gelled hair who was always saying "bless you, kiddo" with gusto. Goolsbay had known Aaron since he was a thirteen-year-old in Grace's youth group. Aaron knew he could call Goolsbay late at night if he ever needed an ear, like the time his senior year of high school when he had some teenage angst to hash out, or the time in college when a girl broke his heart. Goolsbay was the one who asked Aaron to start helping out during Grace's summer camps. During the 1995–1996 school year, while Aaron was a freshman accounting student at Oral Roberts University, he volunteered as the assistant basketball coach/assistant youth pastor at Grace—Goolsbay's right-hand man.

By all accounts, the first failure to report child abuse at Grace came in early 1996, around the time Josh's molestation began. Dr. Mark Peterson and his wife brought Goolsbay a printout of emails Aaron had sent to their seventh-grade son, who was on Goolsbay's basketball team. One email described the son's genitalia and called him a "stud." The emails were all signed "Love, Aaron"—not, Peterson noted, "Love in Christ, Aaron." (Child abuse experts say that lewd emails constitute abuse.) Peterson insisted that the emails be made part of Aaron's permanent file. Goolsbay agreed to do so, using the exact same logic of denial and negligence that everyone at Grace would deploy in the years to come: Aaron is unprofessional, he's immature, I'll counsel him, and all will be well. (Had Goolsbay followed state law, he would have called DHS or the police.) Goolsbay says he didn't tell any of his superiors about the incident, and the emails were never found in Grace's files.

Meanwhile, Pastor Bob published *One Flesh: God's Gift of Passion— Love, Sex & Romance in Marriage*. "When you have a strong relationship with your mate's soul," the soon-to-be popular book advised, "the relationship with his or her body becomes something fantastic!"

Aaron became Grace's part-time assistant athletic director in 1997, and in late 1998, shortly before he graduated from ORU in the spring of 1999, he was hired as a full-time PE teacher at Grace—on Goolsbay's recommendation.

After Aaron's arrest, Dr. Peterson called Goolsbay to remind him of the emails. Goolsbay was defensive, and the conversation grew heated, Peterson later testified. "CYA"—Cover Your Ass—was "the feeling I was getting," Peterson said.

Long before any sexual abuse came to light at Grace, Dr. Gene Reynolds, a Tulsa psychologist, remembered trekking out to the school on Garnett Road, asked by parents to evaluate this or that kid for issues unrelated to the abuse. He was struck that the administration and staff seemed totally unreceptive to professional recommendations.

"They had their own ideas about what needed to be done," Dr. Reynolds noted.

He ended up examining seven of the Grace boys Aaron had abused. In the boys' pre-teen and teenage years, the early effects of trauma were varied: the gamut ran from severe anger to depression, suicidal feelings and attempts, insomnia, fear of men, panic attacks, feeling like "damaged goods," shame, guilt, early sexual activity and promiscuity, incarceration, and drug abuse. "There were some boys who said they never wanted to set foot in a church again," Dr. Reynolds added.

Late effects of abuse vary individually, but the numbers are grim: victims of abuse are more likely to have trouble in school (a 50 percent chance); more likely to develop substance abuse or mental health problems (one study found 80 percent of 21-year-olds who'd been abused had one or more psychiatric disorders); and 5 – 8 times more likely to experience major depression in their lifetime. Both depression and substance abuse are associated with poor treatment outcomes when patients have histories of child abuse. Men who've been abused as children are 3.8 times more likely to perpetrate intimate partner violence as adults. Adults who've been abused as children are twice as likely to have attempted suicide—and 12 times more likely to commit suicide. The sooner abuse is detected and treated, the better the child's prospects are in the long term.

The men who sexually abuse children—and they are mostly men—
are often the last people on earth you'd ever imagine. About 90 percent
of child sexual abusers are people the victim knows. About 30 percent
of abusers are relatives—a father, older sibling, a favorite cousin or uncle,
the people you trust most in this world. About 60 percent are outside
the family—coaches, teachers, Scout leaders, ministers, neighbors, family
friends, teenage sons of family friends: the authority figures children
look up to. Abusers work their way into positions where they'll have
access to children, so that they become the "not in a million years" people.
This is exactly why state laws do not allow individuals or organizations
to "handle" abuse complaints or suspicions on their own: these bonds
of trust make it impossible to respond to potential abuse with anything
but disbelief. Outside authorities, by comparison, don't have such pre-
conceived notions.

Girls are victimized more often than boys, but boys are more likely
to be victimized by a non-family member. Underreporting is common,
making data hard to come by, but studies suggest 25 percent of women
and 16 percent of men were sexually abused before age 18 (including
peer abuse). According to the American Academy of Pediatrics, "The
children most susceptible to these assaults have obedient, compliant,
and respectful personalities."

At Penn State University, allegations of former assistant football
coach Jerry Sandusky's sexual assault of a child traveled from graduate
assistant to head coach Joe Paterno to athletic director and University
vice president and president. Everyone, it seemed, was willing to report
a coach up the chain of command and assume they'd done their due
diligence.

For decades, Catholics moved their pedophile priests from one
community to another, dumping them on unsuspecting parishes. The
Catholic Church spent the '90s doling out cash settlements to sexual
abuse victims, who were required to sign confidentiality agreements.
The eruption of scandal was to be avoided at all costs. Defrocking was
unheard of: priests had repented, and that was that.

Then, a 2002 *Boston Globe* investigation blew the lid off of everything.
Just as the Catholic clergy abuse scandal was breaking, Tulsa became
likewise embroiled. While the Catholics shuffled their perpetrators from
parish to parish, Grace harbored Aaron. In this way, the evangelicals of

South Tulsa were much like the ultra-Orthodox Jews of Brooklyn, who have kept their abusers within the tight-knit community.

In the experience of Roy Van Tassell, an abuse specialist at Family and Children Services of Oklahoma, Grace was not all that unique among some kinds of religious institutions locally.

"They tend to be more autocratic, more cloistered," Tassell told me, "and there is some anecdotal evidence to say that those communities tend to be at somewhat greater risk."

"It happened because Aaron Thompson was a member of our family," the church's lawyer told the jury during *John Does 1–7 versus Grace*. Family ties both bind and blind, the lawyer seemed to be saying—a truism that fits most communities.

The only assurance of our nation's safety is to lay our foundation in morality and religion [Christianity].

—Abraham Lincoln,
as quoted by the Grace Elementary School handbook

At Grace Fellowship Christian School, everything from "the World"— that is, the secular world beyond South Tulsa—was suspect: Harry Potter, Tim Burton, whatever clothing happened to be in style that year. But students were led in prayer for the World: that the spiritual enemy known as Bill Clinton would be replaced with a godly leader; that Senator Jim Inhofe would be re-elected; that George Bush would lead our great Christian nation and glorify His kingdom.

Federal laws prohibit partisan political activity in churches and other tax-exempt organizations. Yet, Grace encouraged students to volunteer for Republican election campaigns, sometimes offering extra credit. One year, Grace students went on a field trip to hammer lawn signs for Representative Steve Largent, an original member of the C Street House in Washington, run by the powerful and secretive fundamentalist Christian group known as The Family (perhaps best known as the incubator for Uganda's "kill the gays" bill). Former Grace students and parishioners remembered that Largent and Senator Don Nickles, another Family member, were frequent guests at the school. Also a

Family man, Inhofe has graced Grace's pulpit many times. For a number of years, Grace donated money to Christian Embassy, one of The Family's sister organizations that ministers to Washington elites. It was a Christian Embassy evangelist who led Inhofe to dedicate himself to Jesus in a congressional dining room in 1988.

In an email, the office of Winters & King, Inc., Grace's attorney, said the church "has no relationship with Steve Largent, past or present." The email continued, "Grace has no relationship with Senator Inhofe except to pray for him as mentioned in I Timothy 4:1-2"—the same answer they gave for District Attorney Tim Harris. The verse from Timothy reads, "In the latter times some shall depart from the faith, giving heed to seducing spirits, and doctrines of devils." Stay the course, Grace apparently prays for Christian conservative politicians.

"As we go we follow Jesus," went the Grace school song. "His Holy Spirit guides the way." The way was one of structure and discipline: wear pants the wrong color of blue, and you could end up with in-house suspension, be given a pair of headphones, and made to listen to tapes of Pastor Bob's lectures. Chewing gum as a repeat offense could mean a paddling in the principal's office; girls had to kneel in the entryway of the school to make sure their skirts touched the floor; only one What Would Jesus Do bracelet was allowed: excess was vanity.

At Grace, the bodies of the young were policed with the utmost of vigilance. When a ninth-grade girl kissed a seventh-grade boy on the cheek, he was suspended and banned from sports tryouts. Shaming was a teaching tool. When a 15-year-old girl got pregnant, her expulsion was announced to the whole school in chapel, with her younger sister sitting there in the pews. The infractions of children—major, minor, and everything in between—were punished swiftly and severely.

"It was definitely a dictatorship," remembered one Grace teacher who was a church member for over thirty years.

Grace had an application for volunteers to fill out, with a part that asked if they'd experienced sexual abuse as a child. An affirmative answer rendered a volunteer ineligible to work with children. Way back in 1995, Aaron answered "no." But one day toward the end of the summer of 2000 or 2001—Goolsbay couldn't remember which year—on a long car ride to a campground in Tahlequah where Grace held summer camp, Aaron confided in him. The real answer was "yes." Teenagers molested him when he was four. (Aaron later testified that he was molested again at age 16 by a youth pastor at a different church.)

The two talked the entire car ride, over an hour and a half. Goolsbay was relieved when Aaron told him that his parents had found out about the abuse sometime in middle school—it hadn't remained a festering secret. But, at the same time, Goolsbay understood that victimization could be a cycle.

"Aaron, do you struggle with this in your life?" he asked. "Is this ever something that you've duplicated or acted out on?" Perhaps Goolsbay should have had thoughts along these lines back in 1996, when Aaron sent lewd emails to a seventh-grade boy.

"No, no, I would never, ever do that to a child," Aaron assured him.

Goolsbay thought about Aaron teaching every single child at Grace, preschool through eighth grade, including his own children.

"Are my kids safe, as well as every other kid safe?" Goolsbay wondered to himself.

"I felt like he gave me that assurance," Goolsbay later testified. He told Aaron he was there for him if he ever needed to talk. Goolsbay says he didn't bring up the lewd emails to the Peterson boy, and he didn't think to recommend professional help. After that, whenever they'd see each other around Grace, which was just about every day, Goolsbay would put his arm around him and ask, "How is your heart?"

Around this period, Aaron, as a counselor, molested two Grace students at Camp Dry Gulch, where many Grace kids went.

Despite Aaron's own history as a victim of sexual abuse, Grace continued to let Aaron work with children. Goolsbay claimed he never reported that conversation up the chain of command. Grace purged Aaron's volunteer file in 2001.

———————

In 1998, Laura Prochaska became the computers teacher at Grace. She started noticing that certain boys used to arrive late. Again and again and again, the same boys. She'd ask them where they were, and they'd answer that they had been helping Coach Thompson put away equipment after PE—or at the nurse's office. Then they would sit the entire period, staring blankly at their computer screens without even turning the monitor on. After class, she'd pull them aside.

"What's wrong?" she'd ask them. "Are your mommy and daddy having trouble at home?" To no avail.

Prochaska went to Mary Ellen Hood, the elementary principal at the time. Hood was gung-ho about Christian education as a calling; Grace was her life. She wore a blue blazer emblazoned with the school crest.

"I said, 'I've got some kids who are coming late, they're sullen. I try to talk to them after class, they just stare down at the floor and don't say anything except, 'I'm OK, I'm OK,'" Prochaska remembered telling Hood. (When I called Hood in March 2012 and read her this quote, Hood paused a full five seconds, cleared her throat, thanked me with a "bye now," and hung up.)

At the time, Prochaska said, Hood apparently never followed up. This was all happening while rumors were circulating—malicious rumors, or so it seemed at the time, that Aaron was molesting boys. Without any formal complaints, Prochaska and the other teachers dismissed it as "just talk," she said. "We blew it off, thinking, 'Oh my gosh. What is this? A frustrated kid that wants to get back at his coach? Or a frustrated parent that wanted to attack the coach?' Because he was a man of integrity, as far as we knew."

Prochaska was the unit leader for the Specials Teachers. In retrospect, she marvels that the principal didn't have her monitor Aaron. "I guess Mrs. Hood gave Aaron the benefit of the doubt and thought she could handle it on her own," Prochaska said.

Prochaska didn't know reporting protocol because Grace hadn't trained her to know it: those rumors they'd been hearing of child sex abuse—"smack talk" about Aaron—were grounds enough for a call to outside authorities. Reports to DHS can even be made anonymously. But it was a culture in which the World was not to be trusted or called upon. One's responsibility was to the chain of command.

Under Oklahoma law, the Child Abuse Reporting and Prevention Act, it is a misdemeanor for anyone "having reason to believe" that a minor is potentially being abused to not report it to the Department of Human Services (DHS). (In at least three states, failure to report child abuse can result in a felony.) In some states, the legal requirements to report abuse are limited to certain professionals like health care workers and school employees, but Oklahoma is one of 18 states in which everyone is what's called a "mandatory reporter." The reporting obligation is individual, meaning that it's not enough to simply alert one's superiors and have them make a decision about whether or not to call outside authorities. DHS investigates abuse within the home and refers cases like that of Grace to the Tulsa Police Department (TPD) for investigation. When rumors were spreading at Grace, anyone could've alerted DHS or TPD. Then, hypothetically, TPD would've gone out to Grace to "turn over every stone, ask every question," said TPD spokesman Jason Willingham. "We're going to ask, 'Hey did you ever see anything unusual?' It's the little things that just didn't add up."

District Attorney Tim Harris handled Aaron's case. He never returned my phone calls. I left messages asking him to explain why he didn't prosecute Grace for failing to report child abuse. Harris once said, "As a criminal prosecutor, I look at the Ten Commandments." Harris and Mike King, Grace's lawyer, were classmates of Michele Bachmann's in law school at Oral Roberts University, which promotes a biblical interpretation of secular law in an effort to undo the separation of church and state.

Roy Van Tassell of Family and Children's Services of Oklahoma said failure to report prosecutions were "rare" in his experience. Nationally, successful failure-to-report prosecutions are few and far between. They typically result in a fine of a few hundred dollars, if that. "If any good would come out of any of this," one father of an abused boy at Grace told me, "it'd be that somehow, somewhere, laws would be changed." He suggested a fine of $10,000 for every day someone fails to report child abuse.

There is a big shortcoming in Oklahoma's current law: "reason to believe" can be read subjectively. The statute states, "Any person who knowingly and willfully fails to promptly report any incident" may be charged with a misdemeanor. "As a practical matter, unless someone made an admission ... that they knowingly and willfully failed to report as required by law," a DHS representative told me, "how would we know?"

According to the plaintiffs' lawyers, all Grace had to do to avoid prosecution was say they didn't have any "reason to believe" and didn't "knowingly" fail to report that Aaron was molesting boys. They didn't have any reason to believe it, because they chose not to believe it.

In a recent phone conversation, Grace's lawyer, Mike King, reiterated his interpretation of the law. When an organization receives an abuse complaint, King said, "If they have reason to believe that that report is true, they should report it [to DHS]." Yet, credibility is beside the point. That's for the World to discern.

At the time, Prochaska didn't know about all the parental complaints Grace was receiving. Sometime during the 1999–2000 school year, a father came to Mary Ellen Hood to complain that Aaron had showed up at his house one afternoon, wanting to treat his son to lunch. The family had just moved, and he had no idea how Aaron knew where they lived.

"I don't want my son around Aaron Thompson," he told her, asking for the boy's removal from Aaron's PE class. Hood refused, thinking his concerns irrational: teachers walk students to and from gym class, she said, and there was no way his son would be alone with Aaron. (Little did the father realize, his son was regularly late to Prochaska's computers class. Which is to say he was among the victims.) Hood told the father not to worry: everyone at Grace had known Aaron for years and years and years.

Privately, however, Hood met with head administrator John Dunlavey—instead of going to the authorities. They told Aaron that under no circumstances was he allowed to be alone with children off-campus. None of the other teachers at Grace were informed, and no paperwork to this effect was ever found in Aaron's file.

In September of 2000, a mother called Grace to talk with Principal DeeAnn McKay, who had recently succeeded Mary Ellen Hood. After her son freaked out when asked to undress for a physical, a doctor wondered if there was sexual abuse in the child's past. McKay said she didn't know of anything. The boy was another one of Aaron's victims, also late to Prochaska's class.

Then, in early October, another mother contacted McKay, expressing concern that Aaron was giving her son special attention: an extra birthday cupcake, a kiss on the cheek during gym class to encourage him when he was struggling to finish laps; she'd also seen Aaron play-fully swatting kids on the butt. Then, there was yet another mother who called McKay in October to inform her that Aaron had removed three boys from class, walked them toward the edge of Grace's property, told two of them to stay put, and led Jason Taylor alone into the woods.

Jason's father figure paid Principal McKay a visit in late October 2000. He wanted her to know that Aaron was planning to host a sleepover for a group of third-grade boys after Grace's annual Hallelujah Party. Plus, earlier that year, Aaron took Jason alone to the movies and back to his house afterward. McKay then talked with Mary Ellen Hood, the previous principal. Hood told her that she'd instructed Aaron not to be alone with students off-campus. Hood was surprised to learn that Aaron was now disobeying those orders.

After all this, on October 27, 2000, McKay and head administrator John Dunlavey sat Aaron down for a marathon two-and-a-half-hour-long meeting. (This was a year before the signing of the "do not fondle" agreement.) Dunlavey explained that good Christians often get falsely accused of things, giving examples of legal cases he'd learned about in grad school for Christian school administration at ORU. Dunlavey and McKay laid down the rules: no being alone with children off-campus (maintain "two-deep leadership" as they called it).

"What if I get invited to a swim party at someone's house?" Aaron asked. "Only where there would be numerous other adults present," Dunlavey answered. They instructed Aaron to stop babysitting and inviting students to his house. McKay would monitor Aaron's compliance with the babysitting stipulation by periodically asking him if he was babysitting. Grace ran on the honor system.

There was yet another incident in October of 2000. Zach Sweeney, a first grader, was on the merry-go-round one day at lunch. Aaron helped him off. Zach made a beeline for his teacher, telling her Aaron had touched his genitals. Aaron assured the teacher it must have been an accident; Zach insisted it was intentional. Later, the teacher called Zach's dad. He hung up the phone thinking it was an accident. The teacher said she never reported the incident to anyone else—not Grace, not the police.

Zach had done well in kindergarten at Grace, but something changed in first grade. He started getting in trouble at school, especially for sexually acting out—one of the more common indicators a child has been molested. (Yet, some victims don't have any noticeable behavior change.) Zach suddenly hated school and refused to give his mom, Julie, a reason. "What about PE? You get to run around and play," Julie asked him. "I hate going to PE," Zach answered. Until then, Aaron had been Zach's favorite teacher. He'd been Julie's favorite too. Aaron seemed like the only teacher at Grace who didn't look down on them for not living in a million-dollar home. In fact, the Sweeneys could barely afford tuition, which was about $2,000 per year. Then, too, there were the monthly fundraisers students were required to participate in.

Julie met with Principal McKay, telling her Zach wasn't doing well at Grace, and the financial burden was overwhelming the family. "Have you thought about getting a second job?" McKay asked. Julie explained they'd still be short. "Well you and your husband could both get part-time jobs," McKay suggested. Both Julie and her husband were working forty-hour weeks already. She told McKay they had an eight-month-old baby at home, a boy they'd never see if they followed her advice. As Julie saw it, McKay only cared about Grace losing their tuition money. Colleagues say McKay was a real go-getter, determined to climb all the way from kindergarten teacher—where she began—to elementary school principal. Like Mary Ellen Hood before her, Grace was McKay's life. Blonde, always ready with a fake smile, she was one with the institution: "Grace personified," as one longtime teacher described McKay. To let a family leave the school was to admit Grace was not perfection upon a hill in Broken Arrow. "You should think about what is important to God," Julie remembers McKay adding.

Julie left the principal's office bawling. She withdrew Zach from Grace shortly thereafter. It was then that Zach told her, "There's someone there who is touching kids in their private area." It was Aaron, and Zach was one of those kids. It is painful for her to think back on it, but Julie didn't believe her son. Aaron? No way, not in a million years. It is a common misconception that children lie about sexual abuse. In reality, kids rarely ever do. But Julie consulted with her husband, who told her about the teacher's phone call, and they considered the matter settled. They should have but did not make a report to the authorities—like Grace, except without the whole body of additional knowledge Grace had.

During the whole 2000–2001 school year, Aaron would pop by Grace's after-school program, help himself to cookies, and ask to borrow a boy.

"May I borrow so and so?" he'd tell the after-school workers, and they'd go with Aaron and then come back alone an hour later with a piece of candy.

Head administrator Dunlavey and Principal McKay hadn't told anyone else at Grace that Aaron was not to be alone with boys. At the end of the school year, Aaron decided to have a daycare in his house for Grace boys. This was after he'd been ordered to stop babysitting. McKay knew about it in advance and did nothing to stop it; Dunlavey found out after the fact. Four boys were molested at Aaron's home daycare during the summer of 2001.

"I'm glad to hear it," McKay gushed when another Grace employee remarked that he'd asked Aaron to serve as a counselor at Camp Dry Gulch, where Grace kids went. Two boys were molested at summer camp the summer of 2001.

FIRST ANONYMOUS LETTER

Josh made his parents promise not to tell a soul. They promised. He was in tenth grade. At school, he could not become The Kid Who Got Molested. Together, Josh and his parents drafted the first anonymous letter. Josh had a hunch he wasn't the only one who'd attempted or considered suicide. "This is a matter of life or death for a child or children," the letter urged. "We thank God every day that this did not go unrevealed any longer in our son's life … [He] will not carry this experience and shame into his adult life, as others may." The letter was signed, "Your Brother & Sister in Christ."

Addressed to head administrator John Dunlavey, the letter arrived on August 16, 2001, by certified mail. Dunlavey opened it and prayed, "Lord, what do I do with this?"

Dunlavey photocopied the letter and took it straight to Pastor Bob and Associate Pastor Chip Olin. Instead of contacting the authorities, Olin and Pastor Bob went to their lawyers. That consultation did not lead Grace to go to the authorities, either. Instead, they took the law into their own hands, with Dunlavey as their detective.

Grace installed cameras in the hallways. Dunlavey and Principal McKay walked by the gym a little more often than usual, keeping an eye out. Every Tuesday afternoon, during his weekly meeting with Pastor Bob, Dunlavey would report back what he'd seen: a whole lot of nothing. Grace would later testify that they interpreted the letter as a generic warning: about what and about whom, they weren't sure, but they claimed nobody suspected sexual abuse. They latched onto the ending: "Watch, pray, open your eyes, be discreet, and above all use wisdom. God will reveal the truth!"

SECOND ANONYMOUS LETTER

By October 21, 2001, God had still not revealed the truth. Two days after the "do not fondle" agreement was signed, another anonymous letter arrived at Grace. It was addressed to Ron Palmer, the chief of the Tulsa Police Department, and CC-ed to Pastor Bob and Dunlavey.

"I am obligated by law and by integrity to inform you that I know PERSONALLY that Mr. Aaron Thompson … sexually molested a boy at school." This, too, was written by Josh's parents. They were frustrated that nothing seemed to change after their first letter.

Upon the second letter's arrival, Dunlavey got called into Pastor Bob's office. Dunlavey asked Pastor Bob what they should do. Pastor Bob said he and Associate Pastor Olin would take care of it. Sometime after that, Pastor Bob and Olin discussed the letter with Dan Beirute, their lawyer at Winters & King, Inc.

Dunlavey and Olin called Aaron in for another meeting and handed him the letter.

"I don't know what to say," Aaron told them.

"Some encouraging words would be really good right about now," said Olin. "Like, 'I didn't do this,' or 'I've never done this before' and—or 'that is not me.'" Aaron simply nodded in agreement.

It was a short meeting. Dunlavey and Olin reminded Aaron about the guidelines of the Corrective Action Plan, and then he was dismissed.

TPD says they never received the letter. Later, Grace's lawyer explained to the jury that Pastor Bob and Olin figured they'd be hearing from the police if there was any reason to be concerned.

Dunlavey testified that contacting the authorities on his own pre-rogative was out of the question: Pastor Bob and Olin called the shots. Dunlavey explained, "I don't think I would have done it without them okaying it and putting their blessing on it."

THE ARREST

One Saturday, Lorrie Taylor was driving her son Jason, a fourth grader, home from a basketball game. Her cell phone rang. It was Aaron, and he asked to speak to Jason.

"I love you, too," Jason said to Aaron as he hung up the phone that day.

Lorrie spent the weekend grilling her son about those four words. Jason was defensive and angry. She knew something was not right. Recently, Jason had begged her not to have Aaron babysit him. On Monday, they were in the car again, stopped at a stoplight. She asked him flat out: "Has Aaron Thompson ever touched you in your privates?"

Jason answered yes.

On March 12, 2002, Lorrie met with school administrators in Jason's fourth-grade classroom. She told them what Jason had told her: Aaron had rubbed his genitals in chapel at Grace. Lorrie was beside herself: on the one hand, she didn't think Jason would lie about something like this; and on the other hand, she—like everyone else—didn't think Aaron could possibly have done anything of the sort. Jason's teacher told the group she had interviewed Jason herself, and she believed him. Lorrie watched the associate pastor, the principal, and the school's head ad-ministrator take it in. She was struck that none of them seemed the least bit surprised.

At the end of the meeting, they prayed together.

Lorrie had mentioned Aaron's ongoing babysitting of Jason, which meant Aaron violated Grace's Corrective Action Plan. This required a firm response. But Jason's molestation allegation was a separate matter—and one Dunlavey and Olin would later say they didn't actually believe. They decided to suspend Aaron. Olin then called Pastor Bob, who was traveling.

Rather than contact DHS or the Tulsa Police Department, Pastor Bob decided to confront Aaron upon his return. Olin made some phone

calls—to Grace's attorneys at Winters & King, Inc.: Dan Beirute and
Mike King. The next day, Olin announced that Grace employees were
to bring him any and all documents pertaining to Aaron. (Youth pastor
Mike Goolsbay, for his part, destroyed a photograph of Aaron.) Olin
handed the cache over to the attorneys.

A meeting with Aaron was scheduled for Wednesday, March 20—a
full eight days after Lorrie Taylor's confrontation—"in order to allow
[him] to hear the allegation," Dunlavey later wrote in a letter to the
International Christian Accrediting Association, detailing Grace's
extra-judicial proceedings. During those intervening eight days, Dunlavey
said, "All I did was pray."

Wednesday came around. Associate Pastor Chip Olin, head administrator John Dunlavey, attorney Dan Beirute, and Pastor Bob met with
Aaron in the church's conference room. Olin told Aaron that they'd had
a molestation report from a parent. Olin asked if it was true. There was
a long pause. Finally, Aaron answered yes. They asked if there were
others, and Aaron named two additional boys. Olin beseeched Aaron
to report himself to the police. Aaron hesitated, so Olin called a Grace
congregant who was a police officer. Then, another TPD child abuse
detective called back.

At the end of the meeting, Olin, Dunlavey, and Beirute had Aaron
call DHS to report himself. Pastor Bob had already left the room by this
point.

"I think he had other responsibilities," Olin testified.

TPD arrested Aaron on March 25, 2002. Five days later, Pastor Bob
wrote an open letter to the congregation and parents at the school.

"That such behavior may have occurred and caused injury to children
is unthinkable," he noted. "Pray for the children and the families directly affected, especially for the children."

Pastor Bob's next letter to parents on April 5 began with an apology.
"The time required to focus on these events has made it difficult to
communicate with those who matter to me most—you and your family."
Pastor Bob encouraged parents to be in touch. By proxy. "I have
directed Chip Olin, Associate Pastor, with responding to you directly,"
wrote Pastor Bob. He assured the parents that Grace was "aggressively
developing community resources that will give us guidance to ensure
that this never again happens at our school." But, when Dunlavey and

McKay testified nearly two years later, they said no changes had been made to Grace's child-abuse reporting policies since then.

It should be noted that Dunlavey, along with Principals Hood and McKay, had certificates of completion from "Child Lures," a popular national sex-abuse prevention program offered in conjunction with their law firm, Winters & King, Inc. At public schools in Oklahoma, staff are required to undergo yearly training on recognizing and reporting child abuse and neglect.

THE MONTHS AFTER THE ARREST (2002)

Over a lifetime, the monetary costs of caring for a sex-abuse victim can be sky high. Clergy sex-abuse victims generally expect settlements of about a million dollars apiece. In lawsuits against the Catholic church, attorney fees ate up about 40 percent of the settlements. In 2003, Aaron pleaded guilty to molesting nine boys between 1996 and 2002—sixteen counts of lewd molestation and two counts of sexual abuse of a minor. (Aaron's twenty-five-year sentence ends in 2027, but he's up for parole in 2023.) Long after Aaron's plea agreement, a tenth and eleventh boy came forward and successfully sued Grace for negligence. If Grace's settlements approximated those of Catholic churches, the Aaron Thompson ordeal could've cost them about $11 million, not including the defense's attorney fees.

In the aftermath of Aaron's arrest, faced with a spate of costly negligence lawsuits, Pastor Bob circled the wagons. In 2002, on the advice of their law firm Winters & King, Inc., Grace moved all of their assets into a dummy corporation. A $7.5 million mortgage, $1.2 million in cash, all of Grace's furniture and equipment—everything went into Grace Fellowship Title Holding Corporation. In a letter to Bank of the West, Grace board member and Financial Director John Ransdell explained that the board approved the corporate restructuring in hopes of "protecting the assets of the church in the event of a catastrophic event in the school that resulted in a momentary award exceeding insurance coverage." Ransdell is currently the president of Grace's Covenant Federal Credit Union, a position he's held since 1993.

In court filings, plaintiffs' lawyers alleged Grace had committed fraudulent conveyance, which is a civil offense. All the Grace lawsuits were settled before reaching the stage at which a court might have awarded damages for fraudulent conveyance. Several plaintiffs' lawyers told me Grace's financial maneuverings didn't impact their settlements. But it's the thought that counts. As attorney Clark Phipps explained, it "rubbed salt in the wounds" of the victims and their families.

Plaintiffs' lawyer Laurie Phillips remembered it took forever to assemble a jury for *John Does 1-7 versus Grace*. Potential jurists kept getting disqualified. As Phillips put it dryly, "Everybody in Tulsa has been molested in Tulsa County—or has a sister or a brother or a child who was." Each year, Oklahoma DHS has about 1,700 confirmed cases of child sex abuse, with underreporting a given.

After a grueling seven-week trial, in October 2004 the jury found that Grace had acted in "reckless disregard" and awarded the seven John Does a total of $845,000. The individual amounts ranged from $75,000 to $250,000. It was a pittance, given that each boy paid about $60,000 in lawyer fees that came out of their settlements. The jury found Pastor Bob, Associate Pastor Chip Olin, head administrator John Dunlavey, Principal Dee Ann McKay, and former Principal Mary Ellen Hood had acted negligently. (According to plaintiffs' lawyers, Mike Goolsbay was not a defendant in the trial because his role with the lewd emails didn't come out until late in the discovery process. Goolsbay was named in two subsequent lawsuits.) "Reckless disregard" meant the jury could have awarded punitive damages in the next stage of the trial, but the lawyers settled out of court for an undisclosed amount before then. The court had capped the possible punitive damages amount at $870,000, so it's a fair bet that the plaintiffs settled for less than that.

Seven boys, less than $2 million in settlements. Grace got off cheap, especially considering that, as one boy's mother told the *Tulsa World*, the school had "turned and looked the other way and protected their reputation and not my son." Grace's new children's building almost certainly cost far more than the settlement.

On the Sunday after the settlement, Prochaska and the anonymous "Special T" said Pastor Bob announced the news to the congregation. Prochaska remembered punch and cookies at the end of church services; the anonymous "Special T" remembered a song with a pointed chorus: "freedom, freedom." Thinking back to that Sunday, Prochaska's colleague reflected, "Pastor Bob had the whole church rejoicing over them being free of [the lawsuit]—not praying for the families." Several victims' families confirmed that Pastor Bob never offered them an apology.

JOSH'S LAWSUIT

Josh and his family didn't want to sue. (Josh testified in the John Does' trial but wasn't one of the 1 – 7.) But, with his statute of limitations about to expire on his 19th birthday, Josh filed an extension protecting his right to sue—just in case. Sure enough, shortly thereafter, Grace stopped paying for his therapy.

Josh wanted something that Grace—as a corporate entity deeply vested in protecting its assets—would never give him: an apology; a recognition that he'd been wronged and hurt; an assurance that the people in charge were sorry for failing him. A court could tell him what Grace would not: the school hadn't protected him when they could have and should have. "If Bob had been kind and repentant and just a little heartbroken," Josh reflects, "I would have never sued Grace."

In February 2005, during the discovery period of the suit, Pastor Bob and his lawyer submitted a request for admission that tried to get Josh to "admit that you touched Aaron Thompson in a sexual manner before he first touched you in a sexual manner." Josh was eleven when the abuse started.

Grace also subpoenaed his therapist's notes, apparently trawling for material that would help make the case that Josh had somehow seduced Aaron as a fifth grader. After that, Josh could no longer trust the very person who was supposed to help him heal. He was just start-ing to get to the place where he didn't think the abuse was his fault. But that set him back. Way back.

While Pastor Bob engaged in victim blaming, surprisingly, no one at Grace retroactively labeled Aaron a gay child-molester. This was re-markable for a deeply conservative megachurch that offered "Restoration by Grace," an in-house pray-away-the-gay counseling program.

Josh's entire middle school and teen years were taken up with his abuse—first with the molestation itself, and then with the criminal case against Aaron and the lawsuits and the endless depositions and hearings. It all blended together. The subpoenas were never-ending. He was forced to live it again and again and again. He said what many sexual assault survivors say: the protracted agony of the legal system was yet another assault. During one deposition, as he talked he could see his mom through a window in the door. She was sobbing.

After Aaron's arrest, Josh defected from Grace and spent the remainder of high school in homeschooling. Reading on his own, learning about things like evolution, he marveled at the realization that Bible class, science class, and history class had been pretty much interchangeable at Grace. Slowly, he began to cast off his biblical worldview. The only direct Grace contact Josh had was with John Dunlavey, who was always apologetic and kind when they'd run into each other. So Josh was surprised when Pastor Bob's lawyers contacted him with a message: Pastor Bob wanted to discuss a settlement with him over lunch at Marie Callender's, a home-style chain restaurant.

Josh thought Pastor Bob wanted to say he was sorry for what had happened. He also thought Pastor Bob was taking him to lunch. But it soon became clear that Josh was paying his own way, and Pastor Bob was not there to apologize. Josh ordered a glass of water and watched Pastor Bob eat.

"He quoted scriptures about how I was sinning against God for coming against his church, his ministry," Josh remembered. But Josh came prepared with scripture passages of his own, about the responsibility of a shepherd to protect his flock. The message fell on deaf ears. Josh drank his water. Pastor Bob ate a big meal and ordered dessert.

THE SCHOOL CLOSES

In the year after Aaron's arrest, Grace saw an exodus of students who headed for other Christian schools attached to Tulsa-area megachurches, like Victory Christian Center or Church on the Move. But before long, enrollment stabilized, more or less. Then the economy went bad. At the end of the 2008 – 2009 school year, Grace had 300 kids in grades K–12. The previous year it'd been 400.

In May 2009, Pastor Bob announced he was closing the high school. Nineteen employees lost their jobs. Everyone hoped it would be temporary—as soon as the economy got back on track. But in July 2010, Grace announced it was closing the elementary school, too. After thirty-two years in operation, the church was losing too much money on the school.

Josh's mother broke the news.

"Good riddance," he texted back.

THE LONG ARM OF GRACE

Jeff and Lynn wanted to send their son Gabe to a good Christian school. Gabe had always been an easygoing kid. But somewhere around first or second grade at Grace, he changed. Lynn would pick him up in the afternoon, and Gabe would beat on the dashboard, saying he hated school and didn't want to go back. He started acting out. Over the years, just about every counselor or doctor who looked at Gabe would tell his parents he had all the hallmarks of sexual abuse in his past. Jeff and Lynn guessed Gabe was in denial. Of course, they didn't realize Gabe was one of the boys who were late to Laura Prochaska's computers class.

"My son just got out of jail again," Jeff begins to tell me over the phone, his voice weary. "He got home and lasted two days before he was back on drugs." Jeff and Lynn are the kind of people who strive to keep their driving records spotless.

Once, Gabe threatened to slit his parents' throats.

"That night I found a box blade under his mattress," Jeff remembers. "At that point in life it didn't surprise me. We had been down the path with him so much. We were living with 30 or 40 holes in our walls from him kicking them in." To say Gabe was angry was an understatement.

One year shortly before Christmas, Jeff and Lynn were on yet another psych ward with Gabe. Something snapped, and Gabe threw a chair at a plate glass window, aiming for his mother. On Christmas Day, calling from another in-patient facility, Gabe finally broke down and admitted it.

"Mom," he said, "something did happen at Grace."

———————————

The stipulations of the settlement don't allow Jeff to name dollar figures, but he says it doesn't even begin to cover the cost of rehabs and detoxes and psych wards and halfway houses. A weekend on a psychiatric unit costs $12,000. Jeff and Lynn have paid Gabe's medical bills instead of putting away money for their retirement. Besides Gabe, several of Aaron's other victims have required in-patient treatment of one kind or another.

A lifetime ago, Jeff and Lynn had an account in Grace's Covenant Federal Credit Union. That was just the culture. "You're one for all and all for one, and you're trying to help each other," Jeff explains. "Why not keep it in the family?"

At some point in the phone call, Lynn comes home. She tells Jeff she brought some groceries over to Gabe that day. Gabe's doing well, for now at least, which is all they can hope for. During those times when she's scared of their son, or if Gabe's lashing out and calling her names, or if he's in one of his explosive rages, Jeff tells Lynn not answer the phone: he'll deal with Gabe. But, Jeff explains, she always caves in, wanting to help. His voice becomes soft. I get the feeling Lynn is standing nearby—that Jeff is talking to her now. "She's so tender, and so loving."

In November, Jeff and Lynn renewed their wedding vows and went on a second honeymoon to Hawaii. They love their son, they will be there for him, but now the next chapter of their lives is beginning. "He's part of life, but he's not all of life," Jeff says, determined to make this a reality.

Gabe met his girlfriend in rehab. Last year, Jeff and Lynn helped the couple get set up in an apartment, assembled donated furniture from friends, and paid for the first three months rent. Two weeks after moving in, Gabe was in police custody again: a domestic assault against his girlfriend. They're still together. In March, she gave birth to their son. Then, Gabe returned to jail, serving his sentence for last year's assault charge; mother and child just checked into court-ordered rehab and can't see visitors for a month. "Kinda takes the fun out of being a grand-parent," Jeff wrote in an email shortly before this story went to press.

Julie Sweeney and her husband were not fated to have a second honeymoon. Who is to say what ends a marriage, but the life Julie and her husband had together for fourteen years could only withstand so much. The pressures of the aftermath of Zach's molestation were not among the things they could bear—together, at least. Trusting one's own had been a basic fact of everyday life. Suddenly, everything they took for granted in this world was upended. Abuse is experienced by entire families, and it goes on long after the physical part is over. In the wake of Aaron's arrest, for the parents of the victims, at least two other marriages broke up.

It took Julie nearly a decade to be among Christians again, to conceive of church as a place where healing might be found. "I lost faith in people," Julie says. "I didn't lose faith in God."

If Gabe is one end of the sexual-abuse spectrum, Josh is at the other. Of the two paths, child abuse experts say Gabe's is probably more common. The deck is stacked against abuse victims.

In his teens, Josh was angry: at Grace, Christianity, his parents, everything and everyone—but especially at Aaron and Pastor Bob. "I used to dream of beating Aaron and Bob with baseball bats," Josh remembers.

After settling his lawsuit, around the time he turned 20, a realization set in. All that bitterness wasn't making him the person he wanted to be. So he hit the road, crisscrossing the country, ending up at the 2006 Austin City Limits music festival. It was there that he got a tattoo across the underside of his left forearm: Hebrew letters that spell out "mechilah"—forgiveness. Forgiveness was what Josh wanted: not the Christian concept of forgiveness, but more a state of mind—of being at peace with the past.

Forgiveness was a goal, not an immediate reality. Josh returned to Tulsa and made a second suicide attempt. He swallowed two bottles of Tylenol PM and woke up in a hospital bed. "All my family and friends were huddled around me," Josh says. "I was so embarrassed and disappointed that I was still there." He spent the next few weeks on the psychiatric ward, wishing he'd been successful.

By the time he got the tattoo, life had settled down enough for him to mourn just how much of it he'd missed. 1996 to 2006 was Josh's lost decade. He was a little kid, and then, suddenly, he was an adult. Growing up, growing into one's own as a sexual being—Josh had been denied these things. "I couldn't imagine a future without something terrible happening to me."

In the years that followed, Josh worked at letting go. There on his arm, he bore mechilah, a daily reminder. That's what he wanted, especially for himself—for "letting it happen to me," as Josh puts it.

"For a long time I had the mentality of 'I am a child abuse victim,'" Josh says. "Now I have other things. It's not something that defines me like it once did."

At 27, Josh is ready to leave Tulsa. He has always felt years behind everyone else his age. But he's catching up. He was just accepted to a prestigious art school. He'll enroll in the fall. Meanwhile, Josh works a day job and makes art. That's what got him through his teens and into his twenties, and that's what will take him to whatever comes next.

Dick Thompson, Aaron's father, and I emailed back and forth for some time. I wanted to visit Aaron at the Joseph Harp Correctional Center, where he is said to have a thriving prison ministry. The Thompsons were deciding as a family whether they wanted to risk "going public" with their experiences. Christmas 2011 turned into the New Year. There was a much apologized for lull while the Thompsons remodeled their house. Then, I got this email:

> Aaron took a situation that could have destroyed him, but with God's help has received healing, rehabilitated himself, and moved on accepting responsibility and consequences for what he did. Our prayer is that all of the alleged victims have also received healing and moved on with their lives. However, we know that may not be true for all of them. Those who are stuck in the past and resisted God's healing and forgiveness will continue to blame Aaron and others for whatever failures they have in their lives. Being fondled or molested as a child, is a very bad thing, but many, many people who have gone through that have grown up to be very successful individuals and even role models for others, so it is not an experience that cannot be overcome. As with all things that happen in our lives, it's not what happens to us but how we respond that makes or breaks us and/or reveals our true character.

It turned out that Josh did not resent Dick Thompson's character-ization of the long-term effects of abuse as personal failings on the part of the victims.

"Parents always want to see the best in their children," he replied. He was calm. I was baffled.

"You're not angry?" I asked.

"I guess I'm just all out of anger," he said.

PASTOR BOB'S PRACTICAL WISDOM

Photos of Corvettes are displayed on the bookshelf in Pastor Bob's office. One day shortly before Thanksgiving, Pastor Bob welcomed me into his domain. He held forth behind his big wooden desk, wearing jeans and a gray wool pullover that clung to his belly.

"We trusted this kid," Pastor Bob told me. "I'm not omniscient—I'm not like God," he noted. "The church is just people."

Up close, Pastor Bob's skin had a purplish putty quality. His bulbous pug nose was a few shades darker than the rest of his face. Pastor Bob continued, "You never quit trusting people. You just get wiser through the years."

Soon, our conversation turned to Penn State, which had recently been cast into the national spotlight over what appeared to be a child sex abuse cover-up. Pastor Bob hoped there were Believers on staff there to guide the university through the dark times to come. He identified with the school's predicament, he said, for he too had once been accused of turning a blind eye at Grace. He remembered the parents of the victims were particularly accusatory. "When we found out, we fired [Aaron] and called the police," Pastor Bob said. "But it's never early enough with them."

Every day during the seven-week *John Does 1 – 7 versus Grace* trial, Pastor Bob's wife, Loretta, made him a list of scripture to read. He drew spiritual strength from the Psalms on deliverance and protection, espe-cially Psalm 91. "He'll protect you from arrow by day, the terror by night, the snare of the fowler," Pastor Bob recited, his own condensed version. When the jury came back with the verdict, Pastor Bob marveled at the low amount Grace had to pay the victims.

Before long, Grace got back to business as usual, as Pastor Bob always knew they would. He leaned forward slightly and bridged his hands. "Many are the afflictions of the righteous, but the Lord brings you through all of them," Pastor Bob said. "So we came through."

Today, Pastor Bob estimated 50 or 60 percent of the congregation was unaware of what took place at Grace a decade ago. "The Lord moves on. He promises you that," Pastor Bob reflected, smiling broadly now. "The ability to forgive and forget is—" Here he paused. "Divine."

My time with Pastor Bob was up. On the way out, his secretary, Gwen Olin—Associate Pastor Chip Olin's widow—wished me a blessed day.

———————

Back when the lawsuits were underway, Principal DeeAnn McKay was working toward her doctorate in Christian educational administration at Oral Roberts University. Associate Pastor Chip Olin died of cancer in 2007. Now retired, former Principal Mary Ellen Hood lives in Jenks. Since 2007, former head administrator John Dunlavey has been the principal of a private Christian school in South Korea. Dunlavey declined interview requests, saying he wanted others to learn from Grace's ordeal but was worried his words would be "taken out of context."

Mike Goolsbay, Grace's former youth pastor, has his own congregation now, Destiny, a massive stadium of a church with the motto "Loving People." By car, Destiny is about three miles northeast of Grace, a stone's throw as distances go in Broken Arrow. Goolsbay still refers to Pastor Bob as "my pastor." For financial guidance, Destiny's website recommends John Ransdell, the one who was tasked with maneuvering Grace's assets into the dummy corporation. Like Grace, Destiny is represented by Winters & King, Inc.

I asked Mike King how he'd hypothetically advise Destiny Church if they were to receive an anonymous letter exactly like the first one Josh's parents sent to Grace. King gave a little chuckle, answering, "Well, it would depend upon the facts and circumstances."

If anything, the lesson of Grace should be that it never depends.

Just before Thanksgiving, I went to Destiny's Saturday night church service. On stage, Goolsbay sat comfortably on a stool, against a backdrop of neon blue paneling and jumbotrons. A far cry from Pastor Bob's formal pulpit manner, Goolsbay ran his service like a call-in radio show, his speech peppered with "dude" and "sweet" and the occasional "ridonku-lous." He videochatted a housebound congregant set to soft keyboard music; played for laughs with a call to his wife to see if she'd found his lost wallet; and gave a sermon in what he calls his "Perils of Power" series. The message: accountability begins at home, top-down, from parents to children. King David must hold his son Ammon accountable for raping his daughter Tamar. Leaders went unmentioned.

Former parishioners say Grace's heyday was over three decades ago, at the old church building out on Memorial Drive, a few miles west of the citadel on Garnett Road, in the building that was later sold to Higher Dimensions church (where its pastor, Carlton Pearson, stopped believing in hell and all hell broke loose). It was standing-room only back then, with people crammed on a balcony that was really just a half story. That was the heyday of the Word movement, too, when a mega-pastor could take to the pulpit and bring the house down and that's all anybody expected from him.

"Now people want somebody a little more personable," explains a former Grace member who'd been deeply rooted in the church for decades. Others were less charitable in their assessments of Pastor Bob: "no emotion" and "nothing behind the eyes." Tulsa, of course, is a city with ever-multiplying options.

On Sundays, Grace's parking lot is typically half full, if that. The church still offers a kids program, but attendance has dwindled. Peek into the children's building on a Sunday, and you'll find more building than children. Grace's membership appears to skew older, now, toward the retiree set. In the sanctuary/former gym, the big, padded seats are spread further apart, masking the emptiness. Basketball hoops are folded against the ceiling. The gym floor is still emblazoned with a maroon and gray decal of a basketball with the lettering "Grace Christian Eagles," a relic from another time.

Recently, Grace board members gave Pastor Bob a list of thirty things he could do to be more "people friendly."

"Why aren't things like they used to be?" he asked them. He was genuinely puzzled.

The Sunday before Rick Santorum won the Oklahoma primary on Super Tuesday, the former Pennsylvania Senator made a single campaign stop in Tulsa. Santorum spoke from the pulpit of Grace's gym/sanctuary, where he denounced liberals for thinking "the elite should decide what's best for those in flyover country." The crowd cheered and waved their Santorum placards, the word "COURAGE" projected upon the jumbotrons that flank the stage. It was a packed house.

Back in the day, Pastor Bob would say he'd preach 'til he died. But those close to the church board say he's announced he wants to step down soon. His son, Pastor Robb Yandian, will ascend the pulpit. Aaron has fifteen more years to serve on his sentence. The boys are now men.

Grace never built the auditorium they'd planned, the one that would have connected the children's building with the main wing. They constructed what was to be the connecting wall of the children's building out of material that wasn't weatherproof, leaving it vulnerable to the elements. There are leakage problems now. There is also talk of perhaps selling the land in front of Garnett Road just to make ends meet. Then again, maybe things aren't so bad: Grace had a budget of nearly $5 million last year and ended 2011 in the black.

Heading toward the Mingo Valley Expressway on the way out of Broken Arrow, you can see, rising from the hillside, something that looks like a brand new airport hotel. It's stamped with rainbow-colored lettering large enough for passing cars along East 91st Street to read from across an immense grassy field: "Grace Kids."

Inside, a gilded carousel awaits.

MOOD SWING

Spade Cooley, a famous Western swing fiddler turned
wife-murderer, played his last show at Oakland's Paramount
Theatre and then died to a standing ovation

By *Steve Gerkin*

ON A FURLOUGH FROM A CALIFORNIA STATE PRISON, convicted
wife-killer Spade Cooley walked off the stage of Oakland's Paramount
Theatre, basking in the thunderous applause of 2,800 Western swing
aficionados who'd come to see the former fiddle star turned inmate.
Anchoring the first half of the show with his three-song set, a beaming
Spade raised his violin above his head, saluting the cheering crowd. Their
jubilation continued as he disappeared behind the curtain, made a
comment to waiting friends and suddenly slumped to the dressing room
floor. Then he died, to a standing ovation.

Part Cherokee, Donnell Cooley was born into a family of fiddlers
on February 22, 1910, in a tornado cellar on a dusty ranch near Grand
in western Oklahoma. Today, Grand twists in the wind, a ghost town
with only the footings of the courthouse and its vault showing above
the red dirt. Even then, it didn't offer enough to hold Cooley.

At the age 21, Cooley lit for California, arriving in Modesto with "a
nickel in my pocket and a fiddle under my arm." Cooley became a farm
laborer, nighttime fiddler, and card gambler. He claimed he couldn't see
himself "farting down a row of beans," preferring instead a future in
Hollywood Westerns, studio recordings, and radio shows. Playing cards

one night he drew three straight flushes, all of 'em spades, and was ever after known as "Spade" Cooley. Feeling lucky, he left for Los Angeles.

Thanks to the scores of 1930s Dust Bowl immigrants heading down Route 66 to the Golden State, honky-tonks and cowboy dance halls became the rage on the West Coast with the likes of Cooley and the Sons of the Pioneers supplying the tunes. Their brand of music was Western swing, characterized by a southwestern-bred hybrid of folk, bluegrass, hillbilly, swing, and jazz.

Spade ruled Western swing on the West Coast. He was challenged by Bob Wills, who brought his Texas Playboys to LA to make a play for Spade's steady gig at Bert Phillips' Venice Pier Ballroom. A battle of the bands took place on the pier with thousands crowding onto the huge dock. Ever the bulldog, Spade crowed that he'd "show who was the king in this here sunny state." Spade won and thereafter proclaimed himself the "King of Western Swing."

With his bandleader style, Cooley was a Benny Goodman in cowboy duds. Likewise, he suited his dozen band members in $500, custom-made Western wear and gave them spiced-up nicknames like Deuce, Cactus, and Smokey. Wills stuck to the old-fashioned band configuration that often included horns, and the more traditional get-up of cowboy suits and neckerchief ties. But more than clothes separated their styles.

Shelby Eicher is bandleader of the Tulsa Playboys, a Western swing band playing monthly at Cain's Ballroom in downtown Tulsa, where an over-sized photo of Spade looks down on the crowd. Eicher, ever a student of swing music, says, "There are fundamental differences between Spade's and Bob's music. Bob had a foot squarely in the blues world and allowed the fiddles to draw more on their ethnic fiddle-tune style. Spade arranged his fiddle section to have a more violin quality.

"The other great difference to my ear is that Bob had access to great songs, many written by Cindy Walker. Spade's material was a little tongue in cheek, and this may have been due to his work in Hollywood. Both men had great bands and were somewhat bigger-than-life characters. Bob Wills had a charisma in my opinion comparable to Elvis Presley, which is a valuable quality that set him apart and added to his legendary status."

Both held dear to the whiskey bottle and paid for it. Wills was known as a binge drinker who'd miss entire performances due to his drinking. He suffered several heart attacks before dying of a stroke in 1975. With his huge success going to his head, Spade was always difficult to handle, but his near-constant drinking made him a devil and a half. And his bent toward physical brutality made him a feared man.

Shortly after Cooley's "Shame on You" hit No. 1 on the country charts, a Missouri clarinetist, Ella Mae Evans, sat in with the band. Despite the pleading of manager Bobbie Bennett who protested, "She had no voice," Cooley made the blonde-haired, brown-eyed Evans his lead singer. He liked to introduce her on stage as "the purtiest little filly in California." They soon married and, not long after, her short vocal career ended with the birth of Melody in 1946 and Donnell Jr. in 1948. Cooley retired her and the kids to his Mojave ranch house.

His career, meanwhile, was about to go meteoric. The "Spade Cooley Time" on KFVD radio in LA became a staple of Southern California airwaves. Not long after, Cooley began starring in his own syndicated TV show. He was hired by Republic Studios, appearing in nearly 50 B-Westerns, usually playing bit parts that often showcased his band. He became a local celebrity in a city full of them and enjoyed the trappings of stardom. He'd loan his 56-foot yacht to Roy and Dale Rogers, who'd take family fishing trips to Catalina Island. His closets were lined with 100 custom cowboy suits, 50 hats, and three dozen pairs of boots. All told, Cooley was bringing in $10,000 a week (about $120,000 today).

But Cooley's drinking was getting the better of him. He drank and fired band members in moments of drunken anger. He got fired from his television show after a ten-year run, at least in part due to his drinking. Things hit rock bottom in 1956, when the radio station cut him loose.

Cooley combined the booze with a pathological jealousy. He convinced himself that Ella Mae was sleeping around. He confessed his love for her, hoping for reassurance. She sat quietly, offering no rebuttal or consolation. With no concrete proof of her straying, Spade became delusional about her supposed betrayals.

His stock continued to plummet when rock 'n' roll came in and danced on the grave of Western swing. The recording contracts, studio calls, and concert bookings dwindled to nothing by 1960. With a reported $15 million in the bank, the little man with the big talent redirected his entrepreneurial ambition to real-estate development.

Licking his wounds, Cooley left his Encino townhouse on fabled Ventura Boulevard and moved in with Ella Mae and the kids, whom he'd kept cooped up all those years at the ranch. Living there put him closer to his new venture, Water Wonderland, a project aiming to cash in on the success of the 1955 opening of Disneyland. Cooley envisioned an eighty-acre park with a lake for boat races, fishing, shops, a big swimming pool and a set for television production.

Being closer to his wife made it easier for Spade to keep track of her movements. Through his alcohol haze, every man was her potential lover. Interrogating her every moment, demanding she confess her extra-marital affairs, he abused her, first with words and later with fists.

By this time in 1961, Cooley began chasing his whiskey shots with uppers in the morning and downers after nighttime boozing. He became disoriented and wildly abusive, forcing Ella Mae to send the kids away to live with a nearby friend.

Ella Mae was in a local hospital recovering from a hysterectomy when Spade caught her on the phone with another man. "So what?" she said. "Now you know." Cooley asked a Wonderland associate if he knew anything about Ella Mae misbehaving. He told him of a man called Bud Davenport and took him to his trailer home in Granada Park.

Cooley confronted Davenport, who gave nothing but guff, so Spade smacked him in the kisser. When he got home and phoned Ella Mae's room, she wouldn't take his call. He called a friend and nurse, Dorothy Davis, and begged her to tell his wife that, "I love her with all my heart."

Ella Mae came home and, for a time, things were calm. It wasn't long, though, before the physical and emotional outrage reached new levels, for both of them. Plied with pills and booze, their thoughts became muddled, adding to the tension. They went back and forth about divorcing, with Ella Mae alternately digging in her heels then yielding. For her trouble, Spade gave her a beating. Then, he'd sober up and say how much he loved her. Finally, Ella Mae cracked.

They went for a drive, and a long talk. Angling for a divorce, Ella Mae confessed to giving a man named Bud Campbell $600 because, "I thought I was in love with him." Spade drove on, numb from the drugs, the drink and the pain. Ella Mae demanded he drive her to her parents in North Hollywood and Spade acquiesced.

He pulled up to the house and she got out of the car, alone. A confused Cooley rolled down the window to say goodbye but, instead, begged her for a second chance. Tormented by the powers of love and drugs, Ella Mae climbed back in the car.

He headed for home. Disconsolate over what might be in store, Ella Mae pushed open her door and leaped from the moving car. "I just want to die," she told Spade, who held her in his arms. "I just want to die."

He wanted to drive her to a hospital but she refused. They went back to the house no longer a home, its rooms strewn with half-eaten hamburgers, rotting apple cores, and multiple pill bottles on the bed stand—pills for tension, pills for nerves, sleeping pills, and phenobarbital.

The next morning, Cooley tried in vain to get back to work. He paced anxiously between drinks. Martin, his only remaining associate, took note of Cooley's bruised hands, which looked more like those of a street fighter than a fiddler. Ella Mae walked into the room wearing a dirty robe, her face discolored and in obvious pain, and slumped into a chair.

Martin knew he had been beating her. Disgusted, he left the house. "I can tell you things now," she said, raising her eyes toward Cooley.

She began with Davenport, of how she'd become a recruit for his free-love cult near Los Angeles. Cooley responded by yelling, his anger ricocheting off the walls. Drunk out of his mind, Cooley went off on Ella Mae.

———————

Fourteen-year-old Melody walked in the house around 6 p.m. A blood-splattered Cooley met her at the door. "You're going to watch me kill her," he said, pointing a gun between her eyes. "If you don't, I'll kill you, too. I'll kill us all."

Ella Mae lay still on the carpet. "We'll see if she is dead," he said. Bending down, he touched his burning cigarette to her skin not once but twice. She didn't move or make a sound.

The phone rang. As Cooley turned to pick up the receiver, Melody ran out the door. He had called several friends to come to the house, telling them Ella Mae was hurt. Eventually, he phoned for an ambulance. Five hours had gone by. As she was loaded onto a stretcher, the driver recalled Cooley saying, "I love you. Please, don't be dead."

The coroner reported that Ella Mae had strangulation bruises and deep, dark contusions on many parts of her body. She died from blood gushing out of a ruptured aorta. Cooley was formally charged with first-degree murder. At trial, the prosecutor called it a "murder by torture" involving stomping, beating, and strangling.

Following weeks of testimony and a break to treat Spade for a heart attack, a jury convicted him on August 19, 1961. Cooley, against his attorney's recommendation, withdrew his insanity plea, opening the door to a possible execution. Instead the judge sentenced him to life in prison, which ordinarily meant the forbidding, hard-time San Quentin. But, with his long history of heart problems, Cooley was assigned to the medical ward of the California state prison at Vacaville, just east of Napa Valley.

Cooley became a model prisoner, found religion, built fiddles in the hobby shop and taught inmates to play. By 1965, he began to show contrition for his wife's murder. In 1966, Ronald Reagan became governor of California. In the 1950s, he'd appeared on Spade's TV shows numerous times. "It seemed like only yesterday those two were clowning around and laughing it up backstage," remembered Bobbie Bennett, Cooley's manager.

A mutual friend in the B-movie business asked Reagan to pardon Cooley. Reagan balked at an official pardon, but the California parole board unanimously recommended Cooley's parole for February 22, 1970, his 60th birthday. Reagan signed the special release papers, telling Bennett he was "repaying an old debt."

Four months before his release, Reagan authorized an interim release allowing Cooley to travel to Oakland to make his first public appearance in nine years. Heading for what he thought was a concert for other inmates, Cooley lit up another cigarette and shuffled out of his elaborately furnished private cell at the Vacaville prison, wearing a borrowed suit several sizes too large. He entered a surprise party thrown for him by high-up prison officials and his former manager Bennett. A bigger surprise was being escorted to a black limousine.

Only told he was playing for an outside benefit, the bewildered Cooley arrived an hour later at the back door of a large auditorium in a jam-packed parking lot. "Must be rasslin' night," Spade said. Escorted to a small dressing room with a pencil-drawn sign scrawled with a misspelled "Cooley" taped to the door, he changed into one of his old, high-dollar band suits Bennett laid out for him.

"Two minutes to show time, Mr. Cooley," a stagehand yelled through the door. "Okay, son. It's a deal," he replied, sweating and scraping nicotine off his front teeth and upper lip. Spade, Bennett, and his old pal and emcee for the event, Chill Wills, walked to the curtain together.

An off-stage announcer introduced Wills, who strolled out to center stage. "Y'all fasten up yer stirrups and cinch-down yer saddles," he growled, "'cause y'all 'bout to take 'nother wild ride with our good ol' fiddlin' friend, the King of Western Swing, Spade Cooley!"

A stunned Spade stepped onto that Oakland stage to play in the "Grand Old Opry Spectacular" benefitting a local sheriff's association. Prior to his first note, Spade thanked the deputies for "the chance to be free for a while." The sold-out auditorium cheered the three songs Cooley played with the 24-piece band, including "Fidoolin'," a "San Antonio Rose" tribute to Bob Wills, and his signature closer, "Shame on You."

Leaving the stage to thunderous applause, he greeted friends and reporters behind the curtain. "I think it is going to work out for me," he said.

With the standing ovation ringing in his ears, he retired to his dressing room to change out of his sweat-laden suit. When he failed to make a curtain call, Wills and Bennett forced open the door. Cooley was naked, sprawled out on the dirty concrete floor where he'd collapsed, holding the broken fiddle neck in one hand and a picture of Ella Mae and him in the other.

Wills announced to the audience, there would be no second half of the show. As the band struck up the sad cowboy dirge, "Goin' Home," Chill Wills told the hushed crowd, "Spade Cooley, is ... is, well, podnahs, he's dead."

THREE

MINDING THE CENTER

SILENCE OF THE GOATS

A group of city women take a class in field dressing, learning
to kill, skin, butcher, and cook a goat, all in an effort to preserve
hunting heritage

By *Spring Houghton*

I EAT MEAT. But I had never killed an animal to eat its meat. I had
always relied on other people, strangers, to kill and process and package
my meat for me. Until I killed a little goat in November, with a few of
my girlfriends.

We left Tulsa at night and drove the winding roads into the prairie
forest of Lake Tenkiller near Tahlequah to camp and take classes on
outdoor living. The classes were offered by an organization called Women
in the Outdoors, which is a part of the National Wild Turkey Federation.
Their goal is to teach outdoor skills to women, and their mission is to
conserve the wild turkey and to preserve hunting heritage. The target
demographic is the Sarah Palins.

Our interests diverged from most of the middle-aged soccer mom
huntresses, but our goal was nonetheless pretty straightforward. We
wanted to be bad-asses.

We signed up for classes like Primitive Cooking, Blacksmithing,
Pine Needle Basket Weaving. We wanted to be well-prepared if a zombie
apocalypse should come; if the shit hit the fan, we wanted to be able to
eat while on the run from zombies. We also wanted to know how to
make utensils and containers. We wanted to be ladies in possession of
practical knowledge, with iron sporks doubling as weapons.

We also signed up for a class called Field Dressing. Here we would learn how to cut meat from animals without puncturing intestines, and how to cut off hides for clothes and shelter in the most efficient way. This is where we would confront our complicit role in the slaughtering of cute animals. If we couldn't deal with the meat from its source, we were thoughtless carnivores. We wanted to be thoughtful carnivores.

We would be empowered and cease, as farmer and philosopher Wendell Berry says, "consenting to an economy that exploits women and men and everything else." Our hands and bones and muscles would fuel our industry. We would help each other and share. We would become one with all living things and with the land. We would separate ourselves from those Americans among us who, he explained, "are far more concerned about the desecration of the flag than we are about the des-ecration of our land." We would learn how to make spoons that would never bend or rust because we, too, had felt frustration that "industrial workmanship is certainly worse than traditional workmanship, and is getting shoddier every day." Free from the dependency of destructive, soul-depleting concrete capitalism. Wendell Berry would be proud.

We would win the coming zombie apocalypse and save all our friends. And we might even become super-human. We would fill our souls, worship ourselves, and become holy.

Without church.

———————————

It's cold near the lake in the middle of November. We set up our tents in the face of a freeze warning. Black night with stars clear and perfectly spaced, like tiny white polka-dots on black velvet. We built a fire, sat in folding chairs, and talked. About jobs, about personal philos-ophy, about food, about eating meat, about parenting, about boys, about girls. We drank Coronas and ate sunflower seeds.

Not one of us slept an entire hour that night, mostly because we were so, so cold. I tried curling up in a fetal ball to conserve heat. I wrapped things around my head and ducked into my sleeping bag. Then my toes got cold, so I covered them with my quilt and a small pile of clothes I couldn't identify in the dark. Then my butt got cold, so I wrapped a scarf around my pelvic area like a bandage. Dozed off. Then wild dogs started barking.

And in the morning, I drank shitty coffee and ate a bite and went to the workshop called Field Dressing. I imagined in my head when I signed up for this class two months prior that there would be a dead but fairly clean deer hung up in a warehouse of some sort, and the instructor would have a knife that s/he would pass around and give each of us a turn cutting something.

But when my friends and I got to the designated meeting spot, there was a trailer full of 10 live, quite cute goats. Their owner, who had raised them from kids, would show us how to kill, skin, and butcher them herself. This was what she bought them for. After they had grazed her pasture as living lawnmowers, they would become food. Goats are prized because they eat a quarter of their weight in weeds and brush—vegetation that cows snub—daily. She appreciated them for their low maintenance, easy demeanor, and appetite.

She shot the first one through its head very precisely to sever the spinal column. She explained the technique humanely. After each goat was shot, we would take turns with the knife, cut the jugular vein, then the carotid. She asked for volunteers. I waited.

One portly 60-something lady turned her head away from the killing scene and toward me and commented that she "didn't realize how much this would affect her." I tried to look strong, but I couldn't help but hug her. I tried to distract her with awkward interview questions. She told me she had been a school teacher but was now retired. She wore a fanny pack and a florescent baseball cap, and she appreciated the small talk.

She shot them one by one. After each shot, a thud, then we students each took a turn with the knife. When it was my turn, I grabbed the knife from my friend's blood-caked hand. The knife was bloody, warm, and sticky; clumps of fur stuck to the blade.

You have to push pretty hard to puncture animal skin. The goat was dead, but its lungs still had breath. I felt like I was pushing the knife too hard. I stupidly thought I might hurt something. I tried to snap out of my emotions by cussing at myself; I told myself that the animal was already fuckin' dead, I just had to cut its blood vessels to let the blood out so that all its organs would stop. Get on with it already. I knew the science, but it took me a few seconds to steady my heart. When I finally sliced through the layers and opened the first vein, blood ran down to the rocks and dead leaves and soil, and steam rose from the blood. Then I flipped the goat's head, heavy with death, and cut the other side.

We cut 10 jugular veins and 10 carotid arteries in all. Then we carried them all by their feet, one lady on the front legs and one lady on the back legs, to a pile of wood so their bodies could finish bleeding out. This took about an hour.

Then we loaded the corpses in the truck and rode with them to the place where we would field dress and butcher them. Once they were all unloaded, we cut them open delicately so as not to puncture their stomachs or intestines or bladders because we didn't want to taint the meat. Then we lifted out their hot, heavy bowels. We set the heart and liver aside. The portly lady called them the "best parts." We cut the hide away from the muscle. We spread the goat body until it resembled a snow angel, and then quartered it. Leg meat, neck and shoulders, back, then ribs. This meat went directly to the kitchen. We sawed off the feet and heads. These parts went to farm dogs. Done.

And half a day later, maybe we didn't become super-human. But we felt like better humans. It felt better knowing how much energy goes into bringing one pound of meat to a kitchen, and providing that fuel with my own hands and heart. It felt good to have my friends helping me cut away connective tissue and saw bone. It felt good to be able to take over the butchering for my breastfeeding friend when she needed a break to go pump milk for her baby back home with the father in midtown Tulsa. It felt good to see all types of women: one who had to use a fake name because she was in a domestic violence protection program, a mother convinced to come live in the outdoors for a few days by her gutsy 11-year-old daughter, retired women, city women, straight women and lesbians, religious women and non-religious, conservatives, liberals, and near anarchists.

To have retreated from computers, neck cramps, disjointed moods, and the monotony of a completely predictable weekday routine, even if for a weekend, felt smart and peaceful and like having found a church where I finally felt at home.

IN THE COMPANY OF GIN

Go on a 'martini safari' with the man who wrote the book on it

By *Mark Brown*

BARNABY CONRAD III POINTED OUT THE HOME OF THE MAI TAI, its entrance obscured by palm fronds and banana trees.

"That's the old Trader Vic's room," he said, handing his keys to a parking attendant. "It's now a pretty popular Vietnamese restaurant."

Le Colonial, it's called, and it manages to fit. When it was Trader Vic's, the area known as Cosmo Place, between downtown and Little Saigon, was a nightlife destination. According to a website that tracks tiki culture, Queen Elizabeth II experienced her first-ever anywhere restaurant meal at Vic's in 1983, as guest of the Reagans, no less. She drank a Tanqueray martini. That Vic's closed in the early '90s.

We walked up Taylor Street to the Bohemian Club. It was Thursday—bohemians' night out. Before dinner, we drank a No. 209 martini at an oak bar long and polished enough to have 10 pins at the end of it, surrounded by large oil paintings and the soft roar of men not at work. I stole a couple of paper napkins off the bar, the club's owl logo teetering across them.

I'd spied the No. 209 tucked among the other gins. It's a newish brand, produced locally in a distillery down at Pier 50, very near the spot where Barry Bonds Jr. used to plunk home runs into the bay. A couple of sips in, I spotted the bottle next to it: Junipero, a small-batch offering from the folks who also brewed Anchor Ale, another San Francisco product.

"Hmm," I said. "Maybe we ordered in haste."

"I know Fritz," Barnaby said, referring to Fritz Maytag, who'd resurrected the old Anchor brewery and then sold it after an award-winning run. "He's 75 and in great shape. Beefy, not obese, you know? You know, like he could have played quarterback at Cal-Berkeley back in the day."

He suggested a trip up the coast to meet Maytag, but I suggested we drink a Junipero instead, as an after-dinner nightcap. The club ranks were beginning to thin and last orders being taken. I wondered if anybody would awaken the older gent I saw napping earlier in the library, his body sunk into the puffy, tan leather of a club chair. I thought of him being left there, like Corduroy, to be discovered in the wee hours by a security guard making rounds.

"Next time," I said about Fritz, sipping the Junipero and making a mental tasting note I soon forgot.

"Anyway," Barnaby said, chinking glasses, "welcome to San Francisco."

He'd grown up here, in the shadow of his writer-saloon keeper father, drinking ginger ale at one end of the bar while the likes of Tyrone Power and Ava Gardner drank gin at the other. Dad Conrad named his bar El Matador, after a novel he wrote on bullfighting called *Matador* became a surprise bestseller. He chronicled those days of wine and roses in a delicious tell-all, *Name Dropping: Tales From My Barbary Coast Saloon*. (A dozen years before, though, he'd published a memoir of a different sort—*Time Is All We Have: Four Weeks at the Betty Ford Center*.)

With writers and drinkers, the olive often doesn't fall far from the tree. Conrad III followed in his father's footsteps with a fistful of books. One of them, *The Martini*, published in 1995, caught the front end of the wave that stranded 'tini menus across American bartops, recipe books in the stacks at Borders, and faux-vintage cocktail shakers on the shelves of Pottery Barn. It was my martini manifesto, a reference guide and devotional in ice-cold words and pictures. Its cover—a tightly cropped photo of a martini glass, its bowl glistening with the droplets of mid-chill—was the model of perfection I pictured when shaking at home during what historian Bernard DeVoto called, and Conrad quoted, "the violet hour."

The same year he published *The Martini*, Conrad met Maurice Kanbar, who couldn't drink more than two martinis without getting a headache. (Conrad's own theory, from page 120: "Even if there's no driving to be done, two's a pretty good limit.") Having the wherewithal and now the need, Kanbar invented SKYY, the quadruple-distilled, blue-bottled beauty that overran the vodka market in the 1990s, in large part because of that cobalt bottle, which he had to get produced outside the country because, he explained, "making glass is a dirty business. You have to have smoke and glass and ovens. Americans don't want to do that. They want to sit at a computer."

But the SKYY wasn't the limit. With his non-compete clause expired—he'd sold SKYY off to spirit conglomerate Campari in 2001—Kanbar now peddles Blue Angel (in a clear bottle of brushed glass), another ultra-distilled spirit in a market he helped saturate.

Kanbar's inventiveness manifests itself in all manner of productions—*Hoodwinked!*, the animated hit film; an 85-cent pair of eyeglasses he wants to distribute pro bono in third-world nations; *Hoodwinked Too! Hood vs. Evil*; Zip Notes, in which he put the adhesive in the middle so the paper wouldn't curl—but, in 2005, it ran to a few square blocks of downtown Tulsa. Kanbar now owns 16 buildings worth of it.

Always a bookish sort, Kanbar's properties have included, almost since its inception, Council Oak Books, the Tulsa publishing house struggling to make it in the world of Kindles and downloads. (As of December, the firm had relocated to San Francisco.) With Conrad, he'd launched a new imprint on Council Oak, Kanbar & Conrad, though he couldn't remember when or how he met his new partner.

"San Francisco is basically a small town, and he's a writer. I like writers. If Barnaby Conrad is a writer, then I immediately have a compatibility with the man. Writers are my guys."

Mine too, especially when they fall in with guys who buy up downtowns in their spare time. You know, when they're not distilling spirits and publishing books. I'd been looking for a reason to get back to San Francisco. Now I had a couple.

"You know he was a tummler?" said one-time columnist Bruce Bellingham.

I pictured Maurice in circus tights, floating beneath the big top. I wouldn't put it past him. I shook my head.

"Not a tumbler," he said, reaching for something to write on and finding it in his breast pocket in the form of a sealed envelope. "It's one of my many medical bills. I had a heart attack in June 2010 and now I have $94,000 in medical bills. And there goes one of them."

Bellingham took another sip of wine, scribbled something on the envelope, then handed it to me.

"A tummler, for you Gentile boys, is a man who's hired in the Catskill Mountains to break up the party before an opening act. So, he's really like a clown. Like Jerry Lewis. It'd be like me going from table to table, 'Hi, ya, how ya doin'!' It's a Yiddish term for a troublemaker. Someone who stirs it up."

Barnaby took a sip of his Blue Angel martini—a gin man segueing into vodka out of homage, I assumed, given that we were in Perry's on Union Street, Maurice's favorite spot, and he was to have been here with us. Kanbar calls a Blue Angel martini a "BAM," believing that a drink without a name is a bottomless well. ("The key to the business is a call," he said. "Like a Cosmo.") Barnaby downed his in an effigy-like salute to its absent inventor, while I paced myself with a Sierra Nevada.

"He wasn't a kid—maybe 19 or 20—and he's been a tummler ever since," said Bellingham. "But, he's cultivated tummling into a finesse. Of course, no one around here knows what a tummler is."

Bellingham wrote columns for the *San Francisco Examiner*, and with San Francisco newspaper icon Herb Caen.

"I wrote jokes for him. I'd send him jokes everyday by fax. Puns, political metaphors. I sat in Herb Caen's office while he was ill and went through 59 years of his column, all gathered in leather-bound books. The *Chronicle* owns them. I thought, 'Where am I going to begin?'

"They had so much fun. You and I cannot imagine. Barnaby can tell you."

Caen and Conrad Junior inhabited a time in San Francisco when the word saloon was a term of endearment. When books were books and men were men and martinis were gin. You can still get a drink there, but the way the old boys—and their sons—tell it, things have all but dried up.

"Single women with dogs and fast-food restaurants and nothing else," Barnaby says of the future city by the bay.

Writer Rebecca Solnit, in her *Infinite City: A San Francisco Atlas*, plots 21 bars on a map of the city's legendary "6 a.m." saloons, so named for the hours they kept in order to better serve the dock workers leaving the graveyard shift. Service and software have replaced shipping, but the bars remain.

Beyond the living proof, there are the dead. Novelist Jack London had a San Francisco saloon mix vast quantities of martinis and ship them to his getaway in Sonoma. "Professor" Jerry Thomas, hands-on author of *The Bar-Tender's Guide*—an 1862 classic that predates them all—made his mark at the Occidental Hotel on Montgomery Street. Thomas makes a good case (particularly for a deceased) for inventing the martini, or at least being its missing link.

Bellingham was in purgatory when Kanbar bailed him out. A local charitable house received a big gift for taking care of Bruce between gigs, courtesy of the man with the golden arm.

"I've not been upset with one gift that I've ever given," Kanbar told me. "But if you asked me about business deals, oh God, have I met snakes."

We left Bruce and Perry's for Bix, next stop on the "martini safari" I'd been promised and was doing my best to make a good show of. We drove up Laguna, jumped over to Broadway, and headed downtown.

Gold Street hides between Sansome and Montgomery, a few blocks in from the Embarcadero. It was called Gold Alley back in the day, when the burlesque clubs and watering holes of nearby Broadway teemed with all that was then rustic and possible about San Francisco. When Streisand was playing the Purple Onion before she was Streisand, and newsmen like Caen had the equivalent of 10,000 Facebook friends, all of it earned in the saloons and restaurants and nightclubs within earshot of here. It's around the block from City Lights Bookstore on the diagonal at Columbus. Chinatown is near, as is American Zoetrope, Francis Ford Coppola headquarters, where the ground-floor café proffers Coppola's own wines at a relative steal, and tempting plates of radicchio *treviso*, spaghetti carbonara, and pizza *quattro formaggi*.

"This is Gold Alley," Barnaby said, pulling into a lane too tight to turn around in, and promising to tell me later about the time he shot a .44 out into the bay standing right here. I looked up over a warehouse roof to see the white apex of the TransAmerica Pyramid. That, the neon of Bix, and the headlights of the sedan were the only lights glowing.

We crowded around the bar at Bix, a restaurant I'd known only from an image in *The Martini*—of other people crowding around the bar at Bix. In the book, author Conrad, proprietor Doug "Bix" Biederbeck, painter Mark Stock, art dealer Martin Muller, Herb Caen, and others smile over a caption labeled "Neo-Martini Culture in San Francisco." In the foreground sits a very large bowl of crushed ice sprouting chilled cocktail glasses like so many spring crocuses.

Biederbeck likes his martinis cold, versus large, and to that end he serves them in small, tulip-shaped glasses, the gin cold enough to induce shock. "Here," he said, retrieving my cocktail from the bartender. "Drink that and I'll get you another."

I sipped, squinting at the peal of competing conversations, and a piece of the city's still-strong drinking culture revealed itself to me. Towering shelves of spirits glistened from the backlit bar. Fit, robust men in white jackets shook and poured in a dizzying blur of glass and ice and steel. The musty smell of Argentine malbec forced its two scents—strawberry and spice—on an air already perfumed with heavier tincture. Older, moneyed-looking women brushed skirt hems with young, honey-eyed vixens while their collective men pushed empty glasses back for refills.

"You about ready for another?" Biederbeck asks me. "No, wait … Let's have a punch!"

Like a good barman, he'd recently found Amer Picon through a London purveyor and purchased a case. Its orange essence and dry bitterness begged for a punch, the definition of which varies, even among liquid historians. Two non-wavering components tend to be the presence of fruit, and the mixing of batches versus glasses at a time. (*Esquire* drinks writer David Wondrich outlined all the tasty possibilities in his 2010 book, *Punch: The Delights [and Dangers] of the Flowing Bowl*.)"When the case showed up," Biederbeck said, "there were only 11 bottles in it. My tariff, I guess. Here … "

He handed me a glass of punch and I turned to watch the band, all ivory pings and bracing snares and throat. The bigshots of old-school jazz play here, not that I'd know them by sight or sound. But Biederbeck, true to the name, is a student of both jazz and the drinks that tend to mingle in its presence.

Over the piano, singing a tune of its own, is a painting from Mark Stock's *The Butler's in Love* series. It's the first thing you see when you enter Bix and the last thing you take in before you pass the velvet curtain on your way out. It dominates the space the way the Eiffel does Paris, no matter the vantage point.

In "The Butler's in Love–Absinthe," the butler—a barely veiled Stock—leans into a jade-green wall, gazes at the lipstick staining an empty absinthe tumbler, and resigns himself to a life of subjugation and unrequited love. He hangs with his back to the crowd, which likewise pays him little heed.

Between Picon punches, Barnaby showed back up from somewhere down the busy bar. I'd been trading John McEnroe stories with a tennis fan named Renée Richards (not the U.S. Open Doubles finalist of sex-change fame)—she knew him in high school, I peed next to him in a New York theater. Anyway, I'd lost track of him.

"Here," he said, handing me yet another punch, "I got you another drink. We should probably eat something. I realized I hadn't eaten anything all day except a piece of lemon meringue pie for lunch."

I stood two-fisted with my back against a marble pillar that stretched to the second-floor ceiling. A single window in a whole ceiling of them was opened to the late-January night. Oh, to be a bat in that belfry. Caen is dead, and Biederbeck a little thicker through the middle, but Bix is about as much like a photograph in a favorite book as a place can be, meaning every bit as good as you prayed it would be lest you feel your faith wavering. Of course, it could have been the cocktails. It always can.

Earlier, I'd asked Barnaby where Team Martini held court before the days of Bix. It was Alfred's.

Forgotten, but not gone—having moved from its original location over the Broadway Tunnel to Merchant Street, in the shadow of the Pyramid—Alfred's is a steak joint in the pre-Fleming's sense, meaning ripe, aged cuts smoked over mesquite and big martinis and Manhattans cold and keep-'em-coming. Kerouac ate there (and knowing him, drank) and wrote about it in *The Subterraneans*. Among old souls, Alfred's was the nostalgic choice in an environment of New Age imbibing.

"Everybody was drinking white wine and then going to the bathroom to do cocaine," Conrad said. "Well, we didn't want that. We wanted to do our thing out in the open."

There was a time when Barnaby Conrad III was among San Francisco's most notorious bachelors, eligible and elusive at once, as likely to be in his attic painting, or at the bar drinking, as he was being seen on somebody's arm. (A lot of that time is scheduled to come out in April, in a book titled *The Bachelor's Progress*, which his editor called "a sort of Tom Jones romp.") But then he married Martha Sutherland, an authority on contemporary Chinese art and a CIA operative of 18 years—two passions that must have played out strikingly when she found herself in the midst of Tianmanmen Square in 1989. But then she married Barnaby Conrad.

Of the lumber Sutherlands, she is, whose TV ads once employed country comic Jerry Clower in all his big-bellied bluster. Playing the Kevin Bacon game, that put Clower and Conrad at too close a remove for my comfort and taste. Yes, I had done the fanboy thing and chased my favorite writer (on ice-cold gin drinking, and absinthe's "green fairy" wings, anyway) all the way to the top of Pacific Heights, sometimes called "Specific Whites" for the exclusive group that dwells there.

I'd chased him to a watering hole in a book where writers and drinkers mixed like vermouth and gin (or more likely vodka) in my mind. Yes, I was ashamed. But I was also on assignment.

"San Francisco is a drinking town," Conrad said, balancing a glass of Amer Picon as he might a combustive nitrate or some tonic of eternal youth.

I drank to that.

IRONS IN THE FIRE

How Oklahoma State University fueled the rise of the PING
golf club dynasty

By *Beau Adams*

MINUS THE INVENTION OF THE STEEL SHAFT IN THE 1930S, golf
clubs had barely changed in decades. Irons were forged of steel. They
were muscle-backed and dipped in chrome, and woods were an incon-
sistently milled teardrop of persimmon wood glued to the bottom of a
shaft. The most popular putters of the day resembled a smaller version
of their iron cousins, lower profile with less loft.

Then, in 1966, came the PING Anser. The Anser was invented by
a GE aeronautics designer named Karsten Solheim. Its moniker was a
bastardization of "answer," the missing "w" born of the necessity to fit
the name in the space afforded on the club—evidence of its designer's
rigid aesthetic of form follows function.

The son of an immigrant shoemaker, Solheim grew up in the Ballard
area of Seattle. Currently crawling with cyclists, foodies, and hipsters,
Ballard was more of a fishing village in the early 1900s when Solheim
and his family immigrated.

He was never a great student, at least not early on. His grandson,
Andy, recalls a story told to him by his grandmother: "In fact, there was
a time when he decided that he was going to study and do well on a test
and he did. But then his teacher basically accused him of cheating."

Under-challenged in high school, Solheim applied to the University of Washington and was accepted to its engineering program in 1931.

He'd never make it through the course work, leaving the college after only one year to help in his father's struggling shoemaking business. Luckily for Solheim, there were just as many lessons to be learned in the private sector.

"When Karsten went back to work for his father making shoes, he found that he had a new competitor who had opened a shop across the street," says his son John Solheim, current CEO of PING. "This guy was undercutting his prices and taking his customers, so Karsten decided he would lower his prices as well and start using less expensive material to build shoes and make repairs."

This experiment failed miserably and Solheim nearly sank the family's business. In a bold redirect, he decided to start using the *best* quality materials he could find. Though it drove the price of his product beyond double what his new neighbor was charging, he found that the market responded favorably and within a couple of years he had put his competitor out of business.

Solheim kept looking to the future, and for an opportunity to again study engineering and design. In 1945 he got his break. What the Depression had stolen, WWII would give back.

———————

After Pearl Harbor, materials, supplies, and engineers were suddenly in great demand. The University of California offered a 10-week crash course in aeronautical design through an extension program. Solheim enrolled and finished the course work in five weeks.

In 1945, he took a position with Ryan Aeronautical, the engineering team that had designed Lindbergh's *Spirit of St. Louis*. Solheim was a project engineer for the first tricycle landing gear that made it possible for airplanes to safely land on aircraft carriers. He developed systems that would guide the Atlas missile for another company, Convair.

Solheim worked for a host of engineering and design firms through the '40s and '50s. After the war, while at GE, he was the lead on a design team that not only invented the first portable television but also perfected the "rabbit ears" antenna. "GE thought that they would build about 40,000 units," recalls John Solheim, "but the design was so popular that they built over 4 million." A Chicago firm would accept the credit for perfecting the rabbit ears. Solheim decided this would be the last time he invented something that he didn't manufacture himself.

Solheim's military, aeronautic, and industrial design experience had turned into a career. Although chiefly a tennis player, he was persuaded to take up golf by his workmates at GE.

"Some of his engineer friends invited him out to play without realizing that he had never played before," says John. "They were on the second tee before he had finished up on the first green."

Like a lot of golfers, Solheim struggled with putting. But rather than throw clubs, he deconstructed them. His engineer's mind told him that the design of the putter seemed off. The shaft met the club head at the wrong junction, and the weighting of the club seemed haphazardly scattered throughout the design plane. It was as if almost no practical thought had gone in to the making of this contraption. With no sensible putters on the market, Solheim decided to build his own. He borrowed $1,100 and holed up in his garage.

The name PING owes itself to a bizarre attribute of Solheim's initial putter design, which he called the 1A. Built from a prototype of sugar cubes and popsicle sticks, the 1A was weighted on either end and had a gap between the face and the back of the club which upon striking a ball provided for a xylophonic tone. The 1A was a success by design standards, but golfers resisted it. It didn't look like anything else on the market and it made a strange sound.

In order to get his putter to market, Solheim moonlighted by promoting his product to industry leaders. He was a regular at tour events, hanging around the practice greens, diagrams in hand, ready to prove his design to those who would listen.

Eventually, Solheim would redesign the 1A into the more aesthetically pleasing Anser. Through sheer persistence he struck distribution deals with pro shops and convinced several touring pros to use the putter on tour. His true genius for marketing came from his decision to imprint his company's contact information on each club, much like a design firm would tag each page of a blueprint. "You've got to remember," says John, "we didn't have the Internet; we didn't have anything. So what Karsten did was put his address on every golf club—cast in. And we'd get letters from all over the world requesting our products because of that."

An up-and-down pro named Julius Boros won the 1967 Phoenix Open, sinking the winning putt with a PING putter, sending orders through the roof. Solheim then turned his attention to the other clubs in the bag.

———————

At age 25, Texas-born Mike Holder had taken the reins of the Oklahoma State University men's golf program in 1973. A gifted amateur golfer, Holder earned medalist honors in 1970 at the Big Eight Championship while playing for OSU. During his coaching tenure, OSU won eight national championships. Additionally, he coached his way to 21 conference titles, a number bested by only one other coach, Forrest Clare "Phog" Allen. He and his players have amassed more individual and team awards than is worth mentioning, but if it wasn't for football, Holder may have never found his way to golf.

"It was in the seventh grade. I played football that year and the school told us that if we wanted to play football the next year, we had to play a spring sport," Holder recounts. "So I said, 'Alright, what sport ya got?' Well, they only had golf and track—they didn't have baseball or anything else. So I was a little pudgy kid, and I'd been around track but it wasn't my strong suit. My dad had a set of golf clubs in the garage. I'd never seen him use them, but I'd seen them in there, so I asked him if I could borrow them and try out for the junior-high golf team.

"So he took me out in the backyard and he told me to keep my left arm straight and he kind of showed me how to hold the club."

Holder would make the team at Sapulpa Junior High School and golf would make him forget about football. "I kind of liked it right off the bat," he says, his eyes pointed toward the ceiling in his office. "You didn't have to be the fastest or the strongest guy." And although playing golf that spring semester meant he was eligible to play football the next year, Holder can't even recall if he did.

What he does remember is becoming a dominant force as a coach in the world of college golf. Mike Holder was to college golf what Mike Krzyzewski is to college basketball. His teams were perennial contenders, and known for being top-notch athletes. He insisted on it. They did aerobics at 6:30 a.m. weekdays. They did push-ups and ran stadium stairs to atone for miscues on the course. Holder held team qualifying rounds in the midst of spring storm season, in an effort to cultivate mental and physical toughness. Holder-coached teams were the trend-setters, the innovators, sometimes even the laughingstock of the league for their unorthodox regimen. That made them the perfect target for PING.

In 1976, club manufacturers weren't in the habit of courting amateur programs. "You might be able to get a set of clubs at wholesale or something if you were a really good player," Holder says, "but mostly a college golfer had to purchase his own equipment." PING's offer to outfit his team was of interest to Holder, but he had reservations. Namely, the look.

"They were ugly," Holder says with a puzzled look on his face, even still. "I didn't like anything about them. They were offset at the hosel, which kind of made them hard to line up. The finish was dull instead of shiny. The whole thing seemed wrong."

Unimpressed with the current design, Holder sent the PING representative, Gary Hart, back to the drawing board. "I said, 'Look, you're a great guy and it sounds like you have a great company, but no one wants to use your clubs—they're too ugly.'"

By 1978, Karsten Manufacturing had made significant improvements to its irons and introduced the PING "Eye" series. This got Holder's attention. "In 1978, David Edwards won the NCAA Championship while at Oklahoma State playing with PING clubs and a PING golf ball. By 1979 or 1980, everybody on our team was using them."

The Cowboys won three national championships in the '80s and two in the '90s carrying PINGs. The golf world was paying attention. Sales of PING clubs took off, no small thanks to OSU. "It meant a lot," Holder says. "It gave them credibility."

"It was hugely important," says John Solheim. "For us to be able to get into Oklahoma State at the time, there was no question that they were the number one golf program in the country. As soon as other teams saw Oklahoma State use our equipment, then they had to have it. And as soon as they went home, the kids at the clubs saw it, and they had to have it."

Players weren't the only ones noticing PING's rise to domination. Traditional manufacturers like Wilson, Titleist, and Hogan found themselves saddled to a club design that was seen as stale and unsophisticated. Their sluggishness in the boardroom was getting them trounced on the fairway. Absent a design and engineering mind as capable as Karsten Solheim, they threw themselves on the mercy of the court—the governing bodies of professional golf.

In 1988, both the USGA and PGA disqualified PING irons manufactured over the previous two years. To qualify, a player would either have to play a PING club that was manufactured before 1986 or switch to a different club. The rule hinged on a negligible discrepancy regarding groove placement on PING's most popular iron to date, the PING Eye 2. The argument was that the design created an unfair advantage by enabling players to impart more spin on the ball. In golf, more spin equals more control.

Solheim would spend the next couple of years in the courtroom instead of the design studio battling to keep his clubs in the hands of professionals. He pleaded his case with zeal, looking more like a mad scientist than an executive, a subtlety not lost on the staid, conservative governing bodies of golf with which he had filed repeated injunctions. Solheim was an outsider in every way. It allowed him to approach club design with a different perspective, and it lost him footing with golf's good old boys.

"I have no question that there were some of the old guard that got together on that," says John Solheim of the controversy. Though the current CEO is reluctant to name names, he will admit that "during the groove issue there were some people who kept prodding the USGA—a lot."

It's worth noting that the PGA, which carried on its court battles with PING long after the USGA reached an agreement with the club maker, was feeling considerable pressure from its sponsors to continue questioning PING's viability. The PGA derives a sizable amount of income from club makers. Although its stated purpose as an organization is to protect player interests, a quick perusal of their current website yields motion ads from Titleist in the top two advertising spots.

———————

The legal battles of the early '90s took their toll on PING and Karsten Solheim. John says his father's inherent fight came, in part, from his heritage. "Part of that Norwegian that's in you, your mind sticks on something and you can't get it out of [there]." Karsten's grandson, Andy, has an additional theory: "A lot of what got to him was that some people questioned his integrity." For people to believe on any level that he was trying to cheat through design would have been the ultimate insult to Solheim. Ultimately, PING would be recognized as having no malicious intent regarding it's nonconforming design and the clubs would be grandfathered in and allowed for play. But the damage had been done.

In 1995, John Solheim made a move at a board meeting to replace Karsten as company president. He had previously broached the subject with his father. "He wouldn't have anything to do with it," he says. "But he knew he was slipping. So I told him at a board meeting that I would like to nominate him as chairman and I would like for him to nominate me as president. He and my mother discussed it for a few minutes and then he did it."

Karsten Solheim remained chairman until his death in 2000 from complications of Parkinson's disease. His children and grandchildren continue to run the company, which has not only regained its position atop the golf equipment industry, but has continued to attempt to emulate the innovative spirit of its founder. Concepts such as perimeter weighting, investment casting, and custom fitting matter today because of Solheim.

Holder, now athletic director at OSU, says they broke the mold after they forged Solheim. "There's not gonna be another one. Karsten was pretty special. There was nothing conventional about him. He was a genius."

WHERE THE BUFFALO DRIFT

A *flâneur* drifts toward downtown Tulsa in a way the city's
founders, politicians, and planners never intended: on foot

By *Russell Cobb*

MAYBE IT WAS A GIMMICK, but I'd prefer to call it an experiment
in semi-urban psychogeography: Walk as far as possible through Tulsa
in a single day, feeling my way through the city with only my two feet.
Psychogeography is a discipline on the margins of academic acceptabil-
ity, in part because it's entirely subjective—how could you possible
measure the effects of a landscape on someone else's emotions?—and
because its origins stem from a radical political agenda. For the French
theorists who invented psychogeography in the 1960s, an unplanned
walk—a drift—through a city could set off a chain of events leading to
a revolution. The high-water mark of this project was the Paris General
Strike in May 1968, when slogans like "take your desires for reality" ruled
the day.

There were a number of obstacles to my experiment: First of all, I
wanted to survive, so this precluded certain parts of the city where pedestrians are routinely mowed down. In fact, the very day I set out on
my journey, an elderly woman was struck by a car while trying to cross
21st Street. If a walk to Med-X could kill you, I might want to take some
precautions, like seeking out neighborhoods with ample sidewalks.

Just off Cherry Street, there were unbroken sidewalks for blocks.
Then, they randomly ceased in front of some houses in Maple Ridge,

only to resume a couple of houses later. Who maintains these sidewalks? Why do some houses have them and others not? The patchwork of sidewalks resulted in a sort of hopscotch in and out of traffic. At one point, I nearly hopped on a decomposing squirrel that must have been rotting on a 19th Street sidewalk for days. The only other person I saw on this particular stretch of the walk was a 30-something monk—at least he was dressed like a monk, wearing an ankle-length, hooded black habit and rosary beads—walking a Jack Russell terrier.

Another obstacle was determining a final destination. Every journey implies a starting point and an ending point. Where was I going? I traced old streetcar routes, courtesy of Michael Bates, who has mapped Tulsa trolley lines onto a Google map. I thought about walking one of these lines, but most of them ended after a mile or two. I wanted something with more of an epic sweep to it. I considered walking the old Sand Springs Interurban line, but this prospect depressed me, thus predetermining my psychogeographic experiment.

I threw out all these options and opted to become a *flâneur* in the drift of the city. The *flâneur* is a bit like the American buffalo: a creature who moves randomly across the landscape, picking out bits of food here and there, digesting on the move. Unlike the buffalo, though, the *flâneur* usually inhabits the densely packed streets of the big city, moving against the grain of a consumer society. Nobody really thinks of Tulsa as a big city, but a quick glance at Wikipedia reveals that the Tulsa metropolitan area has a population of just under one million souls—about the same as mid-19th century London and Paris, the cities that gave birth to the modern *flâneur* in the works of Charleses Baudelaire and Dickens.

"An idle man-about-town," Merriam-Webster defines the word, perhaps with a note of disdain. The *flâneur* is, after all, a French creation, a by-product of Parisian splendor and squalor. He is one who strolls about the city not looking to acquire knowledge or consumer goods, Walter Benjamin once wrote, but to experience a city as a work of art. Most people interested in pedestrian issues want to get from point A to point B without getting run over or mugged on the way to work. I was more interested in loafing, seeing what secrets the city might reveal to me that I never noticed in three decades of car travel.

The voyage started out with promise: a mild, bone-dry December day just after Christmas, the kind of day that brings the earmuffs off the dog walkers and prompts the joggers to doff the leg warmers for sporty shorts. A day, in sum, that should have pushed the citizens off their couches and into the streets. Cars swarmed around the Brookside QuikTrip, but I was on foot. Crossing 36th Street, humanity disappeared. I walked for two blocks, waiting for my first encounter with a fellow pedestrian.

There's a website that has developed an algorithm for walkability—walkscore.com—and it claims that Brookside is one of Oklahoma's most walkable neighborhoods. Walkscore.com talks a big game: walkability is not only the answer to climate change, it says, but the ability to walk your neighborhood also corresponds with a longer lifespan, a smaller waistline, and higher property values. In fact, Brookside is supposed to be Tulsa's model for pedestrian-automobile encounters, with what urban planners call "textured crosswalks" that "make the pedestrian space easy to determine for a motorist."

A stylish shop on the west side of Peoria caught my eye. Scandinavian-looking kitchen instruments posed in the windows, urging this buffalo-*flâneur* across one of these model crosswalks made of bricks.

In Canada, where I live, cars screech to halt when the pedestrian dips his toe into the river of traffic. Pedestrian right-of-way is a sacred concept, even in suburbia. I waited patiently at the crosswalk, trying to catch the gaze of motorists, hoping to shame them into stopping for me. As I do in Canada, I stuck a foot in the street to let people know I was serious about getting across the road, but no one stopped. I started to count the cars blazing by me and got to 28 before a pick-up truck stopped and gave me a finger wave, urging me across. But then I was stranded in the right hand lane, with the left lane still buzzing with traffic. I must have looked like one of those squirrels that can't decide whether to dart across the road or retreat to the curb.

Hey, lady in your green Volkswagen bug with a daisy in the flower vase, surely you will stop for me? No. You, the bearded Volvo driver with the fading Obama/Biden bumper sticker, surely you will help a brother out? If I am regarded at all, it is as a crazy person. I am positive that a stray dog would have had more luck crossing Brookside than me on its model, textured sidewalks.

Finally, I am across, but there is little to keep my attention. It's almost noon and I want to at least make it downtown. I pick up my pace and walk for almost a mile before I encounter my next pedestrian, the monk (Is he Benedictine? Eastern Orthodox? What is doing *here*?), who gives me a wise nod, just past the decomposed squirrel. I catch a glimpse of a lowrider on a bike struggling up the hill on 21st Street, and that's about all the humanity I see for the next half hour.

"I am moving to Tulsa from Denver and am wondering if it's safe to walk the streets," someone on city-data.com posted. Someone else replied with this warning: "I think the biggest hazard of walking repeatedly to and from work in downtown Dullsa (oops, I meant Tulsa) is getting killed or injured by boredom."

———————

I am at 18th and Boulder at 12:43 p.m., but there is still no sign of life on the streets. I am getting hungry, so I stop in The Treehouse for some barbeque. It's toward the end of the lunch rush, but I am the only diner in the place. My journey is starting to take on a *Twilight Zone* quality. Three employees hover around me, making idle talk about the weather.

I pick up the old Main Street trolley line and spot my first post-lunch pedestrian outside New Age Renegade, a gay bar that seems much less formidable in the bright, early afternoon sunshine than it does at 2 a.m. I shuffle along behind my fellow walker for a few blocks before he stops to examine the stranger following him downtown. I consider catching up with him to explain my experiment and possibly interview him, but he sets off in a sprint across the street. Now we are walking parallel to one another down Main Street. We make it to Ninth and Main before he is sufficiently freaked out to take off running again, this time in a westerly direction down Ninth Street. This is also where I see only the second pedestrian since lunch, a homeless-looking woman who stops me to ask for some change.

"Do you do a lot of walking around here?" I ask.

"Naw," she says, "I'm just trying to get some change to get the bus back to my apartment."

In the heart of downtown—"The Deco District" they have apparently rebranded it—I spot a few people actually walking places. One guy stumbles down a staircase adjacent to Orpha's Lounge and nearly falls on top of me. Now I am a true *flâneur*, I think. I am anonymously adrift in the big city with its big buildings. But the thing that really appealed to the *flâneur* par excellence—Charles Baudelaire—is nowhere to be found:

> The street about me roared with a deafening sound.
> Tall, slender, in heavy mourning, majestic grief,
> A woman passed, with a glittering hand
> Raising, swinging the hem and flounces of her skirt.

Where are the "agile and graceful legs" that obsessed the Bad Boy poet? "The sweetness that enthralls and the pleasure that kills" is nowhere to be found. A half a mile north, I encounter a couple of teenagers making out at the Center of the Universe, but that's about as sensual as my voyage gets. The City of Lights, Tulsa is not.

I've made it downtown by 3 p.m. so I set off for Greenwood, imagining the blaze of madness that engulfed Tulsa 90 years ago. There are plaques on Archer Street commemorating the businesses and residences destroyed in the Riot, sometimes three per block. How long have these plaques been here? Once again, I am the only pedestrian in sight, begging the question: who ever reads or notices these small plaques in the sidewalk? I walk up and down Greenwood, my head buzzing with noise of I-244 and thoughts of the Riot. A man with a three-legged dog is talking on his cell phone.

I cross back over the track and spot a couple of pedestrians heading into McNellie's. It's almost 4 p.m. and my legs are weary. The drift is pulling this buffalo-*flâneur* towards the bar, so I follow the couple inside. I take a seat by the window, watching for others caught in the drift of the city. After a few minutes, the Edward Hopperish loneliness wears off and I am simply bored. I check my iPhone and text my wife. I need a ride home.

TROUBLED WATERS

In September of 2012, This Land Press published a three-part series about water—how we store it, how we use it, who owns it, and who wants it back. This is the first story in that series, explaining the history behind Oklahoma's water wars.

By *Ginger Strand*

On Memorial Day weekend, Lake Sardis' Potato Hills South campground is packed with groups of guys in pickup trucks—the kind of guys who travel with just the essentials: boat, pole, radio, beer. Potato Hills South is an Army Corps of Engineers Class B campground—no sinks, no showers, pit toilets. But if you follow the trail that starts behind the picnic table at campsite #1, an easy 15-minute stroll will take you to the Potato Hills Central Class A campground, populated by families and retirees in RVs, the kind of people who travel with boat, pole, radio, beer; plus chairs, rugs, gazebos, televisions, small dogs, satellite dishes, and carved wooden signs identifying themselves—"The Scudders: Josh and Patty"—to fellow campers. The trail leaves you right behind the shower building, meaning you can avail yourself of Class A hot water for the pit-toilet price.

As you hike the trail in quest of water, you'll see mosses growing beneath cedars, along with prickly pear cacti. Cacti and moss co-existing: it's an apt symbol for Oklahoma's hybrid hydrology—one foot in the arid West and the other in the flood-prone East—a geologic fact at the root of the "water wars" currently brewing over this very lake. Like several other big reservoirs in Southeastern Oklahoma, Sardis is a federal project, and multiple faraway cities hope to dip a straw into it. In June

2010, over a year before releasing its 50-year Comprehensive Water Plan, the Oklahoma Water Resources Board sold "storage rights" to 90 percent of the Sardis water to Oklahoma City, which plans to build a pipeline and pipe Sardis water 200 miles and 600 feet uphill. The move triggered a lawsuit from the Choctaw and Chickasaw nations and a threat of litigation from local activists.

Understanding what's at stake in the water wars—which will ultimately reach well beyond Lake Sardis—requires taking a look not just at Oklahoma's unique climate and landscape, but its equally unique history. Water disputes are common across the West, ever more so as populations grow and the climate becomes more extreme, but Oklahoma's stand-offs are unlike the rest, because here the problem is not—or not yet—scarcity.

A STATE IN TWO WORLDS

Oklahoma has more eco-regions per square mile than any other state—from arid western plains to tallgrass prairie, cypress swamps and Ozark forest. The western half of the state is part of the arid West—the land beyond the 100th meridian that John Wesley Powell declared no one should try to farm. The eastern half of the state has frequent rainfall and robust prairie rivers that tend to flood in the wet season. It's not uncommon for part of the state to be awash in floods while another is parched with drought.

Oklahoma's history is marked by both extremes. Not long after the Dust Bowl, the Arkansas River swelled to eight miles wide and swallowed whole towns. The problem has never been that the state doesn't have enough water: it just doesn't necessarily have water when and where it needs it.

The state's variable hydrology means that its water laws are also a hybrid. Oklahoma recognizes riparian rights—the form of water law (common in the East) holding that property owners have the right to reasonable uses of waterways abutting their land. But it also recognizes prior appropriation—the doctrine whereby he who diverts the water first wins the right to continue diverting it. In the water-poor West, prior appropriation dominates because most landowners do not have access to water except by diverting it.

Today Southeastern Oklahomans are crying foul, citing their property rights to the beds and banks of their waterways. Activists and tribes are trying to point out the pitfalls of trying to reboot the natural order. But massive human intervention is the only way agriculture and urbanization can happen in arid regions. America's West has embraced a frontier mentality that enjoys moving water around. Visit Hoover Dam and you're greeted with soaring triumphal sculptures and booming recorded voices touting the Bureau of Reclamation's accomplishment. There's a heady whiff of ozone wafting by: the smell of man triumphing over nature. For much of its history, Oklahoma has breathed the same air.

KERR'S LEGACY: LAND, WOOD, AND WATER

"It is in our power," wrote Senator Robert S. Kerr, "under the watchful eyes of God, to determine the physical form of the world in which we live. We can make it a paradise of 'land, wood, and water,' or by neglect, permit it to become a desert. The choice is ours."

Kerr, a mountain of a man with a good-old-boy grin, was born in 1896 in a log cabin in what was then Chickasaw territory. An oilman and a wheeler-dealer, he became governor and then a powerful senator for the young state. In his memoir, he summarizes his vision for Oklahoma with a quote from Brigham Young: "The earth is the Lord's, and the mission of man is to subdue it and make it fruitful."

Subdue he did. Kerr won the governorship on the theme of "more water," promising urban Oklahomans that failure to develop water supplies was a "ceiling on your growth." But even as governor he couldn't accomplish what he could once he had access to federal dollars. Soon after being elected to the senate, Kerr got himself appointed to the Public Works Subcommittee for Flood Control and Rivers and Harbors. From there, he began diverting a huge river of federal cash into the goal of subduing Oklahoma's waters.

When Kerr took office, Oklahoma had three federal reservoirs. Under his administrations as governor and senator, 11 more were built, and when he died, 14 more were approved or underway. The state now has more federal reservoirs than any state save California. Dwarfing the typical municipal reservoir, the behemoths built by the Bureau of Reclamation and the Corps of Engineers hold hundreds of thousands of acre-feet of water. Lake Texoma holds more than two and half million, Lake Eufaula only a little less. One of the last reservoir projects to be approved on Kerr's watch was Lake Sardis.

But for all his talk of making the desert bloom, Senator Kerr's reservoirs served not agriculture, but urban growth. Of all the federal reservoirs built on his watch, nine were used for municipal water supply; only four were used in any part for irrigation. Senator Kerr saw control of water as a means of helping cities grow and prosper. And they did, so much so that Oklahoma City is now turning itself into a water retailer. But in the agricultural parts of the state, farmers were also hard at work reshaping the state by moving massive quantities of water around—using the vast reserves underground to drive the Green Revolution.

MINING THE GROUNDWATER

Two years after Senator Kerr went to Washington and began building lakes, a dour-looking Nebraska farmer named Frank Zybach applied for a patent. The device Zybach had invented would transform farming: the center pivot irrigation system. Throughout the '50s and '60s, Zybach and others worked on perfecting it, and by the '70s, pivot irrigation swept the Great Plains. The high-powered pumps and efficient distribution meant that more water could be pumped up from aquifers than ever before. Farmers could irrigate more land through multiple crop cycles. Today, agricultural and livestock irrigation represents 70 percent of the nation's water usage, and Oklahoma is no exception. Irrigation remains the largest water user in the state.

Pumping groundwater from aquifers is a strategy not unlike using your savings account to pay your credit card bills. As long as you're refilling the account faster than you're spending, all is well. But when water is withdrawn from an aquifer faster than rainfall and runoff can recharge it, the results are easy to predict. Debates raged throughout the second half of the 20th century about whether or not the nation's aquifers were being depleted. Today there's little doubt.

"We've become all too dependent on them, thinking it's a resource that's inexhaustible and that's a ridiculous approach," David Moon told me. Moon, formerly a practicing water law attorney, is now editor of

The Water Report, a policy newsletter that's required reading for many a water geek. I called him in his Eugene, Oregon, office to get a big picture view of the water policy world.

Early controversy over how much the Great Plains aquifers were being drawn down focused on the Ogallala, an aquifer so prodigious it was believed for decades to be inexhaustible. That point of view has recently undergone a radical reversal.

"There is a consensus that the Ogallala, like many other aquifers, is being mined," Moon said. "The use exceeds the recharge. You can say what you want, but you're kind of starting to play on borrowed time."

In fact, the Ogallala, which underlies Oklahoma's Panhandle, does not recharge as readily as most aquifers. Only in Nebraska's Sand Hills are the Plains porous enough to funnel water back into it. Geologists expect the Ogallala to reach critically low levels in the next 20 to 50 years.

But though the Ogallala's depletion has caused enough concern for Plains states to begin eyeing the Great Lakes greedily, it is not the only aquifer to experience a drop in levels. Texas farmers were warned that they were affecting aquifer levels as early as the 1940s. The recent evaluations of Oklahoma's Arbuckle-Simpson aquifer found that an expected 24-inch surplus was 20 inches less than that.

Mining the aquifers is an approach that also hinges on the "he who grabs first, gets most" philosophy of prior-appropriation doctrine. But in this case, the philosophy may die without any change of attitude: the water will simply run out.

'WASTED' WATER

"No man has the right to waste one drop of water that another man can turn into bread," Senator Kerr wrote, quoting Brigham Young again. And in Kerr's eyes, wasting water meant letting it run its course to the sea. Water not taken out and used—for drinking, industry, or irrigation—was water gone to waste. That attitude has shaped Oklahoma's approach to both its groundwater and its surface water. But thinking in the water world has changed radically.

"The mantra of 'Well it's there for use and if it goes out to the ocean it's wasted'—I think we've gotten beyond that," *The Water Report*'s David Moon told me. "The majority of people realize that there are in-stream uses that are necessary. The big shift in the water law is that recreation and fisheries needs are considered beneficial uses of water."

"Beneficial" is a term of art in water policy: it means a use that upholds a water right. In prior-appropriation doctrine, if water is not put to beneficial use, the right to it can be lost. Traditionally, "nonconsumptive" uses like recreation or guaranteeing flows to protect river life have not been factored into water policy. In most states now, Moon told me, that's changing.

"They are either known as in-stream flows or ecological flows and are accepted water rights with the same value as any other water right in most Western states," he said.

Not yet, however, in Oklahoma. One of the most controversial things about OWRB's 50-year plan was its decision to leave nonconsumptive uses out of calculations of water supply availability. "There remains no clear consensus in Oklahoma," the report stated, "on the most appropriate way to balance consumptive and nonconsumptive needs for water." In other words, the state is hamstrung on its own contradictory approaches: should water be tied to the land through which it flows? Or is it acceptable—or even necessary—for man to improve on nature by redistributing water?

"Water is a basic necessity for all life, not just humans but also the plants and animals," David Ocamb countered. "Which is why in-stream flow is vital to consider." Ocamb is director of the Sierra Club's Oklahoma chapter, and he'd like to see legislation to guarantee in-stream flows where they are needed. He thinks the OWRB is moving in this direction. The Choctaw and Chickasaw nations, however, disagree. And once again, unique aspects of Oklahoma's history are contributing to the issue's complexity.

FROM WINTERS TO WATER WARS

As Oklahoma became the nation's 46th state, a Montana lawsuit about tribal water rights was working its way through the courts. The following year, 1908, the Supreme Court decided in *Winters v. United States* that in establishing reservations, the federal government had reserved water rights for tribes, and that those rights did not hinge on the amount of water currently needed or in use on reservation lands. In other words, the Indian water rights were grounded in the property, not prior appropriation. *Winters* has been a foundation for tribal water suits ever since.

But Oklahoma's case is unlike other states', since tribes here own their land in fee simple, rather than living on federally administered reservations. And there has been no clear court declaration on whether reserved water rights can be claimed for water used for purposes not intended by the original declaration. That makes it unclear whether the tribes can claim a water right to protect river life, fisheries, or recreation. The tribes, obviously, believe they can.

In the state-tribe standoff, the old conflict rears its head: will the state stay on the road Senator Kerr led it down, seeking to remake its rivers, valleys, and plains? Or will a new era of water policy dawn in which the goal is less subduing nature than living in some kind of balance with it—even if that means accepting limitations on, say, how much water an urban area can use.

David Ocamb of the Sierra Club thinks the state will inevitably adopt the latter approach. He points out the popularity of fishing in Oklahoma as a sign that the state's citizens value water in rivers and lakes just as much as water in pipelines and sprinkler systems.

"This is not a Republican or a Democratic issue, not a liberal or conservative issue," Ocamb said. "It is just do we want the same quality of life for our grandchildren that our grandparents left for us."

The question for Oklahomans, however, will be which part of the state's contradictory legacy its citizens will embrace: the desire to live in harmony with the natural world, or the equally powerful urge to reshape it so it harmonizes with us.

BEGETTING BATS

Every summer, hundreds trek to Oklahoma's Alabaster
Caverns to witness more than a million Mexican free-tailed
bats simultaneously leave their roosts to embark on a
nighttime feeding frenzy

By *Natasha Ball*

A SINGLE BAT REPRESENTS ONE OUT OF EVERY FOUR OR FIVE
MAMMALS ON EARTH. The Mexican free-tailed bat is the speedster of
the 1,000 species on earth, known to cut through the air at the same rate
as the yellow lines of a freeway vanishing into a rearview mirror. But
the size of their colonies, the largest of which can top the population of
New York City twice over, form a huge target. When humans pave the
way for things like farms, shopping malls, and cave tours, bat habitat is
destroyed. And then there are the flying insects, laced with agricultural
pesticides. A pregnant, migratory Mexican free-tailed bat can eat her
weight in them each night.

While bat tourism is changing some minds, not everyone is sending
off for kits to build backyard bat houses. Daniel Duncan dealt the first
blow to the relationship between human and bats with his *Histoire De
L'Animal* in the 17th century deeming vampiric the animals that had been
embroidered on silk in China, where the sounds for the words for "good
fortune," "blessings," and "bat" are virtually the same. Bats were revered
on this side of the planet, too, starring as heroes in stories told by the
Aztec and Cherokee. By the turn of the 20th century, though, we'd read

Dracula and decided bats were the devil's henchmen, driven from cracks in the earth to puncture the pallid necks of our guardians of virtue.

We'd been bused to the viewing area from Alabaster Caverns in northwestern Oklahoma on a couple of school buses, our heads bobbing along the tops of the brown seats as we lurched through the haze caused by a nearby grass fire on Oklahoma 50. Here, just south of the city of Freedom, bat watching is a spectator sport. We'd all migrated there—the bats from central Mexico, the bat watchers from as far away as Florida. Some of us had heard from friends or family about the bat watch, about the chance to watch the unanimous exodus of a million and a half bats from their roosts.

It's promise enough to draw some 365,000 visitors every summer to Carlsbad Caverns in New Mexico, home to one of the world's largest bat caves. Austin artist Dale Whistler created a rotating 18-foot statue of a Mexican free-tailed bat for display at one end of Congress Avenue, a tribute to the colony there, North America's largest of the urban variety. Hundreds of passes are sold each year to the bat watch at the Selman Wildlife Management Area, on land a short bus ride away from Alabaster Caverns in northwestern Oklahoma. Even Governor Brad Henry was intrigued. In 2006, he named the Mexican free-tailed bat the official flying mammal of Oklahoma. Since the first year for the Selman Bat Watch in Oklahoma in 1995, more than 17,000 have made the trip for the show.

It was mid-July, and the temperature had topped 110 that day. The prairie seemed tense, pulled tight by loss of water. Birds of prey glided up and down in spirals alongside the road, like tornados made of hollow bones and wings, waiting for a meal to emerge from the baked, red dust below. We quenched our thirst with iced water from a tailgate cooler, which we dispensed into glow-in-the-dark cups. Tiny black bats had been printed on the sides.

The manila envelope had arrived in the mail from the Oklahoma Department of Wildlife Conservation headquarters in June, the image of a bat with wings outstretched stamped on the front, hovering over the words, "first class bat mail." The headings on the advisories inside were printed in that font I'd seen on makeup packaging at the Halloween stores. "Confirmation," one read. I felt like I'd just gotten my acceptance letter from a secret society.

The office where I checked in for the bat watch was stocked with bat t-shirts and winged children's hats with googly eyes. We waited in line at the front counter, pressed close in the small space 80 feet over a cool pocket of the largest public gypsum cave in the U.S. We were told to report to the dry grass and grayed benches that form the amphitheater outside, where the smiling Melynda Hickman, a wildlife diversity biologist with the state, reviewed the ground rules for the evening as she passed around a bat that had been preserved in a frame, its skin gone ivory and thin like tissue: Adults, you're responsible for your children. There's no smoking on the school buses or at the viewing site. Make sure your mouths are closed while you're looking up, watching the bats. ("Think about it," she said.) If you have a cell phone or other mobile device, put it on a silent mode: "Used to be," she told us, "we didn't have to worry about this because you couldn't get a cell tower down here anyway. But that seems to be changing."

Later, trying to sleep, I crawled out of my sleeping bag. Past midnight, the air still felt like it had rushed from an open oven. I'd ridden the brakes of my car down the hill from the park office after stepping down from the bus, flipping on the brights to alert anything that might have been lurking in the woods around where I'd set up my camp. From where I lay under some netting in the roof of my tent, the Milky Way looked like a road paved through the sky, a mix of dust and gravel, unobstructed by the lights of the nearest metro, which lay on the other side of 140 miles of dark.

Along the road leading back to the caverns office were bulldozers, crawling along the bottom of a shallow, football field-sized hole. It glowed white against the black of the sky. The light from the lamps of the machinery scattered in the floating dust, turning it into a ghostly fog that rose toward an orange sliver of a moon. Right off the surface like that is how most of the world's gypsum is mined. It's in our toothpaste, the drywall, tofu, Kit Kat chocolate bars. It's the white powder that's dusted onto individual pieces of chewing gum to keep them from sticking together. This gypsum, though, from what Hickman understood, was being mined for the oil and natural gas sites in western Oklahoma, which were connected by an invisible circuit that seemed to hum constantly with the traffic of flatbeds and white trucks, with the Chesapeake logo on the driver's side door.

The bulldozers switched to reverse gear, and the rumble of exhaust and the cadence of the warning call flooded whatever sounds might have been playing underneath. The bleat came again and again, down from the RV camps and swing sets on the hill, spilling into the bowl between caves where I camped. When I noticed that the sound had dried up, I realized I'd slept.

When it's time, the mother-to-be Mexican free-tailed bat forms a hammock out of the skin that stretches between her legs and her tail, like a cupped palm, soft and strong. She hangs by her thumbs from the roof of the cave as she gives birth, kept warm by the heat of hundreds of thousands of bat bodies. Her pup, already a quarter of her size, emerges feet first, then climbs her to nurse with its wrinkled lips. She grooms her young, nosing her scent into its pink skin. The two are still connected by umbilical cord as the pup fills its bare belly with her milk. She can identify her pup from as many as 3,000 other newborn pups, which will be left in the same square meter as hers. At dusk the new mothers will leave them clinging to the ceiling of the cave, to each other. The mothers join their aunts and sisters and grandmothers for the evening hunt. There are 17 caves in the U.S. hot enough for this colony, a coven of migratory, pregnant bats. Five of them are in Oklahoma.

Waiting outside are hawks. Some of them are content swooping in on the vermin that the emerging bats manage to stir up. Others have a taste for nursing bats, plucked from the sky—sometimes right out of the cave. And then, of course, was us. Bat caves have been vandalized in ignorance. Barriers have been built into entrances to guard against trespassers, unwittingly affecting accessibility for the bats and the temperature inside the cave. Orphaned pups that aren't adopted by mothers that have lost their young eventually lose their grip and fall to the floor of their caves, sometimes in clumps, since they cling as much to each other as the ceiling of the cave. A certain type of beetle patrols there, through the guano terra, and they can pick clean the feather-light bones in minutes.

It begins late in the winter over central Mexico, where the moths of the corn earworm emerge from the stalks, gravid and bent on migration, climbing thousands of feet into the sky. The Mexican free-tailed bat flies up to meet them, trapping the moths in the folds of their wings before snapping their bodies with their smiling jaws. It's said that the economic impact of these bats is practically immeasurable. A group of bats the size of the Freedom colony will consume up 10 tons of insects each night. The insect force that could cost Texas farmers millions in pesticides and lost crops are headed off by these animals, each of which measures less than a foot across.

The male and female bats are together at this point. It's been a year since they saw each other last. At night, they press north, hunting as they travel. During the day, the males trill and chirp to the females, singing love songs that are mostly inaudible to the human ear. Sometimes, a male hovers over a cluster of females, selecting one seemingly at random from the bunch and, while hanging upside down, mates her without fanfare. But then there's the other way, when a male cordons off a female as a dangerous lover would do, isolating her from her family and friends. Then, he seizes her, digging his thumbs into her fur and pinning her wings so she can't move. For just a few minutes, he whispers into her ridged, wide-set ears.

Once pregnant, the females usually travel to the same cave in which they were born, consuming their weight in flying insects each night along the way, wings beating 12 times every second, since bats can't glide. Mike Caywood, the 20-year park manager at Alabaster Caverns, can smell when they've arrived. "They have a somewhat unique odor," he told us.

The audience was small at the state's first bat watch, made up of naturalists and biologists eager to evaluate the area for tourism. The department is allocated nothing from the state budget. Instead, it cobbles together its operating budget from the money it charges for things like hunting and fishing licenses. The bat watch stirs up enough cash to pay for payroll and the cost of the buses, Hickman said. Ticket sales from the commercial caves like Alabaster Caverns—where the slick mud along the lighted paths is packed hard from foot traffic, and visitors are asked not to touch the soft, clammy walls, soft enough to chip with a human fingernail—goes to the state Tourism and Recreation Department. Weekend visitors to the caves and bat tourists can match the population number on the welcome sign outside Freedom, which hovers just under 300.

––––––––––––––

First, you see them. Then comes the sound, like your pulse when your ears are under water, as a million and a half pairs of long, thin wings swim through the air, pushing the wind behind their long tails with a breaststroke, mixing it with the air we breathe. A few times a bat would drop from the formation and swoop toward us, then lift suddenly out of view, like an acrobat swinging into the rafters, back into the dark. We sat in lawn chairs in the mowed viewing area, snapping the shutters on our cameras, shushing each other. The angry sound of cicadas in the woods behind us ruined the recording I attempted of the deep, almost nauseating sound of the colony in flight. All I could hear on my half-hour of tape were the vibrations of the timpani hidden inside those hard shells, the drumming of another kind of wing.

After we'd arrived at the watch area, a volunteer passed around a sheet of brown foam that'd been cut, she told us, to the approximate shape and size of a Mexican free-tailed bat. On its back was a similar figure, cut from pink foam—it's bald, she pointed out, just like the babies when they're born. A range man named Jerry McLaughlin was our tour guide for the evening. He'd learned the hard way growing up amongst these gypsum caves, he told us, speaking with a feathery lisp, that the water that flows from them are so alkaline that it will neutralize a car battery. He led our group on a nature walk through what he called a patchwork of plant families, which he was disappointed he didn't get to illustrate with a quilt made for the purpose, which he'd forgotten to bring along. We stared at the top of the cliff Jerry pointed out to us, waiting for a sign of the scout bat that would serve as a sort of dimming of the lights for the evening's performance. Jerry whispered to us that if we listened close, we might hear the sound of the bats in flight. He'd never heard it himself. Hearing aids are good, he told us, smiling, but not that good.

Frantic, a flying beetle crashed into my ear. A river of Mexican free-tailed bats had begun to flow through the airspace above us, twisting serpentine against the graduated colors of the sunset, hungry and on the hunt. They formed a column that twisted from the mouth of the hot gypsum cave. The bats were still up there after dark, invisible but electric in the air like radio waves. As the ribbon evaporated, we gathered our water cups and camera bags from the clearing where we'd landed at the end of the tour, a path worn through shoots of little bluestem and buffalo grass. McLaughlin was still whispering: "That might have been the best one we've ever seen."

THE CATFISH HUNTER

A first-time noodler tells all

By *Holly Wall*

I STEPPED CAREFULLY INTO A SMALL, BLACK BASS BOAT WITH FOUR NEAR STRANGERS, one of them offering his hand to guide me into the vessel as it rocked on the dirty, brown surface of Lake Keystone. It occurred to me as I boarded that I had no idea what I was getting myself into. I'd never seen any of the documentaries or reality TV shows that exploit the forays of catfish noodlers—so-called "hillbilly handfishers"—but I'd seen a couple of reporters I knew (or knew of) try it out on the local news and I thought, "Hey, I could do that."

But as the boat began to float away from the rocky shore, I wasn't so sure.

I made small talk with my two new friends, Lacie and Tess—both young, pretty, chatty—thanking them for letting me tag along on their adventure and feeling a little guilty for crashing their party. Then I sized up our guides: one a ranger with the Army Corps of Engineers, the other a biologist with the Wildlife Department. "Huh," I thought, as we chatted about the effort they'd put in to preparing for our little excursion, "they're *smart*."

The pair, Travis and Matt, had spent the previous night and half of that day scouting holes along the shoreline—"running bank," they called it—looking for catfish that we could catch. When they found one, they blocked the hole with a rock, ensuring it'd still be there when we arrived later. After a few minutes of high speeds across the open water, we slowed and approached a rock-strewn bank, then nervously disembarked, our bodies sinking halfway into the water before we found our footing on the jagged floor below.

Lacie would go first, we decided. Matt, who would have been blond if he hadn't shaved his head bald, and whose smooth, sculpted back was a semi-permanent shade of reddish-brown—the side effect of a life spent outdoors—explained to her that he'd hold her hand as they went under water, just to help her find the fish's hidey hole. It would then be up to her to grab the cat by its bottom lip and drag it to the surface.

We were all a little skeptical when she went under, but she emerged 30 seconds later, her right hand still inside the mouth of a 10-pound—no, make it 12—beast, her left arm wrapped around its belly, her curly hair matted and her face aglow with the victory of capture on her first try.

The men "strung it up," puncturing the bottom of its jaw with a sharp, fat needle and then securing it with a shoelace-sized rope.

Next, it was Tess' turn, and she too caught a fish on her first attempt, this one closer to 20 pounds and double the girth of the first.

Matt turned to me, flashing a wide smile that revealed a straight row of perfect white teeth. "You ready?"

I said yes—I lied—and positioned myself on his right side. He took my hand and together we drew in a long breath and let our bodies sink to the bottom of the lake. I didn't tell anyone, but I hadn't held my breath underwater since I was 12 years old, and I was more afraid of drowning than I was of what I would find when I reached blindly into that dark hole.

Matt guided my hand along the top of a flat rock, and below it was an opening. I reached inside and felt something slick and slimy and I immediately pushed off from the rock and thrust my head above water, coughing and rubbing my eyes. (Why had I worn mascara??)

"I felt it!" I gasped, and the others laughed. I went back under, Matt's hand guiding mine again, but this time I didn't feel anything. I couldn't find it.

I came up again, and Matt told me I needed to lie down on the bottom of the lake, either on my side or my stomach, and reach all the way into the hole. I tried, and my hand brushed against the fish, but he was too far out of reach, even with half my shoulder wedged under the rock.

Matt tried, and he couldn't reach it either, which made me feel a little bit better, so he grabbed a fishing pole from the boat while our other guide blocked the hole with his foot. Using the pole, he pulled the fish closer to us, so it was within reach, and when we went under again I felt its head under my right hand. I let my hand slide down the monster's nose and into its mouth. I grabbed its bottom lip—its "teeth"—rough like sandpaper, and closed my fist around it, pulling the beast toward me. It was heavy, and I pulled again, dragging it out of its hiding spot, wrapping my left arm around its middle, feeling it thrash and bite my fingers as we broke the surface of the water.

I squealed and smiled and yelled and yeehawed, ecstatic at my catch—a 25-pounder (OK, 28), the biggest one of the day so far. I couldn't believe what I'd just done, and I was already craving another go.

On my next attempt, which my guides told me would have me going after a smaller but feistier fish, I let Matt take me under the water, and I found the fish right away. I reached inside a smaller hole, in a spot where the water was shallower, and felt the fish glide under my palm. I tried to grab it, searching for its snout, but I came up empty handed, my body still crouched in front of the hole, blocking my prey's escape.

Matt had moved away from me. I was doing this on my own, I'd decided, without really deciding. I furrowed my brow in stern determination and held my breath. My hands searched the water, and again I brushed the fish with my fingertips but couldn't grasp it. I kicked my feet in frustration as I reached farther into the hole. When I couldn't hold my breath any longer, I rose to the surface, still trapping the animal inside.

I didn't wait long before going under again, but as soon as I reached out, I felt the fish glide beneath my belly and out of the hole, its tail flicking me in defiance as it made its escape to freedom.

I cursed when I came up for air but, really, I wasn't bothered too much that he got away. I was proud at having taken control of my catch, at having the confidence to do it on my own. I got a few well-deserved pats on the back and "'atta girls" after climbing aboard the boat, and I accepted them contentedly, unable to contain my wide, open-mouthed smile.

We were done for the evening—and for the season; the flathead catfish, which are the only ones the law allows you to take home and eat after you catch them, would finish spawning soon and vacate their underwater caves. The sun was beginning to set and we could see the dock from our perch across the lake. We'd each had two tries, and while only Lacie had caught two fish, we were all triumphant and glowing, less because we'd caught a few fish and more because we'd done it with our hands, without really knowing if we could do it at all. We'd done it in spite of our fears, and we'd conquered something our friends and families told us we were crazy for even attempting.

And, yes, we'd done it in makeup.

FOUR

PROFILES FROM THE MIDDLE

MR. RAY FITS A SUIT

As he measures and stitches fabric to create the perfect fit,
Tulsa tailor Sherman Ray speaks of surviving Holocaust camps
Auschwitz and Dachau

By *Michael Berglund*

WHEN I WALK INTO RAY'S TAILOR SHOP, I immediately notice the
ordered disorder of the two-room store. Directly in front of me, too near
the front door, sits a table stacked with files and mail and a small radio
propped up on a box. Towards the back of the room, I see a fabric-draped
Singer sewing machine, circa 1950—the first sewing machine, I later
learn, that Sherman Ray purchased when he arrived in Oklahoma City
from Germany. Next to the changing room, a small step stool is positioned
between three large mirrors. The last table I see is loaded with scraps of
tweed, herringbone, and different varieties of worsted wools. And sitting
on the table, in the middle of the material, is Ray, who when I enter is
negotiating a thimble and needle to add a scrap of cashmere to a blazer.

He runs the thimbled hand over impeccably slicked back hair and
looks me over through large-framed glasses that magnify his eyes, which
knowingly search for details that often go unnoticed in casual conversation: Does one shoulder hang slightly lower than the other? Does my
neck crane forward to make my spine curve? Does a 30-year habit of
standing into my left hip make the left leg slightly shorter? All of this
occurs instantaneously as I introduce myself. He's not sizing me up for
a *mano a mano* fistfight. He's measuring me.

I tell him that I'd like to have a suit tailor-made, and that I was interested in gray tweed or a suit with a similar texture. He tells me that he stopped building suits because of the amount of energy it takes, but he'd be happy to alter a suit for me. He chuckles and riffles through a manila folder full of photos, newspaper articles, letters, and trinkets. Ray pulls out artifacts that show me the man he has become: champion weightlifter, avid rower, accomplished tailor.

"I'll tailor the suit so good for you, it'll fit you like a glove," Ray says in a thick Polish accent.

I ask him what kind of suit I should get and he sets down his folder and takes his measuring tape from around his neck and guides me so that my back is facing him.

"Drop your arms," he says. He measures me with lightning speed. "Forty-two is too tight, and 43 they don't make. You'll have to go to a 44. Forty-four might be a little bit too large, but it'll have to be tailored."

He grabs my hand and energetically guides me to the stepstool in front of the mirrors. He checks my inseam and then whips the tape around my waist. "You need about a 35½ or 36 pant. Don't get 34, 36 on the pants. Go to Woodland. Then tell them, 'I will buy it but I will take to my tailor for approval.' See, when you cut it up then you cannot take it back. Then just come over. I'm always open."

Before I leave, Ray shows me one remaining photograph. It's a picture of director Steven Spielberg with his arm draped affectionately over Ray's shoulders.

"See," says Ray, "I was in the concentration camps. Not just a tailor."

A week later, I return to Ray's Tailor Shop with a gray wool suit bought from a department store at Woodland, as he instructed, and I made sure to get a suit that met the size specifications he recommended.

Ray says, "Let me see it."

I pull it out of the bag. Before he even looks at the tag he tells me he can't work on it. He goes over and grabs a suit jacket he's been tailoring.

"You think anybody in this town can do this?" he says, holding up the jacket front. "This is a hand-sewn buttonhole. See? Everything now is made by machine. From China."

Ray takes the newly bought suit from my hands, looks at the tag, and laughs. "China." He takes the jacket off the hanger and hands it to me to try on. We walk over in front of the mirror and shows me how it needs to be adjusted.

"The shoulders are too tight. I have to let out the shoulders, but look." He shows me the inside of the jacket. "Not enough material here. How'm I gonna let out the jacket with no material? Suits like this don't give me anything to work with."

He has me try on the pants. He points to the front pockets, and I see that the outside seams pucker out as I walk. The crotch sits too low. When I raise my arms, the jacket sleeves are too short. Suddenly, a suit that looked slick, modern, and slim-fitting on the rack looks dollar-store cheap. Ray works the material of the suit adroitly, sliding material through his fingers and stopping at all the imperfections: not enough material to let out the sleeve; frayed material on the pants leg; lapels that, because of mass manufacturing, sit unevenly on my chest. He's the doctor and I'm the patient. I ask him how he learned to become a tailor.

"I was trained in Europe," he says. "My grandfather was a tailor. My father was a tailor."

In 1938, when Ray was 12, Russia occupied Poland. Ray lived in a small village near Bialystok, and because of the widespread poverty in Poland, his family survived through bartering rather than money. At 13, Ray began to apprentice under his father after showing him he had mastered a hand-sewn buttonhole. His skills ultimately saved his life.

"When I went to Auschwitz, what would I do?" he asks

Before I can respond, before I can ask, he tells me to take off the suit and take it back. He helps me out of the jacket, but when he hands it to me, doesn't let go. He looks at the cuff of the sleeve and begins to finger it, turning the sleeve inside out to reveal, what seems to me now, poorly sewn stitching. The stitches tack back and forth sloppily, string ends hanging haphazardly, exposing precariousness where one thread, pulled the wrong way, leads to disintegration and ripped seams. Not the arrow-straight line that suggests good workmanship.

"You see?" he speaks softly, hanging onto the arm. "Before Hitler came we were under the Russians for 18 months. Russia took over half of Poland and Germany took the other half. The Russians told my father he had to do hard labor and I said, 'Dad, you stay home because you got to provide and make a living. I will go.' I used to come home with my hand bleeding. I was not used to the work they made us do: shovel mountains to make a road. During wintertime we would go to the forest to cut wood they sent to Russia. But that was not so bad. When the Germans came—that was impossible. They hardly gave you anything to eat. I never dreamed I would come out alive."

That, according to Ray, was in 1939, and was the beginning of the end. Hitler and Stalin agreed to share Poland but, without warning, Hitler forced the Russians out in three days. It happened with lightning speed.

Ray manipulates the jacket sleeve as he talks, exposing its inferior construction. He lets loose the sleeve.

"Well, you take this suit back and get a new suit. A Hickey-Freeman. Or Joseph A. Banks," he says.

I return the following week with a gray pin-striped suit from Joseph A. Banks: a signature two-button wool pinstripe suit with plain-front trousers. When I remove the garment bag, Ray's eyes light up. He shows me the strength and intricacy of the stitching. He sets it down on his material table and shows me the extra material, left for the express purpose of tailoring.

"This I can work with," he says.

I go into the changing room and put on the suit. It swallows me. The jacket fits more like a cloak, and I feel like a young boy playing dress-up with his father's clothes. The pant legs puddle at my feet and if I don't cinch the waist, the pants fall straight to the floor. Ray has his work cut out for him. He has me stand in front of the mirror on the stepstool and sizes me up.

He braces himself to bend down—a wide stance, then bending at the knee while resting both hands on the other knee. He lowers himself slowly until the first bent knee rests on the floor, will-you-marry-me style. He works at the cuff using pins and chalk, marking at the material. I ask him how he was taken to Auschwitz and he stops.

Ray's shop is in the center of a strip mall, and when nobody's talking and the radio's not on, it's pin-drop silent. He looks at the ground without really looking at it. He drops his hands to his side and he's thinking, thinking. It's him and me and the crackly buzz of fluorescent lights that burn color away into dull monochrome. Under this stark whiteness, he schools me in history.

───────────

Ray had lived under the forced labor of the Russians, but the Germans were not so accommodating.

"The Germans put me and my family on a train to Auschwitz," he says. "I was 15 or 16 so that was '41 or '42." Ray had heard rumors that Auschwitz was a death camp, but his family refused to believe him. He begged his family to jump with him from the train.

"They said no," he tells me. "All the time I begged them. They thought they were going to the resort. Every time I think about it I wanna kill myself."

Ray stops talking. He raises his arm. He moves to the other leg and the chalk draws a trail of slash marks on the material to be eliminated. He pauses, hanging onto a piece of loose pant leg.

The Germans, Ray says, left the boxcar unattended because most Poles thought the train led to an interment camp where they would be kept for the duration of the war. They accepted their fate as prisoners of war. No one imagined the human capacity needed to carry out Hitler's *die Endlösung*: the Final Solution.

Ray and four other boys on his boxcar suspected the worst, and they wanted off.

"There was a little window on top of the boxcar of the train," Ray recalls. He had tried to squeeze through it, but his heavy fur jacket wouldn't allow it. He crawled back down, then tried again, this time making it out. A friend threw his coat out after him. Ray and four other boys escaped the boxcar and ran into the wilderness. He didn't realize then that it would be his home for the next year.

"You know, in Poland it gets cold like it's Canada," he says.

He takes pins and begins stabbing at the chalk marks. Purely. Precisely. He pulls the material close to his face. *Stab.* Instinct kicks in while his mind traces outlines of the past he'd rather not recall. *Stab.* He tells me it's a lot to talk about: the farmer who saved his life by providing a single spade but refused any other assistance for fear of retribution. *Stab.* I resist the instinct to flinch as he pulls needles from pincushion to me.

Stab. I trust in his experience as he sticks the pins and tells me more about the year in the forest.

"We took the spade and dug into the ground—about two feet down and then two feet horizontal into the ground," he says. "We make a little place in the earth where we can lay down but we can't sit up. At night, you know, we could get out. But in daytime it was us, staying underground. When the snow comes, we thought it was bad. But then later the rain came and we wish we could have the snow."

He stops stabbing and examines the material closely, running his fingers along the metal dashes that force the pant leg to conform. The pinpoints that poke and scratch safely stay concealed just beneath the surface of the material.

"One of the boys couldn't walk because his legs was frozen," he says. Ray begged him to walk to find food, but the boy's leg had turned gangrenous. Ray and the others eventually took the boy to the ghetto at Bialystok, where the boy's leg was amputated.

"There was no medication. No penicillin. Nothing. Not even aspirin. For Jews, they say let 'em die."

Ray stands back up. First the hands braced on the knee, then the push that shoots the upper body up. He's righted himself and he concentrates his chalk and pins on my shoulders.

"They shot him."

According to Ray, all of this occurred around the beginning of 1943. The Bialystok ghetto was close to his uncle's hometown, and when he and Ray found each other in the ghetto, he convinced Ray to remain there rather than attempting to escape back into the forest. Ray had lost his immediate family and his uncle's presence comforted him, briefly.

The Bialystok ghetto housed around 50,000 Polish Jews laboring under the Germans. In Bialystok, Ray began to realize the extent of the Nazi cruelty. Even physically challenged Germans wound up in the camps and then, not long thereafter, disappeared.

"The trains, the boxcars, was carrying the people to the gas chambers day and night," he says. "Women, young girls—they shaved off their hair and they was wearing wooden shoes. They put potato sacks on them to wear. They looked like monkeys. Killed them all."

It was during this time that Ray was separated from his uncle and shipped to the concentration camp at Auschwitz. It was 1943, when Ray was just 17.

Ray maneuvers himself behind me and I feel the weight of his hands on my shoulders. He pinches the shoulder material and lifts up. He holds the material from each shoulder between his thumbs and forefingers.

"Too much space, you see?"

I see my reflection in the mirror. He's lifted the shoulders of the jacket so that my head sinks.

The second train to Auschwitz was a different story. "Before, I was from a smaller town so it was easy to escape from the train. This time the Germans was starting to lose the war, so it was worse. You couldn't jump because on every boxcar was the SS with a machine gun.

"At Auschwitz they brought you in ... to vanish," he says. At 15 square miles, Auschwitz was the largest concentration camp, and the Nazis divided it into three sub-camps: Auschwitz I acted as the base camp; Auschwitz-Birkenau was the main extermination camp; and Auschwitz-Monowitz enforced hard labor. In all, Auschwitz housed a total of 1.1 million Jews, 960,000 of which were killed. Ray was one of the few who survived the second camp, Auschwitz-Birkenau.

"OK. Now you can step down."

I step off the chair. Ray grabs the back of the jacket at my lower spine and pulls the jacket tight against me. I fall back because I'm not ready for the force of the pull, the firmness with which he holds the coat. In the mirror I see him hunched over, marking the coat with his chalk. Lines and Xs, from the base of my neck to the small of my back.

"When I got there, in Auschwitz, they asked for tailors, shoemakers, bricklayers," Ray says. "I was making uniforms for the SS—you know, the riding breaches. Everything had to be tailor-made. Everything had to be done perfect. You had to do it right or boy watch out. And when we got through with the uniforms we were making civilian clothes. I was 16 or 17 by then. If I wouldn't have been a tailor they would've killed me, too."

The lump in my throat prevents me from swallowing. I look at him in the mirror, bent over, measuring, marking barbed-wire Xs down my back and it's with the hands the Germans forced him to use 67 years ago on the back of an SS officer. One who killed the elderly, gassed the women and children and gypsies. His meticulous hands make the same Xs on me now as they did back then and I wonder at the weight of his hands, at how much they endured, and I wonder if the SS officer really believed in the solution to the *Judenfrage*—Hitler's "Jewish question"—or if he defied the illogic and appreciated the precision of the hands making Xs on his back, and I imagine each X marks another day of life for Ray in a place where a wasted day is another day of gained breath.

"Auschwitz was big," he recalls. "It was an old Polish cavalry camp. And the barracks they changed for the prisoners. Put some beds in that we lived in. Three-story beds. Everybody engraved their names and their town in the wood of the bed. On every bed you saw it. Everybody would take a little knife and engrave or they'd do it with little pencils. And every time I get up in the morning I wake up praying, and when I go to bed, too, if I'm still alive. I never dreamed I would make it 90 years."

It's the carved name that recalls his identity, and the commitment to prayer to a God against whom he can measure himself, that kept Ray going. His main drive, his mantra even today, is "Never give up." When others succumbed to their despair, Ray encouraged them to reject the anguish that paved the way for death. Hunger propelled the despair, and Ray never gave up finding various sources for food. In the middle of the night he'd risk certain execution and creep out of his bunk and sidle alongside the barracks until he reached the kitchen, hoping to see the window cracked with food on the sill or nearby counter. Numerous times he'd filch a potato or two and make his way back to his barracks. Hunger pervaded each breath, and Ray says during the day and all night everyone dreamed about food, which meant that food was the goal, that hunger trumped risk, that life without food couldn't be living.

"You have no idea what hunger means," he says. "The biggest punishment if you want to punish somebody: Don't feed 'em."

He grabs the pants at either side of my waist and tugs. More chalk stitch marks moving down my hips. More pinning.

"Auschwitz was nothing but killing. When people went in, the music was playing because people was screaming. You know, in the barracks the walls was thin and you could hear the screaming. So the music was playing so you couldn't hear the voices. You saw in the chimneys not smoke, but flame—like they were shooting fire. And a lot of times they was making—from the flesh of humans—soap. The called it *reden Juden* fat: RJF. From human flesh. When you went to take a shower they gave you something that looked like a rock. But it was made from humans. They'd shave off the hair to make mattresses."

The pincushion he wears around his wrist has moved its way up his arm. As he moves to take another pin out to stick into the suit, I see, perched on the elastic band that inches up, on the soft inside of his forearm, a bird that looks like Tweety crossed with a macaw.

"Everybody used to ask me about the numbers," he says. "I got sick and tired of it, so I covered it. It didn't matter what in the hell it was because it wasn't doing me any good."

When he tells me B2526, he lets me look close to try to see it, but the tattoo artist executed his job perfectly. No trace of the number.

When the Germans began losing ground in Poland because of the advancing Russian troops, the SS implemented a plan to move healthy prisoners to Dachau, a concentration camp located in Bavaria, Germany. In order to keep the prisoners from escaping during the transportation, the Germans told the Jewish prisoners they were exchanging them for German prisoners held by the Russians. It was a lie, of course. The ruse worked.

Some of the railroads to Dachau had been bombed into disrepair, which forced the Germans to take longer routes.

"It was three or four days on those goddamn boxcars," Ray recalls. "You have a bucket if you want to take a leak. You cannot describe it. Ninety, a hundred in a boxcar like sardines. It was packed. Had to stand you know? You cannot forget. Never. Never. You talk about punishment. In an American jail it's a pleasure. They got a television, they got a bed. They're treated like a human. But over there? They didn't give a damn. They wanted you to die."

Eventually, Ray made it to Dachau, where he was assigned a new number: 19465. They put him to work making parts for the Luftwaffe. He was assigned an impossible work shift of heavy manual labor: 12 hours for the day shift, and 12 hours for the night shift.

"In case you run away they looked right away on your arm," he says. "But we didn't have civilian clothes. Everybody was in blue and white stripes so that nobody could run. They had electric wires, and outside the wire was ditches with water. Nobody could escape. If you would escape they would catch you."

In Dachau, the slightest physical ailment meant certain death. On a regular basis, the SS inspected the prisoners' bodies by calling them out of bed in the morning and forcing them to assemble, naked, and stand motionless for 30 minutes. The winters proved most detrimental because those who exhibited any symptoms of a cold or flu were dealt with severely. After the liberation of Dachau, Ray asked his doctor how he survived, and the only explanation the doctor could provide was, "You was young."

In the mirror, I'm all white-dashed stitches held together with pins. The tailor gives me one more going-over, carefully examining how he's refigured and put the suit together. He steps back, satisfied with his work.

"I never dreamed I would come out alive," he says. "I weighed 75 pounds. Skin and bones."

May 2, 1945, changed everything for Ray.

"That's when there were white flags in the villages, hanging from the rooftops," Ray recalls. "It was snowing in Bavaria in the forest. They was marching us through the forest. They were trying to get rid of us. Russians and Jews in the thousands. And all of a sudden we look, and nobody's there. The SS is gone. The Russians were running to the dead horses along side of the road and cutting the meat and eating it. You have no idea what hunger means."

I take the jacket off. First one arm, then the other, carefully slipping the material off my body to avoid the potential pinpricks while at the same time maintaining the newer, more form-fitting shape of the jacket crafted by Ray. He takes the coat and carefully hangs it, then the pants.

"You know, when the war started, I had a family. They went to Treblinka in the beginning. But young and old, they got killed. When it was over, I was all alone. I was hoping maybe I will find somebody. After the war I went in the German museum and looked at the booth for Poland. The walls in the room were covered with lists of who was left alive and who is gone. I never could see anybody from my family. All of them gone."

He takes the hung suit and places it on a rack next to a row of similarly pinned and white-dashed clothing, all standing at attention and waiting for Ray to reshape them permanently. He tells me to come back next week for the finished suit.

When I thank him, he replies, "Who shall ask, shall receive. Whatever you need, I will give it to you."

LEON'S LAIR

A former paperboy remembers the day Leon Russell moved into
the Aaronson mansion in Tulsa's Maple Ridge neighborhood

By *Matt O'Meilia*

I THOUGHT MY CHILDHOOD WAS PRETTY NORMAL until I started
telling people about it. I thought, for instance, it was normal for every
kid in the neighborhood to be Catholic and for every family to have a
minimum of five kids. Imagine my surprise when I learned in school—
Catholic school, of course—that Oklahoma is only 7 percent Catholic.
I thought, *How can this be?* It was also normal to have a house in the
neighborhood you could go to anytime you felt like it and get candy
from a woman you really didn't know, but it was OK with all your friends
and all the parents because she was The Candy Lady.

And it was normal to have a father who made his living in the
backyard, in a three-car garage he converted into a studio, where he
painted pictures all day and people came over to buy them. One day I
was mowing the backyard when a car pulled up and out stepped a
mountain of a man. I stopped the mower and the man asked where my
father was. When I said he wasn't home, the mountain thundered, "Tell
him Sampson came by. Will Sampson." Of course you can sell artwork
from your backyard to people, including famous actors, and make enough
to send five kids through private schools and college. This didn't seem
strange. I mean, no stranger than a rock star moving onto my block.

I grew up in Tulsa, in Sunset Park, which is somehow located within Maple Ridge South. Neighborhood divisions barely make sense to me now, and definitely didn't when I was a kid. Growing up I had no idea that my neighborhood had an official name. I simply lived on Sunset Drive, a street that is only four blocks long and travels parallel to numbered streets, which I now realize is not normal for Tulsa. People asked where I lived and I said, "Sunset Drive." No one knew where that was, so I clarified: "It's by Woodward Park." Everyone knew where Woodward Park was.

In the early '70s the predominant neighborhood topic was Dutch elm disease, which was destroying our elms—at the time the overwhelming majority of our mature trees—at an alarming rate. We lost seven trees on our property alone, and the introduction of sunlight where there had once been unrelenting shade transformed the whole look and feel of the neighborhood. Then something else quickly changed the topic of conversation and psychologically altered the neighborhood: a rock 'n' roll legend at the apex of his fame had decided to move into the old Aaronson mansion at 24th Place and Woodward Boulevard, a monstrous Georgian-style home on two acres, built around 1920 by oilman Lionel Aaronson.

Leon Russell was coming back to Tulsa one more time.

————————

The teenagers in the neighborhood were flipping out. The parents, even if they didn't know who Leon was, heard "rock star" and saw the writing on the wall: every kid in the neighborhood was about to get hooked on heroin.

I was 10 in 1972, so the name Leon Russell didn't ring a bell. I was into rock music as much as a 10-year-old could be. I had started playing the drums around that time, was already listening to the records my older siblings played—Beatles, Stones, Doors—but Leon's music had yet to trickle down to my ears. It was about to.

My brother, my friends, and I used to roam freely together throughout the neighborhood, and one of our favorite hangouts was the backyard of the Aaronson mansion, although we didn't call it that. It was simply the big house with the empty swimming pool and the beat-up tennis court. Next door to the west was my friend Jeff Heckenkemper's house, and next door to the east of Leon's future home lived the Shackelford family, where Ted Shackelford of *Knots Landing* fame grew up. My house was around the corner from Jeff's, two doors away.

Jeff's side yard offered easy access to the Aaronson property, via the vine- and weed-covered tennis court. There wasn't a fence, so in our minds that was permission to trespass. I don't remember ever seeing anyone in the house or on the property before Leon moved in. If it was occupied, the owners (the Mathews family last lived in the home before Leon) couldn't have easily spotted us in one of our favorite hideouts—a bushy area at the corner of the property by Jeff's front yard, hidden from the street by a brick wall, where we liked to hide and lob snowballs at cars going up and down Woodward Boulevard. During the summer it was our station for shining flashlights in the eyes of the drivers. Anything to make a car stop and chase us. But that little hideaway was no more after Leon moved in.

The first sign of a rock star in our midst was the massive brick wall being built around the property. One day we were outside playing football in Jeff's front yard when we saw the new owner walking the perimeter, inspecting the wall's progress. The image of God in our young minds was like that of most people: an old man with long white hair and a beard. Suddenly there was a slightly younger version of God walking among us, only he wore teardrop mirrored sunglasses. Mrs. Hecken-kemper was outside and went over to Leon to introduce herself. We interrupted our game and followed her. Leon was friendly, right neighborly, and shook all of our hands. He had a very weak grip and a puffy, ashen hand.

"Any of you guys play music?" he casually asked.

"I play the drums," I squeaked. The other guys giggled. Leon then said one of two things to me: either "All right" or "Right on." I can't be sure; all I knew is he was saying something directly to *me*, in reply to something *I* had said to *Him*, I mean, *him*. And he said it with a hint of encouragement, of mild enthusiasm, which led me to believe that Leon would be asking me to come over and jam with him sometime. Sure, the guy who had recently stolen the show in a concert with George Harrison, Eric Clapton, and Ringo Starr would simply die to have a 10-year-old kid lay down the beat for him. This would have made perfect sense in my perfectly normal childhood. But, inexplicably, Leon never called.

I saw Leon again a few months later when I went with my mother to buy tennis shoes. Leon was there, shopping where all the great rock stars shop for shoes: Kinney Shoes at 51st & Peoria. He was by himself, and my mother approached him to introduce herself and then me, which made me roll my eyes and shake my head because Leon and I were already well acquainted, had musical kinship. But Leon acted like he'd never met me! Man, these bigshot rock stars.

During the legendary Tulsa residency of Leon Russell, everyone who was anyone stopped in to visit the Master of Space and Time. Joe Cocker graced the 'hood, J.J. Cale paid visits, Clapton and his bandmates dropped by—sightings reported by every kid in the neighborhood. From his attic window, Jeff Heckenkemper spied on Leon, and one day he's pretty sure he saw Leon and George Harrison ambling through the backyard. It's highly plausible, since George played his first and only concert in Tulsa in 1974, and would have surely looked up his old band-mate from The Concert for Bangladesh while in town. Other sightings strain credibility, like the time we were sitting on Jeff's front steps when we *think* we saw Paul and Linda McCartney drive up in an old white Cadillac. Whether my imagination was working overtime or not, this was the day it really hit me that our new neighbor might be somebody pretty important.

In the summer of 1973 an invitation came in the mail to all of the neighbors: Leon was having a party to meet everyone—or so my parents interpreted the invitation. The catch was it would cost $7 per person to attend. "What kind of crazy thing is this, charging neighbors to come over to your house?" exclaimed my parents in words to that effect. So, my family didn't go, and for years I was under the impression that you had to pay to not only see rock stars perform, but also to visit with them in their homes. In reality, the event was a fund-raiser by the Maple Ridge Association to help pay for legal action against the building of the Riverside Expressway (successfully opposed, thank goodness), and Leon had graciously allowed the Association to use his house as a meeting place. He was on tour at the time so he didn't attend, which further rankled my parents.

My chance to establish a long-lasting friendship and working relationship with Leon finally came, I thought, when I inherited my friend Bobby Alexander's paper route in the fall of 1973, when I was in sixth grade. Bobby was starting high school and wouldn't have time for his afternoon delivery of the *Tulsa Tribune* anymore, so he bequeathed to me the route that included my friend Leon's house. Because the house sat way back from the street and was hidden from view by brick, the routine was to simply heave the paper over the wall in the direction of his front door. Every day the routine included hearing the paper land on the ground with a *thwap*, followed immediately by the sound of guard dogs barking and ripping the paper to shreds. Every day I wondered why Leon took a paper.

Because my route had only 54 houses, I collected the $1.95 monthly subscription from each customer in person. Tips were better that way. But collecting from Leon always required at least two or three attempts. Sometimes the doorbell went unanswered. Sometimes a voice came over the intercom saying to come back because nobody had any money, which even a naïve 10-year-old didn't buy. Then, just before the 15th of each month, the mandatory deadline before paper service was suspended, somebody finally came to the door and coughed up the dough.

But it was never Leon. Every month during my two and a half years on the route—or several times a month, in this case—I would ring the doorbell and hope Leon would be there and have a free minute to pay his paperboy and maybe give me some insight into life, wax nostalgic about his days as a lad in Lawton and an adolescent in Tulsa, those carefree times when the world wasn't so demanding of his talents and forcing him to live in a fortress. Maybe some tips for an aspiring drummer. But no. Every month it was someone different who finally came to the door, more often a young woman than a man—groupies, perhaps, or relatives, or backup singers. The one I vividly remember was a tall, skinny woman with long, straight hair who sniffled a lot and asked me if I would like a brownie. "They're freshly baked," she added. I considered it for a second, but then imagined my mother's reaction if I told her I had eaten a brownie from Leon Russell's house. "No, thank you," I said, feeling, suddenly, intensely nervous. But it was nice of the girl to offer.

When I started high school, I turned the route over to the next kid, and a year later, in 1977, Leon sold his place and moved to California. Tulsa was great for Leon when he was an anonymous high school kid at Rogers, but being a celebrity here proved to be a burden. The police suspected Leon of being connected to "local drug activity" and questioned (some would say "hassled") him about it. He was sued for allegedly backing out of some investment deals. Then he almost burned his house down.

I remember the night the fire trucks came screaming down Woodward Boulevard to Leon's house. A blaze had damaged part of the second and third floors, and opened a hole in the roof. The neighborhood assumption was that Leon and his friends were having a pot party and caught the house on fire. Pot was the only drug my friends and I had any concept of at the time, and a vague understanding at that, so our logical minds concluded that pot was to blame, what with all that lighting of the reefers and the bongs that those pyromaniac potheads are always doing. But I don't know what really happened. Probably not that.

Charlie Holmes, a local attorney, bought the house from Leon and owned it for about ten years. It was acquired by a real estate developer who tore it down one early morning in November 1987 to the unhappy surprise of the neighborhood. According to John Brooks Walton, resident authority on Tulsa's historic homes, among Leon's many modifications to the house was the installation of a recording studio in the basement that caused some structural damage to the home. Some say the damage was irreparable and razing the mansion was the only solution, but others disagree.

Either way, it's gone now, and four large homes occupy the property that was the focus of the neighborhood's attention for many years.

In all of our discussions about Leon while he lived in the neighborhood, the subject of *why* he moved there never came up, at least that I can remember. I mean, of all the mansions in Tulsa, why that one? My crazy artist father, at age 84 still working every day in the backyard, indirectly provided the answer years later, when I was in my 20s, by taking me to the Celebrity Club at 31st & Yale to see Tommy Crook play.

Dad said, "You're not going to believe this guy." And for once the old man was right: I didn't believe it when I saw Tommy then, and I still don't believe it now. The Buddy Rich of the guitar—that's the best way I can describe him. It was during one of the many evenings I returned to marvel at Tommy and his magic fingers that he, in between sets, told me this story:

In the late 1950s, Tommy was in a band with Leon, then known by his real name, Russell Bridges. In 1958, Russell Bridges and the Starlighters were booked to play a private party at the McClintock home, 1151 E. 24th Place in Tulsa—also known as the future home of Leon Russell. The band's lineup rotated on occasion, sometimes including guitarist J.J. Cale and/or bassist Carl Radle. For this gig, the band's namesake was accompanied by Tommy, drummer Chuck Blackwell, saxophonist Johnny Williams, and bassist George Metzel.

They were teenagers, fresh off of a tour with Jerry Lee Lewis, so they had reason to be full of confidence when they rolled in the driveway right up to the front door in their big, black, '53 Chrysler "funeral car," as Tommy put it, with the band name emblazoned on the side in big white letters—you know, like they owned the place. The party's host was aghast that the group had the nerve to arrive at the *front* door, being hired help and all, and directed the boys with a few harsh words to go around to the back. This didn't sit well with any of them, particularly Leon, who vowed aloud to show those rich bastards someday by coming back and buying the place.

Thanks for taking revenge on the establishment, Leon. It made my childhood pretty special.

WHO'S AFRAID OF ELOHIM CITY?

An exclusive journey into the mysterious community at
the center of several Oklahoma City bombing conspiracies

By *Joshua Kline and Lee Roy Chapman*

BAD MEN ARE DRAWN TO THE CITY OF GOD. The Southern Poverty
Law Center calls it the meeting ground for America's most sinister
extremists. Many Oklahomans regard it as the most dangerous and
mysterious place in the state.

For 30-plus years, a small, isolated community in Northeastern
Oklahoma has been the subject of endless scrutiny. Law enforcement
agencies and conspiracy theorists insist that Elohim City is a breeding
ground for neo-Nazis and anti-government militias hell-bent on over-
throwing the "Zionist Occupied Government" (ZOG) of the United
States. The most damning accusation suggests Elohim City played a
central role in the planning and execution of the Oklahoma City bombing.

When asked if she'd ever had the chance to visit Elohim, a woman
with the *Stilwell Democrat Journal* deadpanned, "No, we like to breathe."

"I find them to be quite upstanding citizens of my community," says
Adair County Sheriff Austin Young.

A sharp, stern man with a military presence, Young has the towering, no-bullshit persona of a Clint Eastwood character. His white hair
is neatly cropped, his eyes maintain contact and rarely blink.

"What I read in the papers, I never experienced that with them," he says.

Young says that, as game warden of Sequoyah County (just south of Adair) in the early '80s, he once received a report of poaching that ultimately led him to Elohim City, where the suspect resided. As he approached the entrance of the community, he was met by Elohim City founder Robert Millar and several armed guards. Young politely told Millar that the weapons made him a little nervous.

"Robert said to me, 'Well, you have a firearm, don't you think that makes *us* nervous,'" the sheriff remembers. "So I unholstered my weapon and placed it in my vehicle. And then he sent the armed guards away."

This encounter began a 30-year rapport between Young and Elohim City. Young ran for sheriff in the mid-'90s, when neo-Nazis, a German Nationalist, the Midwest Bank Robbers, and Timothy McVeigh were supposedly frequenting the compound.

"I campaigned in all parts of the county, including Elohim, and as far as I know, they supported me," Young says.

Shortly after the Oklahoma City bombing, a rumor spread that members of Elohim were planning a terrorist attack in Stilwell during the town's annual strawberry festival. Young called Millar and asked him point blank if the rumor was true. Millar answered, "Of course not. We would never do that." The strawberry festival went off without incident.

After offering his opinions ("they're not violent, not resistant, not how the media paints them"), Young suggests we go straight to the horse's mouth.

He dials up John Millar, pastor and de facto leader of Elohim, and son of the community's late founder. When Millar picks up, he explains that he has a couple of journalists from Tulsa who wish to visit Elohim. But instead of waiting for Millar to respond, Young offers the receiver to us.

"You're not interested in repeating all those lies that were told about us?" Millar asks. And then he invites us for a visit.

———————

Stephen Jones is a towering figure in Oklahoma's legal community. Over his 46-year career as a defense attorney, the Enid native has represented a slew of high-profile pariahs and controversial characters, including anarchist Abbie Hoffman, serial killer Bobby Wayne Collins, suspected SLA radical Harawese Moore,[1] and, most recently, indicted Tulsa Police Officer Jeff Henderson. But it was his work as Timothy McVeigh's court-appointed defender for which he's best remembered.

"When the Oklahoma City bombing happened, it didn't surprise me at all," Jones tells us one Saturday afternoon in his Enid office. "I was shocked that it was Oklahoma City. But that somebody would blow up a building and kill a lot of federal employees? That wasn't a surprise at all. I had sensed for some period of time that there was a significant alienation of people in the Great Plains. There was a genuine hatred of the federal government, a hatred of the Clintons. I had not seen anything like it since I worked for the republican state committee in Texas when the Kennedys were in office in the early '60s."

Jones believes that this anti-government sentiment reached a tipping point on April 19, 1993, when ATF and FBI agents assaulted another eccentric religious community: the Branch-Davidian compound in Waco, Texas. When the siege was over, 81 men, women, and children were dead.

"You have the primitive evangelical community," Jones says. "And the defining moment for a lot of those people—and this narrows down to Elohim City—was the assault on the Branch-Davidians... Tim McVeigh told me that he sat in a Bradley tank; he knew what those tanks could do. And those images of that tank punching holes in that building, for several million people, probably more than 10 million people, that was a Biblical prophesy come true."

McVeigh watched closely, first on television and then in person, as the nightmare at Waco unfolded. This proved to his breaking point. Disturbed by what he witnessed, McVeigh began to plot his own revenge on behalf of the Branch-Davidians. Two years later, his vengeance became a reality when 168 people, including 19 children, died in the Oklahoma City bombing.

---

1 Coincidentally, like Jones' most famous client, Moore was also accused of bombing the Murrah building. In 1998's controversial tome on the OKC bombing, *The Oklahoma City Bombing and the Politics of Terror*, author David Hoffman writes, "In the mid-'70s, Oklahoma resident Harawese Moore was convicted of planting an incendiary explosive device outside both the federal courthouse and the Alfred P. Murrah Building."

It's well documented that Jones did not buy the government's conclusion (re-enforced by McVeigh himself) that McVeigh conceived and executed the bombing almost entirely alone, with only the most minimal assistance from Terry Nichols and Michael Fortier. Jones believes the government was desperate for swift, quantifiable justice and chose to focus only on developing an airtight case against McVeigh and Nichols rather than fog the issue of their guilt by fully exploring the possibility of a broader conspiracy. Jones does not believe the evidence against Elohim City provides a sufficient answer.

"There is no smoking gun that shows involvement of any of the people in Elohim City," he says. "There is certainly, in two or three instances, against the backdrop of this, a pretty convincing case that *some* people *in* Elohim City may have been involved."

For the man who spent years studying every tiny pebble of the mountainous evidence, Elohim City is just another "what if?" scenario, doomed to float in the ether, a question mark whose answer is forever unknowable.

He agrees, though, that Adair County is a poetic fit for the community.

"Throughout the history (of Eastern Oklahoma), there has been more chicanery, isolationism, parochialism, xenophobic attitudes, distrust of outsiders, 'We settle things our way,'" he explains. "So Elohim City, yes, is comfortably located. Very comfortably. Historically, it blends in."

You won't find Elohim City on any map. The FBI has dedicated an incredible amount of time, money, and manpower to investigating and monitoring the town's activities. Yet, this idyllic hamlet (known to its residents as "God's City," the Hebrew translation of Elohim) remains well hidden, impossible to find without the assistance of one of the few people in the world who've actually been there. Some reports reference Fort Smith as the nearest town, others Sallisaw, Muldrow, or Stilwell. They're all more or less right, but also dead wrong: Elohim City is not "near" any town; its 400 acres are situated as far as possible from nearby civilization.

The western edge of the Ozarks begins here in Adair County, a sparsely populated spread of bucolic communities with a mere 22,000 residents (43 percent of whom claim Native American blood) over 577 square miles. The pastoral beauty of the majestic, unpredictable terrain stands in stark contrast to the rural poverty that plagues much of its population. Roadsides are often littered with garbage—discarded, empty cans of Busch beer, cast-off plastic grocery bags, cigarette butts—and road signs are peppered with bullet holes. Gutted shotgun shacks and ramshackle houses with landfill front yards rest precariously next to forests of resilient pines and dead, twisted post oaks. Multitudes of modest white churches adorned with hand-painted signage offer a point of communion for residents to congregate and socialize.

Underneath the surface malaise and natural wonder of Adair lies an explosive history, one that informs Elohim's existence. This is the heart of the Cherokee Nation, the last stop on the Trail of Tears where 11,000 Cherokee Indians were forcibly relocated. The area's history is America's history, fraught with instances of revolt and rebellion, of fierce individualism repeatedly clashing with a government status quo. This is the territory where Cherokee general Stand Waite held out against Union troops, making him the last Confederate general to surrender at the end of the Civil War, thus ending the South's campaign for secession. It's the home of Ned Christie, a Keetowah Cherokee traditionalist falsely accused of killing a federal marshal. When he wouldn't surrender, a posse of hired guns from Fort Smith pushed a burning wagon into Christie's fortified home.

The James Gang hid out here, as did Belle Starr and her bunch, the Dalton Boys, and Charles "Pretty Boy" Floyd. In 1977, Gene Leroy Hart, a Cherokee, was accused of the brutal rape and murder of three girl scouts in Mayes County. Hart was a violent local fugitive who'd previously been convicted of raping two Tulsa women. Despite the public outcry, a Mayes County jury acquitted Hart.

Today, the Cherokee Nation is humble home to small-town Oklahomans, many of whom are largely untouched by 21st century development. The landscape is wild and primitive, and self-governance is necessary for day-to-day survival. And the area's legacy of isolationism and individualism continues, carried on in large part by Elohim City.

For five miles, a dirt path snakes alongside a mountain. Then suddenly you see it: a poster featuring the Ten Commandments tacked to the silver gate of a barbwire fence. Nearby, a mangled, abandoned mailbox limply hangs, begging to be put out of its misery. Several hundred yards later, the incline abruptly levels as the trail penetrates the outskirts of Elohim City.

Serenity permeates the village. The day is bright and sunny, and the view of the Ozarks is breathtaking. For all the violence and racism assigned by outsiders, the town feels more like a spiritual oasis than a terrorist compound. There are no armed guards waiting. A small terrier roams free while children play in the road. A quirky collection of huts, trailers, and cottages spread across the property intermingled with several hulking, alien-like stone structures whose bubbled, dome roofs betray the off-kilter eccentricity of their builders and inhabitants.

A modest cottage rests on the side of the town's only artery, its Main Street. A tattered, faded American flag waves in the front yard not far from a child's jungle gym.

The portly, white-haired man on the porch is John Millar.

"Y'all get lost?" he asks, smiling, in a country drawl. His tone is relaxed and friendly and he invites us in.

Millar's home could be a model showroom for Pottery Barn—simple, clean, and elegant, with hardwood floors and a modern kitchen furnished with contemporary appliances. The décor is exact and unobtrusive. On one wall hangs a large digital clock, on another a faux-rustic bronze piece etched with the phrase "The Destination is the Journey." Framed photographs of family on coffee and end tables are given ample room to breathe. You could mistake the locale for middle-class suburbia.

Millar settles into his chair.

"So, what do y'all wanna know?"

———————

In 1973, an ex-Mennonite pastor from Canada named Robert Millar, acting on what he believed was a vision from God, moved his family from rural Maryland to a large patch of land nestled high in the Ozarks, a mere stone's throw from the Oklahoma-Arkansas border. Elohim City was conceived as a spiritual city of refuge for followers of an obscure offshoot of Protestantism called Christian Identity, which teaches a racialist, Eurocentric take on Old Testament fire-and-brimstone piety. Though the elder Millar's vision that prompted the move could be called "apocalyptic"—he claimed to see future wars, natural disasters, and civil unrest—John Millar maintains that Elohim was not created to be a spiritual bomb shelter.

"We didn't come out here to escape like some people do," Millar tells us. "They think the world's going to explode or fly away or something, and that's their right to believe that. But that's not our vision. Armageddon is not our vision. We came out here to express what we feel the Holy One, or God, is wanting to express through us. And so our hearts are turned towards the heavenly spiritual realm."

The pastor insists that his community is focused on heaven alone. Not the government, not a race war, just peaceful communion with the Creator. He cited factoids—"None of us have ever been convicted of a felony"—and repeatedly renounced the idea that they're a hate group. "People think that because we believe in Christian Identity that we hate other races. We don't teach hate. We don't put up with that."

Millar is polite, generous, and accommodating throughout the interview, never once taking the hardline on any issue. The idea of a "white-separatist compound" conjures images of a completely autonomous community forbidden from interacting with mainstream society; this is not Elohim City. When Millar speaks of politics and morality, his ideas have a surprisingly libertarian, live-and-let-live bent to them.

Many of Elohim's residents, for instance, hold jobs in town. The children are homeschooled in communal fashion—most of the parents take an active role in the education of not just their own kids, but in their neighbors' as well; it's Hillary Clinton's "It takes a village" concept realized in the most literal sense. Weekly trips to town to eat at local restaurants, visit the library, or see a movie are not uncommon. The homes even have Wi-Fi. There's little difference in living conditions between Elohim and your typical Bixby or Sand Springs outliers.

Millar does acknowledge that Christian Identity's racially charged theology is at odds with modern notions of equality and color blindness.

"We teach that the scripture is against intermarriage with other races," he confesses. According to the Oklahoma Department of Commerce,

26.3 percent of marriages occurring between 2008 and 2010 were between two people of different races, ranking Oklahoma second in the nation for interracial couples. "[Intermarriage] is a big issue; most of your churches want to promote that. We think that's totally unscriptural. That doesn't mean we hate them, not at all. We think you destroy both races when you marry in."

The core philosophy of Christian Identity is an uncomfortable mixture of traditional Judeo-Christian mythology and a passive form of modern white supremacy. Elohim residents observe the Sabbath on Saturday, and many adhere to the ancient dietary restrictions of the Old Testament, though Millar is careful to point out that it's not a requirement. According to Identity, when ancient Israel fragmented, the tribe of Judah, "God's chosen people," migrated to northern Europe and eventually the U.S. In other words, the true Jews, according to Millar and Identity followers, are Caucasians.[2]

"That might sound really strange to you," says Millar. "But we believe that your Scandinavian, your Germanic, your Anglo-Saxon, your Celtic people, are different waves of immigration that came through. They're really all cousins and they're part of the same people from ancient Israel."

———————

Since the OKC bombing, three things fueled suspicion about Elohim's complicity: the company Elohim founder Robert Millar chose to keep, the testimony of a government informant named Carol Howe who infiltrated the community, and circumstantial evidence suggesting that Timothy McVeigh may have been in contact with Elohim residents in the months leading up to the bombing.

"For over a year we were scrutinized by the FBI," Millar tells us. "We didn't like it, but we thought it was the duty of the federal government to chase down whoever did that. So we were scrutinized sideways, every which way you could think."

———————

2   References to the Christian Identity belief can be traced as far back as the Declaration of Arbroath on April 6, 1320, in which 37 Scottish Chieftains wrote the Pope asking for assistance in Scotland's battle against England.

Millar maintains that the residents of Elohim never held a violent agenda against the government, nor any desire to participate in some apocalyptic religious battle. But according to Mark Hamm, a professor of criminology at Indiana University, in the early '80s the peaceful residents and elders of Elohim became radicalized as they developed a rapport with a similar white-separatist group from the northern Ozarks called The Covenant, the Sword and the Arm of the Lord (CSA). Unlike the benign Elohim City, the members of CSA didn't just passively distrust the U.S. government—they were stockpiling weapons and conducting rigorous military training in order to overthrow it. Furthermore, CSA had close ties to the Order of the Silent Brotherhood, a shadowy organization of bloodthirsty neo-Nazis who fashioned themselves as Aryan Warriors in the tradition of the Phineas Priesthood.[3]

From Hamm's 2001 book *In Bad Company: America's Terrorist Underground*:

> Originally a pacifist community, Elohim City began a long, slow tilt toward militancy following Millar's 1982 address before another far-right group's gathering—the Covenant, the Sword, and the Arm of the Lord's national convocation at CSA headquarters in nearby Bull Shoals Lake, Arkansas. It was there that Millar met CSA founder James Ellison, a militant neo-Nazi who would later join forces with Robert Mathews' Order in what was to become what is called the War of '84—a campaign of terror against ZOG including a series of assassinations, fire bombings, and robberies.

---

3 In the Book of Numbers, upon discovering an Israelite man and a Midianite woman copulating, the Jewish warrior Phineas bludgeoned the couple with a spear as punishment for the interracial relationship (race-mixing was expressly forbidden by God). For the execution, Phineas was rewarded by God with "an everlasting priesthood." Many militant white supremacists believe that they are called by God to carry on this legacy, and it's been speculated that historical figures such as John Wilkes Booth and Jesse James considered themselves to be Phineas Priests. Robert Mathews and his organization the Order of the Silent Brotherhood are among the most violent recent examples of men committing heinous acts of murder and mayhem under the banner of the Phineas Priesthood.

"Millar taught CSA about God, and they taught Millar about guns," said a former CSA member to a reporter.

The FBI considered the CSA to be the "best trained civilian para-military group in America," and was closely monitoring its activity.

On April 19, 1985, exactly ten years prior to the Oklahoma City bombing, the FBI surrounded CSA and demanded the surrender of Ellison, who was wanted for conspiring to acquire automatic weapons. For four days, a tense cold war ensued as Ellison refused to surrender. Robert Millar traveled to the compound under the guise of negotiator, but according to Ellison's right hand man Kerry Noble (who ultimately renounced the CSA and now writes and speaks on the dangers of right-wing extremism), Millar was actually there as a witness in the event that the government drew first blood. Later, the newly militant Millar be-moaned the fact that Ellison ultimately surrendered peacefully.

"Jim was wrong to surrender," Millar told Noble while visiting him in prison. "He should've shot it out with the feds."

Millar also served as spiritual adviser to Richard Wayne Snell, one of CSA's most violent members, who was put to death for the murders of a black state trooper and a pawn shop owner whom he believed to be Jewish.[4] During the trial, Millar testified as a character witness on Snell's behalf. Snell was executed on April 19, 1995, in Fort Smith Arkansas, twelve hours after the Oklahoma City bombing and ten years to the day after the FBI's siege of CSA. Millar and his son John later retrieved Snell's remains from the state and ultimately buried him in Elohim City.

When asked about his father's relationship with Snell, Millar's tone becomes sharp.

"Snell's body is here," he says. "I went to pick it up with my dad, his remains, at the request of his *wife*, okay?"

---

4 In 1983, Snell, Ellison, and Noble traveled to Oklahoma City to case the Murrah Federal building as the potential target of a CSA attack. However, during preparations, the men interpreted a weapons malfunction as a sign from God and the plan for attack was canceled. There's been some conjecture that the Murrah building may have been chosen as the target of the April 19, 1995, attack as a tribute to Snell, who was scheduled for execution the same day.

By forging a relationship with Ellison, Snell, and the CSA, Elohim City effectively laid the foundation for the scrutiny, suspicion, and rumors that would plague the community in the years to come, reaching a fever pitch in the mid-'90s.

"We didn't know Timothy McVeigh," Millar insists. "Never heard of him until the bombing. No connection whatsoever."

In the grand jury indictment of McVeigh, the government alleged that the plotting of the bombing began in early September of 1994, while McVeigh was staying at a motel in Vian, Oklahoma, less than an hour away from Elohim City.

"It is true that Tim McVeigh was there that day, that's what the hotel registration shows, and it is true that that's off the beaten path for him," Jones acknowledges. "Tim McVeigh almost never went to Eastern Oklahoma via Western Oklahoma."

It's believed that during this time, McVeigh was in contact with members of the Aryan Republican Army (ARA), a ragtag group of white supremacists who executed a series of bank robberies in order to fund anti-government activities (earning the media nickname "the Midwest Bank Bandits"). Evidence suggests the ARA was in Elohim City at the same time McVeigh was in Vian. The exact nature of McVeigh's relationship with these men (Pete Langan,[5] Richard Guthrie, Scott Stedeford, Kevin McCarthy, and Michael Brescia) and, by proxy, Elohim City, is foggy. People like Mark Hamm hypothesize that the ARA helped to fund the bombing with their loot and used Elohim as a sort of safe house, an idea known as the "theory of multiple John Does." In Hamm's book, ARA leader Pete Langan, who is currently serving a life sentence plus 35 years for his role in the robberies, is interviewed extensively and appears to be honest and forthcoming about his criminal activities. But he denies any connection to the bombing, and he minimizes Elohim's

---

5 Langan was the ARA's unofficial leader and a self-proclaimed member of the Phineas Priesthood. Upon Langan's arrest in 1996, authorities discovered that his toenails were painted pink and his entire body was devoid of hair. It later came out that Langan was a transsexual who, when not robbing banks, cross-dressed and lived as a woman named Donna.

significance as anything other than a spiritual refuge. McVeigh denied the existence of accomplices to his dying breath. It's argued that there are a multitude of potential reasons for both men to lie, but the fact remains that nothing has been proven.

In March of 1995, the government had planned to raid Elohim City based on ATF informant Carol Howe's allegations.

Howe, a 24-year-old Tulsa debutante-turned-skinhead trophy queen, was brought to Elohim City by her boyfriend, white supremacist and would-be celebrity of the militia movement, Dennis Mahon. A former Imperial Dragon of the KKK, Mahon was now leader of the White Aryan Resistance (WAR) in Tulsa.[6]

Jones calls Mahon a "freakshow," a "burlesque figure of comedy," a man prone to "making extreme statements and engaging in extreme acts of self-promotion." John Millar calls him a friend.

"I don't know what he's done in his life," Millar demurs, when asked about Elohim's relationship with Mahon. "He seemed like a decent man to me. I agree with some of his thoughts. Not all of them, not by a long shot, but I do agree with some of his thoughts."

Mahon had plucked Howe from her privileged existence and taken her as a lover and protégé. He delivered her to his friends at Elohim for spiritual indoctrination, but she'd already been contacted by the ATF and turned into an informant. Upon her arrival, she began reporting her findings. She claimed Millar and company were stockpiling weapons, preaching increasingly aggressive anti-government rhetoric, and, most importantly, discussing plans for an attack of some sort. This seemed to confirm the government's worst fears: Elohim City was a powder keg of anti-government rage, a place where, in Hamm's words, "every resident down to the smallest child was armed and dangerous" and "underground

---

6 In February 2012, Mahon was convicted in federal court of a 2004 bombing in Scottsdale, Arizona, that injured Donald Logan, a black city official. Mahon's sentencing hearing is May 22; he could face up to 100 years in prison. Evidence against Mahon was produced in large part through information provided by Rebecca Willams, a government informant who met Mahon and his twin brother Daniel (who was also tried but acquitted) at a Catoosa, Oklahoma trailer park in 2005.

bunkers held vast stores of ammunition, grenades, and explosives, even chemical and biological weapons."

Howe's was one of the more sensational puzzle pieces of the bombing case. When investigative reporter J.D. Cash broke her story in the *McCurtain Daily Gazette* during the Terry Nichols trial, a national media feeding frenzy ensued. She was profiled in numerous magazines and newspapers, interviewed by Diane Sawyer, frequently referred to by reporters as "glamorous" and "beautiful."

In linking Elohim to Oklahoma City, many conspiracy theorists point to Howe's testimony in the Nichols trial, in which she claims to have witnessed Timothy McVeigh's presence at the compound. From the court transcript:

Q. Now, are you familiar with what Timothy McVeigh looks like, Ms. Howe?

A. Yes, sir.

Q. Have you seen photographs of Timothy McVeigh?

A. Yes, I have.

Q. Did you ever see Timothy McVeigh at the Elohim City compound?

A. I believe I did.

Q. All right. When did you see him?

A. It was in July of 1994.

Q. Okay. And where did you see him?

A. He was at a section of the compound walking across a lawn near the church building.

But Howe was problematic. She had a history of lying. Her stories were inconsistent and contradictory, and with more attention each story grew more elaborate.

"Like many former Soviet spies that come to the United States, Howe's story tended to get better over a period of time," Jones says now. "And then there's always new revelations as (informants) think they've been abandoned or forgotten or they want to increase their stipend or whatever. They remember something new." Jones says he discounted everything Carol Howe said after she acquired an attorney and was thrust into the spotlight.

The FBI's March 1995 planned raid against Elohim never materialized due to growing doubt on the government's part over Howe's credibility. Furthermore, Howe was ultimately deemed unreliable and her testimony in the Nichols trial was thrown out, making it unavailable for consideration to the jury. Mention her name to Millar, and you can almost see the blood boiling beneath his skin.

"They wouldn't even use her testimony," he says with incredulity. "She's so unstable *they wouldn't even use her testimony*. That's one of the things we don't appreciate about our government. They use people who are unstable, give them money and finance them to do unethical things. And that's what they found—she was so unethical they wouldn't even use her as a witness, okay?"

Another difficult question regarding Elohim's connection to the bombing centers around Timothy McVeigh's relationship with a German Nationalist named Andreas Strassmeier. Strassmeier wore fatigues and a swastika, was obsessed with firearms, and lived in Elohim City. McVeigh met Strassmeier at a Tulsa gun show in 1993.

"There was a lot of speculation on how they made contact," Millar says. "We don't know. We have a little over a hundred residents, and if they go to a gun show or a movie or a restaurant, I don't know. I don't want to know. I'm not interested. But I don't want them doing anything illegal, okay? And we make that very clear."

In Kingman, Arizona, shortly after he'd rented the Ryder truck he would eventually convert into a weapon of mass destruction, McVeigh used a calling card to dial Elohim City. McVeigh asked the woman who answered if he could speak with "Andi the German."

According to Howe, Strassmeier was the community's head of security, though Millar vehemently denies this.

"Never—he was here, but he wasn't head of Elohim City security," says Millar. "He liked playing with guns, so maybe he thought he was head of security and wanted to walk around with that. We let people think what they want; we believe in freedom. But we never gave him that position of authority."

The question of plausible deniability looms large over Elohim. The racialist ideology of Christian Identity and the geographic seclusion of

Millar's community no doubt attracted men with agendas, but are the community's elders responsible for the behavior of every guest that passes through? For his part, Robert Millar quickly expelled Andreas Strassmeier from Elohim City soon after he became aware that the FBI was looking at Strassmeier for possible ties to McVeigh and the bombing. Strassmeier ultimately fled to Germany and was never prosecuted.

———————

"I have a niece who's going to a local college," Millar tells us. "She wants to be a lawyer. Her criminal justice professor was talking about terrorists and the Arabs and the Muslims, and then he said, 'Well, we have (terrorists) right up our hill from here, and if you go up there, they hate other races and they're liable to just shoot you for anything.' And my niece raised her hand and said, 'I live up there! That doesn't happen!'"

Millar is clearly vexed by this judgment. He points out that in the 38 years of Elohim's existence, nobody's ever been shot on its property, unlike the surrounding communities. "But because of the stigma and because of us not being politically correct in the eyes of the media, we have a professor in the criminal justice class who throws us in with the terrorists. I don't appreciate that, and he will hear from me. That just happened two weeks ago, okay?"

He pauses, then adds: "You can write that: 'We've never had anyone killed here.'"

Before we depart, Millar gives us a tour of Elohim's new sanctuary, still under construction. The reverend leads us into the beautiful, cavernous chapel, built with the hands of the residents. He apologetically explains that he would normally show us their current church, but the community has no doubt already congregated, and reporters aren't allowed to sit in on their services. Outsiders still make the community uncomfortable.

After the tour, we say our goodbyes and Millar leaves us to find our own way out. With its residents all gathered for service, Elohim City is a ghost town. The air is still and peaceful. The warmth of the sun, the soothing hum of the natural ambiance, the majestic view of the Arkansas wilderness—in this moment, it's obvious why these people are here. On the way out, we notice a primitive, white sign mounted on the side of the road, adorned with a bright red spray-painted phrase: "Jesus Saves."

After decades of scrutiny and mountains of circumstantial evidence, the government has still found no cause to take action against Elohim City. A second Grand Jury investigation of the bombing, convened by State Representative Charles Key to examine loose ends Key and others believed the government did not address to satisfaction in its initial investigation, came up empty-handed on the community.

"We have made every effort to try to identify any plausible connection between (Elohim City) and the bombing," it concluded. "In spite of a possible telephone call from Timothy McVeigh to Elohim City in April 1995, we have been unable to find such a connection."

Does God's City deserve to be granted peace? The questions raised by its proximity to violent right-wing extremism will likely continue to haunt the town for the span of its existence. Image rehabilitation is hardly an option, considering the endless documentation devoted to impeaching the community's collective character. It doesn't help that Millar's own sympathies to violent men ensure that Elohim City will continue to attract them. Then again, Millar and his community aren't seeking social acceptance; they want the right to exist peacefully, outside the parameters of mainstream society. Whether or not society allows that is another matter.

THE GHOST OF KAREN DALTON

She was the Billie Holiday of the Enid plains, a near-forgotten
singer who's finally being rediscovered

By *Thomas Conner*

Katie's been gone, and now her face
is slowly fading from my mind.
She's gone to find some newer places,
left the old life far behind.
Dear Katie, don't ya miss your home?
I don't see why you had to roam.

—"Katie's Been Gone," The Band

EVEN BEFORE SHE ROSE FROM THE DEAD, Karen Dalton always
sounded like a ghost.

Her voice was an unearthly coo, a mournful banshee wail, baying
the blues with a clutching patience. The only urgency was in the timbre
of her voice—fairly high, very round, all soft palette, and just shy of shrill.
On first listen, everyone starts in with the comparisons to Billie Holiday.
Eventually, though, you feel the need to get beyond that blurb, to go
deeper, lured by her slow, slow siren call.

"No one sang the blues slower than she did," says Richard Tucker, a
fellow folk singer and Dalton's ex-husband. "It was her sound, her tone.

To me, that's the big thing in her music. Her voice is so distinctive, nobody sounds like that. Madeleine Peyroux a little bit, but she's more 'up', not so bluesy. [Karen] sounds a fair amount like Billie Holiday, and of course you hear that a lot about her. They could've said 'the new Billie Holiday' or 'the country Billie Holiday', and she might have made a bigger impact, sold more records. I told her that back then, but she didn't want to think about it."

He chuckles. "You couldn't tell her anything." Then he *really* laughs at the thought. "Nobody had a clear picture of how to come out of it commercially and make her a known person. Only certain underground people hear her and say, 'Wow'. Nine out of 10 don't get it, but people who get it think she's the greatest thing in the world."

Nearly 20 years after her death, and 40 years after her last commercial recording, Dalton is just now gaining ground as a "known person." She had everything going for her—a signature and authentic sound, moving from Oklahoma to Greenwich Village at exactly the right moment, the vocal admiration of that scene's rising star, Bob Dylan—but none of it panned out, nothing translated into commercial success.

In the 21st century, though, all music is current and available. The temporality of tunes has been abolished. A teenager jumping into the pop music pool today need not dive, because everything's on the surface—Rolling Stones floating right alongside Stone Temple Pilots, The Beatles with The English Beat, Flamin' Groovies and the Flaming Lips—all of it reachable within a smattering of keystrokes and hyperlinked by relativity and shared adoration. Degree of fame is irrelevant, or at least recast and often upended by the number of page views.

So someone like Dalton sounds at once old and new. Hipsters of each succeeding generation have reveled in her rediscovery—boomers embracing a new shoot from old roots, millennials donning another badge of indie identity. She's the embodiment of the surrealistic, out-of-time ambassador in "Bob Dylan's 115th Dream."

"My daughter's been at parties and people say, 'I heard this on YouTube the other day', and they're talking about her grandmother," says Dalton's daughter, Abbe Baird. "She says, 'The other day I was watching this movie, and they were playing Grandma.' Like she was still alive, like she just recorded the song."

Online, in footage filmed in her time, Dalton sounds and seems ghostly, utterly haunting of any decade. A black-and-white clip from a French documentary shot in 1969 (available on YouTube and as part of the new *Cotton Eyed Joe* CD collection) shows Dalton singing Tampa Red's "It Hurts Me Too." She's at a microphone, sitting stock-still. Her straight, dark hair hangs slightly lower than her empty gaze. She plucks a tinny 12-string guitar with silver picks on her fingertips, which glisten just outside of her antediluvian (or merely "retro") lace cuffs. Only occasionally, and barely, does she let a grin slide across her pale, pretty face. It's a flash of humanity—the only sign that she may be more than merely an earthly amplifier for that otherworldly voice.

Look closely, too, and you'll notice the missing teeth. Dalton's story had no classic *Behind the Music* narrative arc. There was no rise to fame before the trouble started. Her life was tumultuous from the get-go, from her days growing up in Enid. She drank hard, she took drugs, she acted out. She was married and divorced twice before age 21, before leaving Oklahoma. Those two bottom incisors stayed behind.

"She was living with a guy who caught her in bed with my eventual stepfather, and she got punched in the face," Baird says. "She used to say she was going to get her teeth fixed when she got to be a big star."

Dalton, however, never got to be a star—and didn't always seem to really want to be.

Like another Okie transplant in the Big Apple, Woody Guthrie, she sabotaged many chances to move her career forward. She hated recording; her first album, *It's So Hard to Tell Who's Going to Love You the Best* (1969), was only captured because producer Fred Neil fooled her into believing the tape wasn't rolling. She never wrote her own songs, performing and recording only covers in an era that valued the individual voice of the emerging singer-songwriter. Releasing only two albums, she never toured.

Saddled with drug and alcohol addictions, she roamed the country for years until even her two children and closest friends lost touch. She had one friend to the end, a country singer named Lacy J. Dalton (yes, she adopted the last name as a tribute), who got her into rehab a couple of times. But those missing teeth and the pain they caused were Dalton's ticket to getting codeine prescriptions. She died in 1993, in Woodstock, New York.

"But she was more than just this junkie person that had a horrible life," Tucker insists. "People have a tendency to think of musicians that way instead of thinking about the music they made. I don't see Karen as a tragic figure but more as a misunderstood artist. There's a lot of good times and inspiring music."

The good times were rooted in Enid, in Oklahoma's red dirt (and, eventually, Red Dirt music) heartland.

Dalton, born in 1937, grew up on three acres near the edge of Enid. The land was big enough to have horses. By all accounts, Dalton loved horses.

"She always had horses," recalls Tucker, now 72 and holed up in Bellingham, Washington. "We had horses [when we lived together] in Colorado. We'd ride all day through the Rockies with the dogs. She really knew horses, too. We went to one big horse sale, were going to buy a couple. This guy had 50 horses in his pasture. She immediately pointed to one horse, which turned out to be the owner's fastest quarter horse. She bought it. She just knew how its legs were shaped or something. She never lost a race—not on a racetrack or something, just in the hills. She raced a pickup truck once and beat it. Even when Abbe was living with us, she had a pony."

To counter her aversion to recording, before retreating to upstate New York to record her second album, *In My Own Time* (1971), Dalton first returned to Enid to fetch her kids and her favorite horse.

"It's no wonder she loved them so much," Baird says. "She had the same wild spirit."

Tucker visited with Dalton once back home in Enid. "Her dad was a welder, her mom was a nurse. They were real Oklahoma people, the whole family having lived there forever," he says. (Dalton's mother, Evelyn, was of Cherokee descent.) "I remember on that visit, her mother picked us up at the bus station. In the car on the way home, after just five minutes, Karen started talking like her mother, talking more Okie. It was fascinating."

"She loved to tease people with that accent," Baird says. "She'd hear people use bad grammar, and she'd put on that act of an Okie hick to one-up them. But she didn't have to act too hard."

"You can hear Oklahoma in her voice in a different way when she sings," Tucker says. "It's that, I dunno, that lonesome sound. It's not a hillbilly sound, it's something else."

"The phrasing, the gospel sound, the haunting minor key," Baird adds. "It's a backwoods thing. Her mother was a staunch Baptist, but they don't believe in dancing, so Mom became a Methodist so she could dress to the nines and go to a church where they were singing all the old songs. 'The Old Rugged Cross,' all those. Plus, that farm of her grandparents'—there was a dividing line in Enid between where the black people lived and the white people, just two blocks north of it. I know she interacted with the whole black community in ways most people—most white people—didn't get to."

Dalton left Enid around 1961. She wasn't clamoring to escape; she just wanted a new adventure. She'd taught herself guitar and was ready to find an audience. At least, at first.

"Enid was a small Midwestern town, and it was the mid-'50s," Baird says. "The only thing to do at night was drive up and down the main drag and try to get a date. Think about what was expected of women then. Most of them weren't even expected to go to college. You got married and had babies as soon as you could. You stayed home and kept house. Karen did not want to do that. She liked to paint and play music.... She went to New York to do that. First, she went to Colorado, then to New York.

"One of my favorite stories about her getting to New York was her discovery of spaghetti. There were no Italians in Enid, no Italian restaurants. She was very excited about it."

Eventually landing in New York City's Greenwich Village, Dalton found herself among the folk music revival of the early 1960s. She started making the rounds of pass-the-hat clubs, singing and playing her 27-fret banjo or a 12-string guitar. Tucker was a folksinger, too, and this is where they met and married.

This is also when Dalton met Jill Byrem, who would become Lacy J. Dalton. She, too, remembers Karen's impact, specifically in a piece of advice she was given. "Why do you think you have to sing so loud?" Lacy, in an interview with London's *Guardian* newspaper, recalled Karen telling her: "If you want to be heard you have to sing softer."

Dylan was coming up through the same scene and often backed Dalton on harmonica. She had an effect on him, too, one he still remembered years later. Early in the first volume of his memoirs, *Chronicles* (published in 2004), page 12, Dylan writes, "My favorite singer in the place was Karen Dalton. She was a tall white blues singer and guitar player, funky, lanky, and sultry …. Karen had a voice like Billie Holiday's and played the guitar like Jimmy Reed and went all the way with it. I sang with her a couple of times."

"Katie's Been Gone" by Dylan & The Band is allegedly about Dalton. A generation later, she also inspired Nick Cave's "When I First Came to Town." Like Dylan, Cave has referred to Dalton as his "favourite female blues singer." Devendra Banhart has proclaimed, "Without a doubt, she is my favorite singer." Peter Stampfel, of the Holy Modal Rounders, later wrote of Dalton: "She was the only folk singer I ever met with an authentic 'folk' background. She came to the folk music scene under her own steam, as opposed to being 'discovered' and introduced to it by people already involved in it."

The posthumous accolades began appearing within the last several years, as Dalton's music began resurfacing—in both reissues of her two records as well as three new compilations of unreleased recordings. *Cotton Eyed Joe* (2007), named after the Bob Wills hit she loved to sing (downshifted into a slow, regretful reading), draws from the tape of a house concert for a small audience of friends from 1962 in Boulder. *Green Rocky Road* (2008) gathers home recordings from 1963. The most recent is this year's chronologically titled *1966*, featuring songs recorded by visiting pal Carl Baron in a Colorado mountain cabin.

"I sing on a few of those, and play," Tucker says. "We were living in the hills outside Boulder. Carl was a friend of ours and loved to come up and jam with us. I didn't even remember it, but apparently on more than one occasion he had a cheap tape recorder and taped it. The quality is not good. A lot of things are so distorted we couldn't use them. Like, she was doing this Leadbelly song, and she'd do this 'Whoop!' The distortion is so horrible they couldn't fix it electronically. … See, none of this stuff was ever meant to be put out. If you were seriously trying to make a recording, you would've done a better job than most of these tapes. They're just things that were captured in the moment, for personal mementos or maybe to help one of us remember parts of the songs. Now they're just these ghosts come back to haunt us all."

After recording *In My Own Time* at the turn of the '70s, Dalton never made another record. She drifted, around the country and deeper into drugs. Lacy J. Dalton claims she had a recording session scheduled for Karen in Texas in 1992, but Karen exited rehab, went back to New York, and disappeared until her obituary the following year.

Tucker last saw Dalton in '67, two years before she was tricked into recording her proper debut album. The two split up in Denver and Tucker never saw her again. Years later, when he sought to remarry, he says he tracked her down in order to send her divorce papers, which Dalton signed and returned without comment.

Even Baird, now relocated to eastern Illinois, eventually lost touch with her mother. "I was married and having children. I called her and told her I was going to be a mom. There was a long pause," Baird says. "Then this voice said, 'You bitch.' … She never met her grandchildren."

Baird says she doesn't mind the revisitations via reissues.

"People keep saying they've come up with more stuff, so I guess she's going to walk the earth awhile longer," she says. "You're never really famous until you die."

THE LAST OF KENTON

A Panhandle outpost fights off ghost-town status, but for how long?

By *Sheilah Bright*

I HAVE BEEN TRYING TO TELL THE STORY OF KENTON, the west-ernmost town in Oklahoma, since last November, when I passed through on a whim and left carrying ghosts. Another me, an earlier me, would have wrapped the story up with loose ends dragging and the bottom exposed. But Kenton won't let me go.

Until the accident, there were four children here. Now, there are three. Ranchers remain bitter about a man branded as a land rustler who reportedly busted up some ranches then high-tailed it out of Cimarron County with the IRS mounting a posse. People hesitate to talk too long about the bad times, the prolonged drought, and some of the saddest days a community has ever known.

Without hope, they say, you got nothing but dirt.

Back in the 1930s, dust and wind rubbed Oklahoma raw. The pox came back last year with a record-book blemish you can't hide: driest year since 1910. Oklahoma's Panhandle lays blistered for miles with a bad case of shingles. Forsaken ranches, ditched schools, crusty storefronts, and drought-crackled fields make it hard to keep your eyes on the road.

"People blaze right past us every day," said Asa Jones as he sat outside the Kenton Museum. "You just wished more people would stop."

Folks like Asa and his wife, Fanny, are why I stopped, and why I kept going back, logging more than 3,000 miles to fuel a borderline stalker infatuation with a town I never even knew existed until seven months ago.

"Kenton is the tail end of the dog," George Collins told me the first night I drove down into the canyon to my tiny cabin at his Hoot Owl Ranch Bed & Breakfast. "Glad you found us."

Only 20 people live in Kenton. Another 20 or so live on the ranches nearby. Nearly all of them have already bought tombstones

———————

In a converted trailer house with a lean-to covered ramp, the faded Kenton Post Office stands sentry as the only retail business still operating in a downtown that once bustled with hundreds of people. Inside the postal trailer, 200-plus patina-rich brass boxes line the walls. Twenty-seven of them are locked and unlocked six days a week as dependable cocoons for birthday cards, sympathy notes, bank statements, and catalogues from stores few residents will likely ever visit. Here on the prairie, 73946 is more than a zip code. It's an anchor in a dry-locked town with no school, no store, and no gas station.

Mail comes in from Clayton, New Mexico, and Liberal, Kansas, because Kenton is the end of the line for both routes. Two mail carriers head out on either a 130-mile round trip to Folsom, New Mexico, or an 82-mile round trip east through rural Cimarron County then up into Colorado and back. Some 500 to 600 certified letters and about 30 boxes hit the road every week. Inside are precious contents—medications, tractor parts, and one-page sentiments from folks who once called the Panhandle home. But it, too, may dry up: The Kenton Post Office is on the United States Postal Service's chopping block.

"The people who live here are either working ranchers or retired ranchers," said Terry Collins, the postal officer in charge. "They get their medicine through here. They get their supplies through here. If they close us, people will have to drive more than 37 miles away to mail a package. They're telling us to expect deliveries to be delayed one or two days because mail will have to be rerouted through Wichita. They call it snail mail now. I don't know what they're going to call it if this happens."

Bonnie Heppard, 84, ran the post office from 1979 to 2009. We visited over steak dinners cooked by Terry, who, along with her husband, George, operates a steakhouse at their Hoot Owl Ranch on Friday and Saturday nights. Everyone around here does more than one job to pay the bills.

Bonnie came to dinner wearing a prairie dress and shawl that she'd made several years ago for the Boise City Pioneer Day parade. I thought she dressed up for the interview, but she didn't know we were sharing a table until she walked through the door. She had simply decided to drive over for a flat-iron steak and determined it was a nice night for a pioneer dress. My two-day dirty jeans bore a rip in the pocket and holes in both knees.

"So, you were the postmaster for 30 years? Or do you call it the postmistress?" I asked.

She smiled and buttered a homemade roll.

"A postmistress is the woman who sleeps with the postmaster," she said.

Bonnie is worried about what will happen if the post office closes. She explains how it's more than inconvenience for her neighbors, which means someone who lives within a 50-mile radius. About the sixth time that someone gave me directions with the words "drive down the road a ways," I realized distance is irrelevant in Kenton.

Bonnie knows most every road in Cimarron County. When she wasn't mastering the post office, she drove a school bus along with her husband.

"It would really create a hardship on this aging community to have to drive to Boise City or to Clayton to get to a post office," she said. "Very few people in Kenton pay their bills electronically or even have a computer."

If the post office closes, Bonnie won't leave. Her best memories live here. So do her worst.

"I remember what the sky looked like on April 14, 1935. Black Sunday, they call it," she said. "I was 6 years old, and a lot of people were out driving around. People did that a lot back then, drive around after church. We were visiting our neighbors. Black clouds, mostly from the north, rolled in together. It didn't rush in. It rolled."

Bonnie's voice skips a bit so she takes a sip of tea, puts down her fork and repositions the napkin lying on her starched dress.

"I can remember even now how quiet it was. I thought it was so strange, the quiet. The chickens weren't clucking. The birds weren't singing. It's as if everything just hushed."

I let several silent minutes pass. Bonnie sifted through the memories of living with a dust so fine it felt like silk on the arms of a 6-year-old girl and a thick blanket of hell for a father trying to farm. She lost a few friends after Black Sunday when their families decided the Panhandle was too unbearable. Her family stayed.

"You always hear about the ones who left after the Dust Bowl," she said. "I want people to know some people didn't leave. It wasn't easy, but with determination, we survived."

Only three children are left in Kenton now. Two kids go to school over the border in Clayton. The other heads to Boise City. Either way, it's about a 100-mile round trip to school and back every day. For the brother and sister going to Clayton, the pickup stop is just past the state line at a volunteer fire station in New Mexico. The Boise City boy has his own chauffeur—a school employee who drives a van out to get him.

It would be easier on everyone if home school and online classes were an option, but there are problems with that equation. Parents are too busy running the ranches to teach school and Internet service is as sketchy as the rain. The same sun sets and rises over Kenton and Boise City, but it does so an hour apart. Kenton is the only town in Oklahoma operating on Mountain Time. It's why folks are continually having to qualify it in our conversations.

"See you around noon, my time," they'll say, "or 1 o'clock your time."

No one knows for certain just where Mountain Time shifts into gear, but some folks thinks it's just up the rise as you head toward Boise City. All three bed and breakfasts—the Hoot Owl Ranch, Hitching Post Bed & Breakfast and Ranch, and Black Mesa Bed & Breakfast—set their days on Mountain Time.

"The sun does not follow the state line," explained Hoot Owl George. "Most of what we call our neighbors are in New Mexico or Colorado. We kinda feel like people have forgotten about us out here."

Two days into my first trip to Kenton, I meet the town's matriarch, 99-year-old Ina K. Labrier.

"You need to meet a good friend of mine. I've been in love with her for years," said George as his wife, Terry, cooked my breakfast.

Not much surprises me by now. The night before, I drove through the Black Mesa State Park and nearly ran over a midget unicorn. When I described what looked like a shaggy pony with bones sticking out of its head, George replied, "I've never seen that thing before. Must be an exotic. Maybe, someone dumped it out here. It happens."

George fell in love with Ina when he was 3 and wandered away from his grandparents' mercantile store in Kenton. He stumbled onto her porch. She fed him cookies until someone came looking for him. I grab a notebook, then decide I might need two. Before we get into the pickup, George decides we should call first to see if she is home.

"She still gets out?" I asked.

"Oh, Ina K. still drives," he said.

I head back to my cabin to grab a third notebook and a camera.

When no one's around to take her and she's ready to go, Ina K. gets into her car and heads toward Kenton or to visit a neighbor. She parks her car right outside a ramp behind her house so she doesn't have to walk far to get into it. She quit driving all the way to Boise City a few years ago, but she thinks she could still do it in case of an emergency. Once she makes it out of her driveway at the 101 Ranch, it's about a four-mile stretch to Kenton. Her neighbors tend to give her a wide berth when they see her coming, more out of respect than necessity.

There isn't a person in town who hasn't eaten her food. When I first met her back in November, she stood in the kitchen with dough stuck to her hands and invited me to a dinner at the community center. She was making whole-wheat rolls—five dozen of them.

Ina K. looked out her window at the ranch that has been her home for 73 years.

"I can't do things like I used to do," she said and apologized for the grease-splatters on the stove and the dust on the piano. "My old hands are turned this way and that, but I try to make do."

On branding weekends every spring, she and her daughter, Jane Apple, cook up two or three pot roasts, 20 pounds of potatoes, and cakes, cookies, or pies. After so many years of boiling, frying, and mixing, Ina K. cooks from memory, but sometimes the memories are a tad too bittersweet, and she has to wait until the sadness goes away before she can remember whether she's put sugar in or not.

The family operates The Hitching Post, a bed and breakfast with locations in town at her old house and here at the even older house at the ranch. She came to the Panhandle as a bride on the tail end of the Dust Bowl. She left a teaching job in Wiley, Colorado, to marry Ross Labrier.

"We started out with four head of cattle, and I had three checks that weren't cashable," Ina K. said. "I got $75 a month for teaching, but about half the time I'd have to wait a month or two before the check was good."

For most of her married life, she saddled up a horse and rode with Ross to herd and feed the cattle. She carried Jane in a sling in front of her until the girl turned about 3, old enough by ranching standards to ride a good, steady horse. Today, some of the kids who grew up eating Ina K.'s cookies are in their 70s. They still drop by to see what's cooking in the kitchen or call to ask if she needs anything from town. Last summer, she was still hanging her laundry outside to dry. She called her neighbors or family to let them know she was headed outside. If she didn't call back in the time it took to hang a sheet or two, someone came looking for her.

"My walker leaned over in the hallway once, and I couldn't get to the phone so I just slept on the floor until morning," she said. "It wasn't bad. I've slept on floors before."

She eats good food, works hard, and takes vitamins every day. Nearing 100, she only takes three medications and seldom visits a doctor. She changed doctors a few years back because Dr. Wheeler in Boise City is slowing down his practice, she told me.

"He's 90 years old, you know," she said.

I'd heard about Doc Wheeler at the Rockin' A Cafe when I stopped in for pie and conversation back in November. A tableful of old-timers were bragging about how the town doctor could still set bones broken from hard falls and stitch up hands caught in the flywheels of tractors.

Someone asked for another piece of pie and then confirmed that I was picking up the tab. When I said "Sure," three more old men slid out of their booth and pulled up to our table.

"Oldest and best doc in the state, but his hands shake some," said Millard Fowler. "I still go see him if I need something."

I tried to catch up with Dr. Wheeler, but he had left for the day.

I was leaned back in a rocking chair on the porch of the Hoot Owl's hand-hewn stone house built in the late 1800s when I heard the legend of Dr. Wheeler and bubonic plague. The story goes that Doc Wheeler once diagnosed a boy with bubonic plague and saved his life. No one else recognized the symptoms. The doctor diagnosed it as soon as he saw the swollen glands and head welts.

"The boy got it from playing with prairie dogs," said George.

Back in my cabin, I rinsed a day's worth of Cimarron County dust out of my throat with some wine I brought with me. It's unbearably dry here—dry as in you can't buy an alcoholic drink until you cross into New Mexico or head back to Guymon. The best rum in the world wouldn't lure me back to Guymon.

Somewhere around 3 a.m., I woke up from this crazy dream of prairie dogs running, really more like skipping, through a cemetery strewn with tumbleweeds. The prairie dogs are about as far from chipmunk-cute as I am from home. I think one of them bared his teeth.

The bottle of Merlot on the table wasn't empty so I couldn't blame the wine. I spent some time tossing the dream bits around in my head, wondering what a dream interpreter would make of snarling prairie dogs then scribbled down "prairie dogs," "cemetery," and "tumbleweed," in a notebook.

The next day when I ventured back into my Internet-friendly patch up on Oklahoma 325, I decided to dispel this wacky medical myth of the plains. I searched for cases of bubonic plague in Oklahoma. It popped up on the Oklahoma State Department of Health website: "Plague is a rare disease in Oklahoma; the last case of human plague was reported in 1991 and was associated with exposure to prairie dogs in the Oklahoma panhandle."

There is no denying the grim reality that more people now reside in the cemeteries of most Panhandle towns than live in them. No one understands the dying pulse of Cimarron County more than Mark Axtell, who along with his wife, Cindy, operates the only funeral home in the county. When the Axtells bought the mortuary in 1987, they conducted 50 funerals a year. In 2011, the funeral count hovered around 20. There were no funerals in February, March, or April this year, then six people died in one week. Hoping someone will die so you can pay the utility bills is more of a Grim Reaper than Axtell wants to be.

The Boise City nursing home shut down several years back so senior citizens unable to make it on their own are now living in skilled nursing centers near their children. When they die, another funeral home gets the business.

Two years ago, Axtell decided he needed to do something to boost his bottom line. He opened a cafe, the Rockin' A. There was no running from the jokes about how he was cooking up something to keep his funeral home from going under. "What's in the stew? Embalming fluid?" He's heard and chuckled at them all. When a *New York Times* reporter came through last summer to do a story on the drought, she mentioned the cafe in her story. It got a lot of attention, but now, things have quieted down, which sits just fine with the locals who stop by two or three times a week for chicken-fried steak and biscuits and gravy.

"My family likes to stick together. We love Boise City. We want to stay here," said Mark. "The cafe may help us do that."

What he likes is the fact that the old men come in for morning coffee, shoot the breeze and then come back in the afternoon to do it again. He likes the way folks will offer to fix a problem with your truck or your tractor or your air conditioner before you even know you have a problem at all. He knows, with one phone call, he could get 20 people to lend a hand for anything he needs.

With his blue jeans, boots, and cowboy hat, Axtell is not your typical funeral director. He doesn't even own a suit. Around these parts, if someone shows up at a funeral in a suit and tie, people know they're from out of town—way out of town. Maybe even from Kansas.

Caskets are more likely to be perched on hay bales than marble platforms. Several times a year, pall bearers climb into the back of a pickup truck to ride sidesaddle with their loved one in a silent funeral procession through small town streets to a country cemetery. People are buried in overalls and Wranglers and housedresses with aprons.

"I conduct a lot of outdoor funerals here in ranch country," said Axtell. "We've carried people to the cemetery by horse and wagon many, many times. A few years ago, I built a pine box for someone because that is what they had wanted, and I couldn't find one in time."

The only hearse in Cimarron County is a black suburban. Mark and his wife used to have a Cadillac, but it got stuck trying to get into one of the country cemeteries so they traded up. A few years ago, someone at a funeral directors' meeting in Kansas asked him to move his $50,000 pickup truck out of sight because it didn't measure up to the pack of jet-black, funeral-pimped Lincoln Continentals hovering in the parking lot. It didn't go over too well with the cowboy mortician.

"Frankly, I don't get along with a lot of people in the funeral business. I just don't agree with some of the practices of the trade," he said. "Some people view the casket room as a sales room. Ours doubles as a chapel. When families come in, we show them the room and let them have privacy. They're going to buy something, but I don't want them to risk the farm trying to bury their dead."

It's another reason I have fallen hard for this shriveled land. People don't dance around how they feel. Nearly everything they say deserves quotation marks. If someone dies of a heart attack or pneumonia or cancer, the burial arrangements are handled quickly since business is so slow. A suicide up on the Black Mesa trail (leading to Oklahoma's highest peak at 4,973 above sea level), or a missing hiker found dead from heat exhaustion exposes a serious flaw in the system. Those bodies aren't supposed to be moved without permission from a medical examiner.

The nearest medical examiner office is 220 miles away in Woodward. The next nearest is 379 miles away in Oklahoma City. Temperatures climb well past 100 degrees in the summer.

"By law, I'm supposed to either embalm, bury, or cremate someone within 24 hours unless there's refrigeration," said Axtell. "The closest refrigeration is in Oklahoma City. The nearest crematory is in Dodge City, Kansas, or Amarillo, Texas. I can't cross state lines with a dead body without a permit from the medical examiner's office."

One night, he got a call to come to the Boise City hospital to talk with a man whose wife had died from a heart attack as they toured the Panhandle in their fifth-wheel travel trailer. The man wanted to load his wife into the trailer and drive back to Colorado to be buried.

(Apparently, it has been done before.) It was a Friday evening. Axtell couldn't reach the medical examiner. He couldn't release the body to cross state lines either.

"The guy was so distraught and didn't want to leave his wife so I let him hook up his travel trailer here in the parking lot of the funeral home," said Axtell. "It took me three days to get that permit. That guy had to camp in my funeral home parking lot for three days waiting to get his wife back home to bury her. It's a crazy, cruel system."

Sometimes, the Cimarron County Sheriff's Department can convince someone at the ME office to give verbal permission over the phone, he said. Most times, people just have to wait it out. When a man committed suicide in his car parked in front of the Keyes School, Axtell and a deputy had to wait with the body most of the day until the examiner could arrive. School officials tried to keep the students distracted, Axtell says, but the kids couldn't help but notice.

Most everyone knows that the Axtell family has paid for a lot of funerals for people with little means. When you rub elbows with your neighbors on a daily basis and serve coffee to them on Saturday mornings, it's tough to put them in the ground without a proper goodbye. He doesn't like to talk about it too much. What he does like to talk about is the goodwill churned up every time a rancher or farmer takes his final plow.

"I can't tell you how many times that we've had a farmer die in the middle of harvest and, before the day is done, there will be 10 combines working his field. Before the funeral is even set, the crops will have been taken to the granary and the payment will be on its way to the widow. It may be after the funeral before those guys will get back to working on their own fields."

If the Axtells can make ends meet by feeding and burying people, they plan to grow old here. When a recent motorcycle rally came to town, they threw up a sign advertising, "Don't miss out on our weekend specials." The sign hung from a crossbeam on a trailer parked in front of the funeral home. The "weekend specials" were offered at the Rockin' A, but the empty heart-shaped headstone sitting on the trailer made you wonder.

"I keep telling my wife," said Axtell as he loaded surplus cafe groceries into the storage room at the mortuary, "we're going to be covered up with funerals in a few years, and then there won't be anyone left to bury."

_____

Cimarron County stretches for 1,834.74 square miles, according to the 2010 U.S. Census. There is still not a stoplight in the entire county. The 2010 U.S. Census breaks it down like this:

County population: 2,475
Population, percent change from 2000: -21.4%
Persons 65 years and older: 22.1%
White persons: 84.7%
Median household income: $34,096
Persons below poverty level: 21.8%
Building permits in 2010: 0

According to Oklahoma Historical Society records, Cimarron County formed soon after statehood in 1907. Once, it was home to 20 post offices and 56 schools. Today, there are four post offices and three public school districts.

The Black Mesa plateau is hailed as a geological marvel. Some 18 tons of dinosaur bones have been quarried from the region. Bird lovers, naturalists, and outdoor enthusiasts share the space with the hundreds of hunters who come here for the antelope, quail, and mule deer.

Most of the time, their presence is welcomed in No Man's Land. There are times when a misguided bird lover takes a wrong turn and brushes up against a bristled landowner who is tired of people who think no fences mean no rules. It explains a certain sign stuck at the end of a five-mile dirt road:

No Trespassing
No Hunting
No Arrowhead Hunting
No Firewood or Post Cutting
No Park Ranger of Ex-Park Rangers
No Forest Rangers
No Archaeologists

No Universities
No Birding
No Biologists
No Conservationists
No Rabid Environmentalists.

It said nothing about no photographers so I got out, stepped over a half-eaten dead snake, snapped some quick pictures and headed back to the Kenton Museum.

———————

Kenton unfurled its story one gritty layer at a time. Every dirt road peeled back another life rut. In a land where men are judged by the quality of their fences and family stories flap on a community clothesline stretching across three state lines, secrets don't dry out for years.

On a blazing afternoon, I found a lone Internet signal up on Highway 325. Two minutes later, the Cimarron County Sheriff's Office found me midway through a text. Before I could push all the water bottles, notebooks, and a black banana off the seat to find my driver's license, I heard gravel crunch and watched the deputy whip out of there in reverse. I jumped out into the dust cloud, shouting "What the hell?" He flipped another u-turn and barreled back off to Kenton. My Internet signal left with him.

The next day, I stopped by the *Boise City News* office to see editor C.F. David. I'd heard he printed the word "vagina" on the front page, and folks weren't happy about it.

"You were in Kenton, yesterday. Heard it on the police scanner."

"What was up with that?"

"They thought you were James Parker. That Range Rover you're driving. People saw you taking pictures and thought you were Parker. Someone called it into the sheriff. Lucky you didn't get shot."

The locals say James Parker rode into town in a Hummer, started buying up the land, ran up the bids at the school land lease auction, built a faux Western town, then hightailed it out of Cimarron County with the Internal Revenue Service hot on his trail. The mere mention of his name causes church-going women to cuss and old cowboys threaten to do worse. It was written up in the *Boise City News*. The litigation saga continues.

Monty Jo and Vicki Roberts, owners of the Black Mesa Bed & Breakfast, hate to see their corner of the state racked with controversy and trouble. They don't like what Parker's presence brought to the Kenton area, but he did answer a financial prayer. One day, Vicki prayed for help after years of shriveling ranch profits. The next day, Parker knocked on the door.

Still, it's hard to ignore how he has changed Kenton. From the front porch of the Roberts' 1910 native rock house, a sagging saloon town stakes its claim on what once was an unblemished prairie.

————————

The 5-year-old girl in the pink cowboy hat held tight to the calf's front legs and blinked back tears as she watched her dad cut off part of its ear, a family friend lop off its testicles, her grandfather plunge a vaccination needle into its neck, and her grandmother sear the ranch brand into its hide.

"I don't like this," she said.

"What's the name of your favorite Brooks & Dunn song?" her father shouted as she swallowed a sob.

"I don't know," she sniffled and scurried to the side of a stone barn where she'd tucked a secret rock a few minutes before.

"It's 'Cowgirls Don't Cry,'" her dad said and gave her a quick hug before grabbing the next calf.

Kinney Jo Apple, the rookie cowhand at Apple Ranch branding day this year, scanned the herd loitering at the far end of the corral. I knew she was counting how many smaller calves were left to brand. She'd always played in the dirt outside the corral on branding day before, but now at age 5, she was on duty, old enough to practice with the runts.

"I think there are only two or three more left," she said. "I hope they are girls."

Castration isn't easy to watch for a newbie, even a 51-year-old one. It's a bloody slice then a sharp tug and another swift cut. The furry sacks get tossed onto the lid of a toolbox so they can be counted after branding to verify the number of steers.

The gooey parts are either thrown into a bucket, the dirt, or the hot plate attached to the branding iron. Branding day calf fries are about as fresh as you can get.

Kinney Jo watched her dad grab some bull balls from the dirt and toss them onto her uncle Leon's back as a joke. A few minutes later, her dad walked over and pulled a prank on her by tickling her neck until she flinched and looked up at me.

"Is there a ball on my neck?" she asked.

About 10 calves later, she had to go back on duty. The calf was a bit more of a bleeder. She cried even more. Her grandmother, Jane Apple, tried to cheer her up with a smile but it was hard to see through the branding iron smoke. Her brothers encouraged her. Her dad made her stick it out until the job was done.

"We don't give up. You can't play until the work is done," he told her, took off her hat and tousled her blonde hair.

Her uncle winked. Her grandfather nodded. Then they went back to roping and dragging and searing and cutting. Two hundred calves needed to be worked before noon. The two hundred calves branded yesterday had worn soreness into the cowhands' bodies. The horses were tired too.

"Ranch life isn't for lightweights," one of the cowboys told me.

About an hour later, I nodded toward the hot plate sizzling with fresh calf fries. The grit adds an unexpected crunch to the warm, gooey middle. A cowboy tells me they're better dipped in batter and fried. It's not an option today. The testicles are Panhandle power bars full of an energy surge to hold you over until lunch. I make it through three bites and toss the rest of the dangling bit onto the ground.

"That count?" I asked the cowboy kicking shit off his boots next to me.

"Might be invited back next year now," he said and heads to whack the testicles off another black baldy.

Someone with ties to the Labrier family name has been doing this since 1886. No one wants to be the last rancher standing, but the rawhide reality is it's getting tougher with every dry summer.

Ross and Ina K. Labrier had one daughter, Jane. She married Bob and had three sons: LeRoss, who'd brought Kinney Jo and two of his four sons down to help from their home in Thomas; Leon, who went to college then came back to the ranch to raise his sons, Clint and Dillon; and Leston, who is mentally handicapped and lives in a trailer on the ranch.

To have a chance to make money in the cattle business here, you need 30 acres for every cow. Across more grass-rich parts of the state, it's two to three acres per cow. Panhandle acreage is running about $500 an acre if you can find it for sale.

If you need to fence it, that will cost you about $4,000 a mile if you do it yourself, says Leon, who has a degree in agriculture business and is now running for sheriff. Feed costs about $250 per cow to get you through the winter before you can breed the cow and sell this year's calf.

"Cattle prices have been running fairly good about a $1.19 per pound for an 1,100 pound steer and close to 1,500 for a bred cow," he said. "To buy in and try to get started, it's probably impossible. I think for people to buy a place and move out here and make a living, ranching would be pretty tough."

Leon's voice softens for a moment.

"I think for Dillon, it might be possible," he said.

I know what he is thinking in the painful silent moments that drip by, but I still bite my lip until it bleeds. It's taken months to understand the story gathered first from a cemetery then from hesitant neighbors and finally from a man still fresh from grief. The truth is that I tried to write the story without scraping off a family's newest wound and asking the kind of questions that make me swallow hard first.

On my second visit to Kenton, I learned the story from people who were there that day. On the third visit—when the family felt comfortable enough to invite me to branding day—I came to understand what it really meant when Dillon's grandfather gave him a heifer to start his herd. About 200 Black Angus calves bleated for their bawling mothers in the adjoining corral yet it was the cries of one black heifer that silenced the crowd. No one whispered a word about the symbolic nature of Dillon's brand—a cross floating above the Apple Ranch logo, but I could feel they were thinking about a day three years before that changed the future of the ranch.

The cast was almost the same on May 14, 2009. Branding season was done so the Apple family hauled out a spread of good food to show appreciation for weeks of hot, dirty work. Out in the yard of Leon's childhood home, neighbors, friends, and family shot the breeze about fluttering cattle prices and the need for rain, conversations rooted generations deep around these parts. It just doesn't feel like branding season without hearing "parched" and "strapped" and "bureaucrats" thrown out.

Leon's sons, Clint, 14, and Dillon, 9, kicked around with the cowboys, who took pleasure in teasing the boys about how much food they could shovel back or some misstep out in the corral where one wrong move could as easily become an injury as a joke. Dillon was still learning what it takes to rope, drag, hold, castrate, earmark, and brand a calf without getting hurt. Clint had already proven he was cowboy tough. Several ranchers threw out compliments about how Clint roped with a quick arm and grappled calves with graceful ease.

No one noticed much when the two Apple boys, raised by their father, went back to the house. The wind whipped up a few dust clouds. The birds competed with the cattle and the stories and the laughter to create an age-old hymn of ranch life on the Black Mesa.

Dillon's cries broke the happiness with jagged sobs. "Clint" and "gun" were the words people remember.

The boy was conscious when they loaded him into the ambulance. A helicopter was dispatched from Amarillo. Just off Oklahoma 325, a dinosaur bone monument marks the land where giant creatures once lived and died. On that day, it guided a helicopter crew to a makeshift landing strip where people stood hoping a boy could be saved.

"They put him on life support at the hospital in Amarillo," says Leon. "The next day, we took him off."

By the time Leon returned home to Kenton, everyone had heard about the accidental shooting. One son dead, another heartbroken. Leon had taught his boys about gun safety since they were toddlers. The family hosts guided hunts as part of their bed-and-breakfast operation. Clint had recently passed a gun safety course so he could get a youth hunting permit. As a 6-year-old, he could shoot a fly off a cow patty with a BB gun.

"He was one of those kids that whatever he did, he did real well," said Leon. "It's tough. For me. For Dillon. For everyone."

Clint was buried in the Kenton Cemetery on a small rise overlooking the town where his family has lived since the Land Rush. The Cimarron Mortuary handled the burial arrangements. Local ranchers lowered the horseshoe-handled casket into the grave with lariats. High on a ridge above them, a neighbor sat silent in his saddle with a riderless horse by his side. When you ask folks about Clint Ross Apple, they mention the boy's happy spirit and how the shadow of the riderless horse seemed to spread across the cemetery as people lingered around the mound of dirt long after the final prayers.

Not far from Clint's black tombstone lies another grave with a marker honoring "Our little cowboy. Swell boy. Friend to all." Labrier "Kade" McMillen, Clint's cousin, died in a four-wheeler accident on the Labrier Ranch in 2003. He was 12.

Five hundred people are buried in the cemetery, but two small graves tell the story of a community's slow ride toward ghost-town fame. Without hope, you have nothing but dirt, they had said.

As I pulled out of the Kenton Cemetery and drove down its lonely streets for what could be my last time here, I wondered how long hope could last.

FIVE

FICTION

THE REVERSE HIJACK

By *Brian Frazer*

"Get the fuck in the truck!"

"You kidding me, old man?"

"If I were kidding would this fucking Glock be pointed at your dome? Get the fuck in the truck!"

Kevin Durant cradled the four basketballs under his massive wing-span and obediently stepped up onto the back of a twenty-six foot U-Haul.

"Got you, too, huh Kev?" came a baritone voice.

"Sure did, Perk."

"Westbrook and Harden are under the tarp playing dominoes sharing a turkey sub."

"Where we headin'? Back to Seattle?"

"Nah. Too obvious. That's the first place David Stern would look. I think I heard the old dude with the gun and the temper mention something about Santa Fe."

"So we'll be the Santa Fe Thunder?"

"He wants us to pitch him team nicknames on the way. There's an intercom on the wall over there."

"This could be really fun," said GM Sam Presti as he folded towels into thirds. "I love the marketing side of basketball."

"How about the Santa Fe Nets?" said a hopeful Nazr Mohammed, seated in a tiny folding chair on Serge Ibaka's lap.

"There's already a New Jersey Nets," proclaimed Presti.

"Yeah, but when they move to Brooklyn in 2012, I heard they'll be changing their name. So we'll only be sharing it for a season."

"How about the Santa Fe Westbrooks?" came a voice from under the tarp.

"A little too on-the-nose. But press the intercom and pitch it," blurted coach Scottie Brooks, stepping out of the shadows. "You never know."

"Dirk, what the hell are you doing here!? You're not even on our team!"

"Thabo Sefolosha called me up and asked if I'd help you guys move. Said there was some free pizza in it."

"Must've been Dwight Howard pulling another prank."

Then the old man with the Glock reappeared, fired several warning shots through the roof of the U-Haul, and said Mapquest had fucked up the directions and he was now moving the team to Little Rock, Arkansas, where they'd be nicknamed the Slammers.

OK, FINE

By *Mary Jo Bang*

It's as if those first three lines had been wired into my brain. As if they'd always been there, since the first flutter of consciousness. The rest of the lines were extraneous. What more could one need after the rousing excess of that famous opening, followed by the later self-soothing appraisal, "You're doin' fine." Not great, not good, just fine. I always found comfort in that lack of pretension.

I sang it for days before we got in the car and once in the car I kept it up until my mother finally said, "One more time, Robbie, and you'll never see it because I'll have your father turn around and drive us straight home." The threat seemed rhetorical at best. After all, our suitcases were in the trunk and we were already halfway there. I hummed the lines under my breath, except the final "O.K." which I fixed midway between a soundless mouthing and a whisper. The lines didn't hold up under the restraint. "O.K." especially needed volume and emphasis. I stopped after three sotto voce renditions. I rolled down the window and leaned my head out. It would have sounded great out there. How loud, I wondered, would I have to shout "O.K." into the wind for it to have the necessary brio. My mother's voice was sharp, "Robbie, get your head back in. And roll that window up. Now." I slid back in the seat. I didn't take "Roll that window up" literally but more as another way of saying, "Don't do it again." I had no intention of doing it again. I formed my mouth silently around the words, exaggerating my facial expressions for drama. I kept it up until we reached the next town, which is when my father turned the car around.

TOM MIX

By *John Crowley*

1968, AND WE ARE GOING TO THE MUSEUM OF TOM MIX. It is in a place called Dewey. "Dewy" is what my father calls my sister. A dewy girl. She lowers her eyes to not see him looking at her. I have my guns on, I buckle them on every morning when I put on my jeans. They have ivory handles with rearing horses carved on them that look like Tony, Tom Mix's horse. My father's name is Tony too. There is a horse on the hood of the car, and my father said we follow that horse wherever it goes. I watched for the horse to turn right or left, to see if the car went that way, and every time it did. But I am older now and I get it. Tony was a trick pony. My mother says that my father is a one-trick pony. Tony can think and talk almost like a person (Tony the horse). The Museum of Tom Mix is Tom Mix, but Tom Mix is much larger than you would think, taller than the statue of Paul Bunyan in that other town. We go around to the back of his left boot, which has a heel as high as I am, with a door in it. We go in one by one. There is a stairway up to the top of Tom Mix, and it is dark at the top. Tony is there, halfway up; then above Tony is the other Tony, after Tony died, and above him another. Far, far up are Tom Mix's narrowed eyes, letting in the light. We are standing together, I love them all, and we wait to see who will start to climb.

THE DEMONS

By *Eddie Chuculate*

Sing with me, sing for the year, sing for the laughter and
sing for the tear

— "Dream On," Aerosmith

Tommy lit the fuse on a long winding snake of Black Cats
and with a crow-hop fired them skyward. The bandolier soared, tail
flapping, until exploding and flashing in midair over the oval pitcher's
mound rat-a-tat-tat. People gawked, covered their mouths. Daddy Rich,
having already sparked a menthol and slipped into alligator loafers,
launched sidewinders that whistled and curled across the grass before
popping like twenty-twos. Redeye lobbed plastic grenades that rolled
toward the other dugout, thundered, and belched smoke. Meanwhile,
Tommy, still in his shin guards, said to the home-plate umpire, who
leaned against a cane near the backstop in awe: "Sir, I'd just like to say
that on behalf of the team and I, your umping sucks as bad as you walk."

I looked back from Daddy Rich's 280 as our caravan left. Smoke
layered the air and paper littered the field like confetti. Groups huddled
and pointed. We blared horns and shot fingers, cussed and cracked beers,

lit more firecrackers. Tommy already had the water bong gurgling. There was a trophy ceremony commencing and I could see our little plaque lying in the dirt on the infield, wrapped in plastic. It was the end of our season and the Good Sportsmanship Award would have to fucking wait. But in our case the axiom was true: There *was* a next year, for we were only 16 years old.

———————

We destroyed two motel rooms the previous night and fled to our knuckleballer's uncle's house in the country 30 miles out of town. We stood in the blinding black asphalt parking lot blinking our eyes or hiding behind sunglasses while Big John surveyed the damage like a Tornado Alley governor. We had ripped phones out of walls, crushed lampshades, bashed in TV screens, and smeared eye black on mirrors. Then we transferred to the other room and started drinking. Tommy, in his long curly locks and perpetual fat lip, rolled a turkey-foot joint, shredding redhead sense onto a Sonic tray, and twisting a monstrous doobie with two smaller prongs at bottom. You could hit either or all three, but I preferred cigarettes and liquor. Tommy, Winger, and Jaybird, the coach's son, shot Tequila/7-Up slammers, then began drinking it straight. That led to arm wrestling, slap boxing, and sucker punching, and next thing you know that room was toast, too: blood on the walls, toilet flooded, closet door caved in, barf on carpet, beers sprayed like fire extinguishers. This was all *before* the championship. No telling what we would have done had we won. Big John said later he kept watch for the cops to show during the game.

———————

"Whose father!" Tommy shouted as the team stood with hands linked in a circle in right field in our pregame ritual.

"Our Father!" we shouted back, then chanted loudly in unison: "Who art in heaven, hallowed be thy name. Thy kingdom come, thy will be done on earth as it is in heaven. Give us this day our daily bread, and forgive us our trespasses as we forgive those who trespass against us. Lead us not into temptation, but deliver us from evil, for thine is the kingdom and the power and the glory for ever and ever. Amen!"

The coaches worked out a strategy to start the game. The Devils' leadoff man was a spray hitter with speed enough to stretch singles into doubles or doubles into triples. He was obviously a base-stealing threat, but not against Tommy, who had thrown out 90 percent of runners that season. So Shack drilled the batter in the thigh on the first pitch, and, sure enough, the runner tried to swipe second and Tommy threw him out by five steps, standing up. Wasn't even close.

———————

It began to unravel on a bang-bang play at first where I was called safe by the base umpire. The dugout exploded in cheers, rattling the fences, and the tying run was at third with one out. I slapped the pat-ented high-five, low-five with Curls, coach at first. But the plate ump walked out onto the field, pointed at me, then rang me up with a fist. Big John over at third slammed his clipboard, where it stuck in the ground vertically like a knife. He ran in to confront the ump, yelling at me to stay on the base.

"Come on, blue! You kiddin' me? You can't call him out from there! He was safe already! Goddamn, are you nuts!" he yelled.

The umpire saw him coming and pulled off his mask, shaking his head.

"Stepped on the plate during the bunt," the ump said, pointing at Jimbo at third and ordering him back to second. "Dead ball, runner cannot advance. Batter is out. Two down. Play ball!"

Coach wasn't prepared for that one. He yelled across the field for confirmation, but I sort of shrugged and turned my hands palms up, like, *Hell if I know*. Big John stretched the argument mainly for show because the ruling was irreversible. That ignited the dugout. We banged the tin roof, whistled, yelled that the umps sucked, were blind, were crippled, were crazy. Our other assistant Stan the Man threw a yellow Igloo water cooler onto the field and got ejected. Big John argued against that, too, and *he* got tossed. The crowd *boooooed* in the July 4 heat, one hick yelling, "Go back to Muskogee and eat another hog you tub of guts!"

Our home-run king Tommy walked up to crush one out. He swung at the first pitch, a solid clank, driving it to deep center, small as a golf ball in the chalk-blue sky. We emptied out of the dugout with our hands in the air, yelling and screaming, because he'd done it a million times all season, but the ball died at the warning track and the centerfielder caught it against the wall. The Devils dogpiled at the pitcher's mound. We refused the traditional postgame shake.

It was out of character for Tommy to react the way he did. He was one of the lowest keys in the piano that made up the melody of the squad. Short and squatty, sort of bow-legged, he was the epitome of a youth-league backstop. You just looked at him and said "catcher." He wasn't the rah-rah type, but led by example, seeming to possess an understanding beyond his 16 years. His physical stature—thick forearms, barrel chest, enormous calves—and reputation as a street fighter commanded respect and a certain amount of awe. Half Creek Indian, he had smooth pecan-colored skin. A car wreck left him with a slightly curled upper lip, a smirk like he'd just been hit in the mouth. So Tommy's firecracker tirade and insulting of the umpire must have came from the heart.

I had known him most of my life. I'd spend weekends at his house while our parents went out drinking together. His sister Hokte would baby-sit us. There were so many roaches in the house that once we spied a solid-white albino specimen crawling across the living room rug. The house itself was a squat, one-story cinder block structure painted azure and called "The Blue Pill." It was only a few blocks from our home field, Sally Park. One season Tommy and I wound up on different teams and I found myself bearing down on him while he stood at the plate, already with the ball. I crashed into him hard as I could, but he held on for the final out of the game. I don't think I even budged him, scrawny as I was. Even then with the fat lip, he just looked at me and flipped the ball back toward the mound.

I hardly saw any of the guys over the fall and winter until spring as I was the only one still in high school at Muskogee. The rest of the team either went to school on the other side of town, had already dropped out or were going to vo-tech. Tommy worked full time. He would show up to practice in jeans and steel-toed boots, just getting off at the cattle yards. The high school coach wanted to know why I didn't play American Legion that summer like the rest of the team, and I said I had moved out of town. Our team was persona non grata to him. To him we were a bunch of renegades who didn't know proper baseball, didn't practice enough, weren't disciplined, weren't drilled in the fundamentals, weren't in shape, smoked, drank, didn't go to school, stayed out late, stayed in bed all day, didn't treat our bodies like the temples they were. Some of us already had kids. Many times Big John would call the high school coach to schedule a game against the American Legion, but the high school coach always refused. For the high school coach it was a lose-lose situation: Beat the renegades, and you should have; lose to them, and it was a demoralizing embarrassment. But during that high school season (on the bench mainly because I didn't play for Legion that summer) I contrasted our summer outlaws against the current high school lineup and the summer guys were as good or better at every position. So after I graduated and the option came up again on which summer team to play, I picked the renegades.

Curls rolled up in his four-door Catalina on the first day of practice for the new season. With the bill of his cap jammed down over his shades and a cigarette dangling from his mouth, he unlocked his trunk to show us two prone fighting cocks. One had just won, he said, and one lost, but both looked half-dead to me, lying on their rust-colored feathers, chests heaving, red and blue wattles vibrating, staring with eyes flat as dimes, but changing colors like a chameleon: black, red, pink, blue. Curls grabbed the equipment bag and unceremoniously shut the trunk as we peppered him with questions: How much he had won, where did they fight, what are you going to do with the roosters? A thousand dollars, none of your business, bury them.

We took the field, playing catch until Big John showed up, fresh off work from Oklahoma Gas & Electric. He gathered us around the dugout, wrote down our names, said we needed to provide birth certificates and buy a cup and insurance, both protections for the family jewels.

"We've got most everybody back this year except Indian and Young-blood," he said, puffing on a blunt cigar, which he threw down and ground out with the tip of his shoe. "Does anyone know a good second baseman?"

I took that as an affront as I played second. As if reading my mind, he quickly added, "You, Cordell, we're looking at you for right field this year."

There was general chuckling and eye averting. Someone said AC had moved back to town, and they'd contact him to see if he wanted to play. We were loaded again.

Sure enough, they played me in right and batted me seventh. Right is where teams usually stick the sorriest player, but in our case that wasn't much of a weak link as I caught anything hit my way and threw out my share of runners. In youth baseball, you can usually gauge teams by how good their right fielders are. We rolled along again, crushing and run-ruling our opposition, until we finally met up with the hated all-black-except-for-one loudmouthed Muskogee Aces, our stoutest competition from last year. Their only nonblack player was nicknamed "Casper."

The game was held under the lights and the whole town came out. The bleachers were full, split right down the middle blacks on one side and whites on the other. Cars lined the fences along both foul lines and around the outfield, fans honking and flashing headlights when their team executed a good play. Sometimes the ump had to call timeout if a driver left the lights on, distracting a batter. The newspaper was even covering the game, a rarity as it usually dedicated all its coverage to the American Legion games, which on an average night might have fifteen fans.

The night games had a different vibe. For one, not many fans came out for the day games: too hot, or if it was midweek, they had to work. The field even looked different. Freshly chalked, the lines stood glaring against the recently wetted red clay dirt; freshly-cut grass was an emerald green, the bases seemed bleached white, the pitcher's rubber freshly painted, even the baseballs had a particular glow under the fluorescence, stark against the bright red stitching. Stan the Man had cleaned and polished our gear, so our red helmets shone, Tommy's catching helmet and shin guards sparkled, and even our uniforms seemed brand new, freshly washed and layered underneath with the bright-white sanitary socks that made our red stirrups flash.

For other games, ones we knew we were going to win by big numbers, say a 15-0 run-rule or 23-3, we horsed around before the game, slapping each other's crotches with our gloves to make sure we had our protective gear on underneath in what is known as a "cup check." Guys smoked cigarettes while playing toss, or didn't even warm up, staying in their vehicles and cranking rock music like "Panama" or "Sister Christian" while the other team went through its pregame infield drills, trying to whip the ball back and forth, catching pop flies. Guys chatted with their girlfriends between fences, still barely half-dressed, walking around in loafers and wife-beater T-shirts, gold chains showing. One time Big John blew his stack and told us to get our shit together or we could coach ourselves. Then we went out and won 20-0. But for the Aces game, players paced the dugout spitting sunflower seeds with a vacant glare, or sat with their heads bowed, concentrating in what looked like prayer. There was no grab-ass. Except for Tommy's occasional pep cry of "Let's shut their fucking mouths for them," or quiet routine strategy like going over who were their fastest guys, there was no talk until the prayer. We warmed up silently with our no-fucking-around looks, playing catch, stretching, doing quick wind sprints.

At our level of baseball, most guys had been playing since they were five years old. At five years old, Muskogee is full of teams, say fifteen or twenty easily. But as the players get older, many quit, becoming disgruntled that they are sorry and play for weak teams. Some choose other sports or quit athletics altogether and start working on cars or doing jigsaw puzzles, maybe Dungeons and Dragons. ROTC, whatever. So at age 10, you have half those initial twenty teams. At age 15, another half. Then by 17, Muskogee only has three or four teams left. So most of us knew the guys on the Aces, if only because we went to school together. Some of us actually played on the same teams when younger. But that didn't mean we were over at their houses having cookies and tea. There was real racial animosity back then, even though we had our "own" black players: AC, Daddy Rich, and Gandy.

We heard the biggest of their mouths, Victor Tollett, say, just loud enough so that we could hear him, "Those motherfuckers ain't shit!" Shack told Tommy on the bench, "If I hit him and he charges me, throw the ball back and I'll hit that fucker again."

"Don't worry," Tommy said.

We lined up along the first base line and the Aces lined third while the press box played a scratchy rendition of the national anthem. I stood with my cap off and hand over my heart watching the American flag on the pole in left field flutter in the southern cool breeze, thinking all the Aces looked huge, like college football players. The umps even looked more official, with creased gray slacks, shiny black Spotbilts, patches on the arms of their short-sleeved blue shirts. My throat felt dry and I was already sweating, although the temp had cooled drastically with that breeze. I had talked Big John into batting me leadoff, and after we lost the coin toss I was the first batter. Curls nodded and clapped at me, giving me encouragement as I warmed up to the left of the plate.

"Light my fire, one-seven!" he yelled.

On the mound, their pitcher looked like he was standing on a mountaintop, his warmup pitches whistling by in a blur. Taking swings, I scanned the crowd for my girlfriend but there were too many faces. I stepped in the box, holding up a hand for time as I dug a little trench with my spikes like I'd seen the major leaguers do on TV. The first ball whizzed past, popping the mitt like a gunshot.

"Steeerike," the umpire said dramatically, crouching and pointing a finger toward our dugout. The Aces fans clapped and cheered.

"First ball strike," I heard the PA man say, even though the wind was whistling through the earhole on my helmet.

"That sounded high," I said in a moment of levity, backing out of the box, taking a swing, saying it mostly to the ground for fear of showing up the ump.

"Right down the middle, Jack. You cain't hit what you cain't see," catcher Tollett mouthed off.

I grounded out weakly to shortstop, but the butterflies were gone. Winger, our second batter, drove the first pitch into the left-center gap, stole second, and scored when Jaybird singled to right. We led 1-0. Horns blared and lights flashed.

We knew we were in a battle, our first of the season. Their pitcher had an overpowering fastball, great curve, and a nasty slider. Unlike other teams, who booted ground balls or let them skip through their legs, the Aces scooped them up slickly and in one fluid motion fired bullets to first, or turned double plays like college teams. While other squads let fly balls drop over their heads, or let them pop out of their plastic mitts, the Aces camped out under them and caught them one-handed, like pros. Or they made running, diving catches, sliding on their chests on the slick grass while holding up the ball for the umps to see. Other teams hacked at balls over their heads or in the dirt, looking like golf swings. Oftentimes Tommy would call time and walk to the mound because he was laughing. He and the pitcher would fake a strategy session with their gloves hiding their faces. But the Aces were well-coached, selective at the plate, hammering balls into opposite-field gaps, drawing walks, dropping down deftly-placed bunts. We were definitely in a battle, but we were game, too. Winger made his own circus catch in left, initially going back a step on a sinking liner before recovering and making a fully-extended diving snare to end the fourth with the bases jammed, saving at least two runs.

"Winger!" I yelled from over in right while horns blared.

So it was tied when I stepped up to lead off the fifth. I had the pitcher's timing down now and surprised myself by lining the first pitch over the right fielder's head where it rattled against the chain-link fence. A standup double had the dugout fired up and the fans clapping. I looked toward the stands but saw only moths and bugs swarming the lights. I was so stoked my chest was heaving and my heart thumped like a caged rabbit's. Curls at third clapped and pointed at me.

"You the man!" he yelled.

I was, however, a little too jacked. I should have called time and dusted off my uniform or something, anything to calm down, catch my breath. But on the first pitch, when I saw the pitcher's lead leg leave the ground and point home, I streaked towards third, hoping to catch the Aces off guard. Later they told me the pitcher calmly backed off the rubber and fired to third. All I knew was the ball was waiting for me when I got there. Eggy Ledbetter, the third baseman, tagged me forcefully during my futile slide, shoving his glove hard into my gut with two hands, saying, "Fool!"

This enraged me. I got up and pushed him as hard as I could, nearly toppling him. I'd known this skinny rat since grade school and for him to call me a fool PO'd me. I'd been made to look like an idiot in front of all those people, in the biggest game of the year. The quickness with which Eggy retaliated, throwing down his glove and rushing me, caught me flat-footed. He tackled me like a football blocking dummy, driving me into the turf. From then on, it was mostly a blur. Their shortstop ran over and dove on top of us while Curls tried to break it up. My face was mashed into the dirt as I reached up to get purchase on anything I could and got a big handful of Eggy's greasy afro. I began to pull to get traction when Tommy came racing over and knocked both of them off me. When I stumbled up both teams were swinging and kicking at each other right in front of the Aces' dugout. Eggy and I stared each other down, panting. The umpires yelled for everyone to "Stop, stop, stop!" while coaches from both teams got in each other's faces, pointing fingers and yelling whose fault it was. The fans hooted, yelling, "Kick their fucking asses!" When the melee ended Tommy and I, and Eggy and their shortstop were ejected. Big John put his arm around me and walked me off the field. It made me almost feel like crying.

"What the heck happened?" he said.

"He balked, John. He lifted his front foot," I said, looking down at my ripped jersey, tonguing the inside of my split lip. I spit blood, lied, and said Eggy had called me a faggot.

"It's an emotional game, son," Big John said, and scruffed my hatless head. "But sometimes you've got to keep it in check." The Aces had captured my cap; it was never seen again.

We had to watch the rest of the game from behind the dugout, eyeballing Eggy and the shortstop on the other side of the bleachers. Instead of a man on second with no outs, there was no one on with one out. We wound up losing our first game since the Devils loss the previous year, 6-5. I blamed it on myself, but to a man every player came up and said shake it off, they would have done the same thing, we'll beat their asses next time.

"I wouldn't let that skinny fag call me a fool, either," Roger said.

Big John took up for me in the article in "Sports" the next day: "He got tagged unnecessarily hard and retaliated. My guy says their kid balked. I believe my guy."

It was the summer of 69—the year was 1984. Most everyone on the club had a girlfriend, or girlfriends, and Daddy Rich and The Glide had kids already. Sometimes Daddy Rich would bring his to games or practices with most people thinking it was his little brother. Baby Rich, we called him. Tommy's girlfriend was always around: games, practices, parties, the lake. It was like they were married. It affected the way he played, too. If they'd had a fight, he'd be pissed off, grouching or being short with us, not talking much, being an asshole. But if things were going well, he was the normal Tommy we knew outside of his relationship: rock steady, confident, offering encouragement, picking you up if you were down. Some guys on the team began to resent his girlfriend, but most of us accepted her because we knew she wasn't going away. Then there were the five or six girls who made it a point to come to every game and practice, hanging around the periphery, even renting hotel rooms for out-of-town games or tournaments, inviting us over. They'd get drunk and we'd want to screw. Each had their favorite players, embarrassing them by constructing pink and baby-blue posters in curly handwriting saying "JAYBIRD ROCKS! MARRY ME!" "BRUFF TUCKER IS ONE HANDSOME MOTHER—" or "I LOVE SHACK!" Many of the guys had been with one or all of them, but would deny it vehemently if accused.

I carried a certain distinction because my girlfriend was much older, had already dropped out of Oklahoma State as a sophomore. She operated an art gallery that sold original paintings and lithographs of her father's, one of the most famous artists in the state who had died at age 26. Digging through her closet I found a diary I didn't know she'd been keeping. Naturally curious to see if I was noteworthy, I flipped through entries until finding the following: *"Cordell has another game today. He looks so cute in his baseball outfit!"* I stood staring at the word "cute," thinking it made me sound like a little kid, not a world-weary 17-year-old. I'd much rather have been described as one handsome motherfucker.

———————

Since the local league only had three other teams, Big John was constantly on the horn arranging competition or getting us into tournaments. When he told us before practice we were traveling to play Stilwell, everyone high-fived, shouted and got in a great mood. It wasn't that we were stoked for decent competition finally, it was because it meant party time on Lake Tenkiller. Stilwell, near the lake, thought it was in position to make a run at a state title, and was skippered by an ex-Cincinnati Reds scout and minor league coach. But they could have worn clown shoes and been coached by Mickey Mouse for all we were concerned. Practice was a blur as we went through the motions, more focused on when we were leaving for the lake, who was going to be responsible for getting the kegs and staking out a camping spot. The game was Saturday at 1; we left Thursday to spend that day and all of Friday at the lake. It was another major holiday for the team—even some parents tagged along, but camped in tents and trailers away from the squad in a see-no-evil approach. Friends, girlfriends, siblings, and hangers-on trickled in over Thursday and Friday as word spread like grassfire around town that the Demons were partying at Lake Tenkiller.

At its height, the gathering had about 50 people, not including parents or relatives who had their own thing going on, and really kicked into gear when Nate the Skate's big brother showed up towing a ski boat and a pair of Jet Skis. I had never water-skied before and about drowned myself trying to get up into standing position, crashing and gulping water until I managed a decent two-minute ski. I was content to kick back in the boat and drink cold beer, feeling the cool spray on my sunburning skin. Tommy and Winger were naturals, sweeping back and forth effortlessly with their sunglasses on and gold chains flashing, jumping the creamy waves, doing one-legged tricks. The black players said Hell naw, I ain't getting in no damn water, but Rich finally waded up to his thighs, smoking a Kool and carrying a quart of Colt .45.

———————

Half of us were still up when the first icicle of light stabbed the sky and laid a golden smear on the still water. The other half were asleep or passed out in or on cars, some in the backs of pickups. The players that actually brought tents were the ones who were still awake at dawn, standing around a pit fire, drinking, joking, and laughing. I finally cashed in my chips and sought refuge in a sleeping bag in the bed of Winger's truck. It was Tommy, with a two-day growth of scruff, who went around waking everyone, saying we had an hour to get to the game. We followed Parrot in his yellow Firebird since he formerly lived in Stilwell and knew how to get to the field. When we arrived, the Cardinals were already doing drills like catching fly balls shot from a pitching machine, hitting cutoff men, and warming up four or five pitchers while we weren't even dressed. Coaches in sharp uniforms wore whistles around their necks, blowing them when it was time for players to switch drills. We dressed out of our vehicles, looking for mismatched socks, missing spikes, cussing for forgetting gear at home or at the lake. Our coaches showed up a few minutes after us, obviously hungover and wearing their usual attire: blue jeans, team T-shirt, and cap. I knew it was going to be a long, hot day when warming up playing catch I totally missed a perfectly thrown ball, sticking out my glove but missing it by a foot. We looked like shit in warmups, throwing balls over heads, kicking easy grounders, missing cutoff men. I heard some of the Cardinals snicker. But we ground through it.

———————

Word was their starting pitcher was already a professional prospect who had been drafted in the 14th round by the Pittsburgh Pirates but turned it down to improve his position in next year's draft. And looking at him I didn't doubt it. He made the Ace's pitcher look like a peewee player, standing about 6 foot 3 and 220 pounds, solid muscle with thick adult arms and huge thighs, wearing the brim of his cap down over his eyes, snarling. I was intimidated by those types, but to the credit of my teammates, they weren't, treating him like any other pitcher we'd pounded all season.

I struck out on three straight pitches I barely saw to open the game. The stud was throwing gas, the sun blinding, and my vision was bleary from staying up all night. But slowly we wore down the intimidation factor. Tommy homered to deep center in the fourth inning, and Jimbo and Gandy both doubled in the fifth. I drew a walk, and several other guys had singles. We had Shack on the mound, who never drank, thank God, and actually had a solid eight hours' sleep. He gave up a few big hits, but wiggled out of jams thanks to our solid defense. It seemed as the game progressed we became sharper, more focused, intent on beating these pompous Cardinals who thought they were from Saint Louis with their fancy pro drills, new equipment, and about a dozen coaches and a training staff.

It was 3-3 in the bottom of the ninth with two outs and the winning run on second with the pro prospect at the plate. I was standing in right, yelling at Shack to keep it up, rock and fire, put him in the books. He

EDDIE CHUCULATE

kicked and dealed, and the prospect took one of the hugest cuts I'd ever
seen taken, missing and corkscrewing himself into the ground, tripping
on the unwind and falling on his ass as bat and helmet went flying. Had
he connected, that ball would have left even *Yellowstone* Park. If it weren't
so fearsome looking I'd of been laughing. Apparently the prospect twisted
his ankle in the process, and there was a lengthy timeout while their
trainers—dressed in matching tan slacks and red polo shirts—looked
him over for what seemed an eternity. They knelt above him, prodding
and touching, twisting and poking. Then the giant got up and ran a few
light sprints down the third base line before everyone deemed him good
to go. I had taken a knee and was pulling and chewing at grass, looking
at the swimming pool and new gym behind me. Stilwell had one of the
best high school athletic programs in the state. Even the field we were
on was pro-like, with walls in the outfield instead of fences, and towering stadium lights, bullpen areas, wraparound stadium seating with
armchair seats instead of bleachers. Painted on the wall behind me was
the advertisement: CHIEF'S BARBERSHOP, DOWNTOWN STILWELL,
LOWERING YOUR EARS SINCE 1966.

The prospect took two more balls from Shack to work a full count.
The runner on second bluffed a steal and Tommy almost nailed him as
he dove back to second. I was thinking about the sign because my dad
was a barber when I heard a loud aluminum clank, snapping up my head
and seeing the ball sailing at me high, over my head. If I had been focused,
I would have anticipated the ball's direction, got a jump and got in position. Instead, I had to make up for lost ground by turning and running
full-speed directly at the wall. The ball was coming fast and seemed to
gain velocity the closer it came. I leaped in the air, caught it, crashed
into the Indian head on the wall, bounced off and dropped it, head
spinning. I staggered after it hearing wild cheering and fired it in but
the runner from second had scored easily, sprinting all-out on the 3-2
swing. I dropped to a knee with my head bowed, then rolled to the
ground, trying to get my bearings. The next thing I saw were the matching slacks of the Cardinals trainers, come to check on me, along with
Winger, Tommy, and Big John. I was OK after a few minutes, but had
sprained my own ankle, so Big John and Tommy walked me off, an
arm hooked under each of my armpits. I hobbled through a line

good-gaming the Cards. When I reached the towering prospect, he slapped my rear and said in a deep voice, "Great hustle, one-seven."

———————

It felt great to get back to Muskogee and start dominating again. Problem was, after running through the remaining three league teams, we had no more opposition and there were two weeks until state playoffs. So Big John got on the horn again and invited the Devils, Cards, and Aces—the only teams to beat us in two years and 46 games—to a round-robin tournament at our place. Everyone considered it a chance to stay sharp during the lull. And since it wasn't league-sanctioned, Big John could charge a three-hundred-dollar entry fee—a chance to make a little money for playoff travel. But the Devils, remembering our farewell fireworks show and decidedly unsportsmanlike display of a year ago, said Hell no. So it was us, the Cardinals, and the hated Aces with a winner-take-all shot at nine hundred dollars and a split of the gate.

It was a lose-two-and-you're-out format with the Aces and Reds playing first and the Demons waiting for the winner. Big John recruited some of us to help run the tournament: getting ice water for the umps between innings, selling admission tickets, raffling off a Pendleton blanket Tommy's mom had donated. I had the unglamorous job of making sure kids who chased down foul balls returned them. The kids got a free Coke, but many preferred the ball, so it was a chore to stay on top of them.

The Aces beat the Cards, so we had 30 minutes before first pitch. Big John was ready to fill in our lineup, but couldn't find the scorebook. After much searching and cussing, he figured he left it at home, so sent his son Jaybird, our shortstop, to get it, and Tommy rode with him. After we stretched and threw long toss, we took the field for warmups. Midway through, Curls walked out and said something to Big John, who was about to hit me a fly. Big John dropped his fungo bat, and Curls waved us in. We pow-wowed near the dugout.

"Hey guys, Jaybird just wrecked going home for the scorebook," Curls said. "He's in the hospital but he's going to be OK."

Curls dropped his head then looked at us behind his shades. His face quivered.

"But Tommy died at the scene."

Some guys slammed their gloves on the ground, some squatted with heads down. Winger walked off alone onto the field with his hands on his hat. Shack jammed his cap over his eyes. AC took off at a dead sprint toward right field, dropped to his knees. Some of us stared at the coach, not hearing what we just heard. Curls took off his glasses and wiped tears with the sleeve of his jersey. His arm shook. Initially disbelieving with a blank face, Beck burst into tears and stalked away, slamming his fists, looking skyward.

"Tommy's dead?" Daddy Rich asked.

Curls only nodded.

"What happened?" Rich said.

"All I know now is they hit a tree over by the house," Curls told us. "Tommy was in the passenger's side and got the worst of it." Curls gave everyone a few minutes, then huddled us again.

"When Big John left for the hospital, he told me to leave it up to you guys. Do you want to keep playing or not? He said he'd understand either way."

Our backup catcher Beck took over.

"Hell, yes, we're playing. For Tommy. End of discussion," he said. "Link up."

Stan the Man joined us and we waited for Winger and AC to return.

"Whose father?" Beck said softly.

"Our Father," we answered in a hushed tone, "who art in heaven, hallowed be thy name. Thy kingdom come, thy will be done on earth as it is in heaven. Give us this day our daily bread, and forgive us our trespasses as we forgive those who trespass against us. Lead us not into temptation, but deliver us from evil, for thine is the kingdom and the power and the glory for ever and ever. Amen."

Some players sniffled, wiped back tears. We walked into the dugout in a trance. There on the bench neatly folded lay Tommy's jersey, spikes and glove. He had only half-dressed for the game before leaving with Jaybird. Everyone—even the Aces, with caps in hands—watched as Beck, spikes and shin guards scraping the fencing, scaled the tall backstop holding Tommy's jersey in his left hand. He climbed to the very top and hooked the hanger on the uppermost link, then twisted it shut.

There was some lineup shuffling with Skunk and T-Bone coming off the bench to fill holes, but with Tommy's yellow number seven flapping in the breeze behind us at the plate and in front of us on the field, there was no way we would lose. I tripled into the right-center gap to lead off the game, and when I beat a close throw at third Eggy said, "Good rip, Cordell. Sorry about Tommy." The celebrations that day were not raucous, but mild. We beat the Aces 7-3, then took care of the Cardinals 10-2 to win the round robin, even though the prospect was on the hill. We hit four homers off him that, granted, would have been routine outs in his spacious yard, but, hey, both teams were playing on the same field. We saved both winning game balls and Curls had us sign them. This time they let me climb the fence and take down Tommy's jersey.

Me, Winger, Beck, Jaybird, Gandy, and AC were pallbearers, and the entire team was honorary. Jaybird was still in crutches, so Shack filled in. Tommy's mom and dad agreed to have him dressed out in full Demons uniform, but in lieu of a cap he wore a classic red bandana. Inside his catcher's mitt that was fitted on his left hand and angled across his chest was one of the signed game balls. Also lying next to him on the maroon satin was a pack of Marlboro reds and a bottle of Jack Daniel's. His service was held outside at an Indian Baptist church near Okemah, in the shade of massive oaks trees filled with buzzing cicadas. The myriad leaves rustling in the breeze made kaleidoscope shadows over Tommy's body. He looked like Tommy, down to the perpetual fat lip. All the Demons were there, some in suits if they had them, but most in their best blue jeans and shirts. It was odd to see them assembled in street clothes. I wore jeans and a new blue Oxford my mom bought me. After the preacher said his words a cassette player was produced and "Dream On," Tommy's favorite song, was played: *"Every time that I look in the mirror,"* it began, *"all these lines in my face getting clearer … Sing with me, if it's just for today, maybe tomorrow the good Lord'll take you away."* As pallbearers the entire team sat with the family in front under the tent while the song played. When it finished, the cassette, inside its case, was placed into the casket. Then the church bell rang 17 times, each succeeding peal not beginning until echoes of the last one faded. The locusts grew silent, only starting up again after the long silence of the last bell.

We loaded Tommy into the hearse and got in for the caravan to the gravesite. Mortuary workers lowered Tommy into the hole and everyone filed by to drop the red dirt onto his shiny silver casket, with the occasional yellow flower tossed in. Then the team took turns with three or four shovels until the hole was filled, sweaty work in the baking sun. Some of us stood around talking as the funeral dissipated.

"Man, I've never *not* known him," said Beck, still tearful. He was shaven and wore a tight-fitting suit. "Same team since five years old. I lost a brother." He had spoken for all of us.

That was the end of the Demons. Even though the state playoffs began in a week, the consensus was we were burnt. Our starting catcher and best hitter dead, starting shortstop with broken bones. Emotionally whipped. No heart for it. There was a team meeting and a show of hands of who wanted to continue and there were no hands. Too old for summer league, I was forced to play American Legion the next year, and it wasn't the same. Too organized. Everybody lumped into two Suburbans for away games. Highlight of the road trips: stopping at QuikTrip on the way back. Riding pine. No fans. No girls. No caravans. No one slept at each other's house on the floor or couch. No one called their teammate's mother Mom. No one helped you fix your car, picked you up for practice, invited you in for a bologna white bread sandwich. That was my last year of baseball. I was getting sorrier and sorrier anyway. Dream on.

INDEX

BY AUTHOR

BY ISSUE NUMBER